NAS Monograph Series No. 1

Series editor Gerald Grainge

The Sound of Mull Archaeological Project
(SOMAP) 1994–2005

Philip Robertson

with contributions by

Jane Maddocks and Steve Webster

BAR British Series 453
2007

Published in 2016 by
BAR Publishing, Oxford

BAR British Series 453

Nautical Archaeology Society Monograph Series 1
Series Editor: Gerald Grainge

The Sound of Mull Archaeological Project

ISBN 978 1 4073 0177 8

© The authors individually and the Publisher 2007

The authors' moral rights under the 1988 UK Copyright,
Designs and Patents Act are hereby expressly asserted.

All rights reserved. No part of this work may be copied, reproduced, stored,
sold, distributed, scanned, saved in any form of digital format or transmitted
in any form digitally, without the written permission of the Publisher.

BAR Publishing is the trading name of British Archaeological Reports (Oxford) Ltd.
British Archaeological Reports was first incorporated in 1974 to publish the BAR
Series, International and British. In 1992 Hadrian Books Ltd became part of the BAR
group. This volume was originally published by Archaeopress in conjunction with
British Archaeological Reports (Oxford) Ltd / Hadrian Books Ltd, the Series principal
publisher, in 2007. This present volume is published by BAR Publishing, 2016.

Printed in England

BAR titles are available from:

        BAR Publishing
        122 Banbury Rd, Oxford, OX2 7BP, UK
EMAIL   info@barpublishing.com
PHONE +44 (0)1865 310431
  FAX   +44 (0)1865 316916
        www.barpublishing.com

Contents

List of Colour Plates, Figures and Tables	ii
Foreword	vi
Acknowledgements	vii
Abbreviations	viii
Location References	viii
CD-ROM*	viii
1. Introduction	1
2. History of the Sound of Mull	4
3. Work undertaken by SOMAP	9
Colour Plates for Chapters 1–3	14
4. Smaller projects	17
Colour Plates for Chapters 4 and 5	33
5. *John Preston*, Rubha Dearg	46
6. Unknown: Scallastle Bay	58
Colour Plates for Chapters 6 and 7	63
7. An integrated study of the *Thesis*: Rubha an Ridire	67
8. Summary and conclusions	84
Appendix 1 – Abridged transcription of Lloyds survey report 3303	87
Appendix 2 – Table of marine species identified on the wreck of the *Thesis*	94
Appendix 3 – List of known wreck-sites and documented losses in the Sound of Mull	96
Appendix 4 – Glossary	107
Bibliography	110
Index	114

*Please note that the CD referred to above (and throughout the text) has now been replaced with a download available at www.barpublishing.com/additional-downloads.html

List of Colour Plates, Figures and Tables
Colour Plates

Plate 1.1	Lochaline 'old pier', and Lochaline stores (Philip Robertson)	14
Plate 2.1	Duart Castle (000-000-110-630-R: © Colin J M Martin. Licensor www.scran.ac.uk)	14
Plate 2.2	Mingary Castle, Ardnamurchan (Philip Robertson)	14
Plate 2.3	A possible harbour below Aros castle, Mull (Philip Robertson)	14
Plate 2.4	Bailemeonach pier, Mull (Philip Robertson)	14
Plate 2.5	Remains of a steamer pier at Salen, Mull (Philip Robertson)	15
Plate 2.6	Rubha nan Gall lighthouse, Mull (Philip Robertson)	15
Plate 3.1	Multibeam sonar leg and position system set up on *MV Gaelic Rose* (Philip Robertson)	15
Plate 3.2	Setting up the survey base-station close to the west pier, Lochaline. (Philip Robertson)	15
Plate 3.3	Pre-dive planning (Philip Robertson)	15
Plate 3.4	Offset survey on the *Thesis* (Philip Robertson)	15
Plate 3.5	Sediment monitoring stakes were used on the *John Preston* and the *Thesis* (Philip Robertson)	16
Plate 3.6	Visitors at the Duart Point wreck interpretation board prior to their dive on the visitor trail (Philip Robertson)	16
Plate 3.7	Online interpretation of the *Thesis* (Barry Kaye)	16
Plate 4.1	Multibeam sonar composite images of the *Pelican* (© Sound of Mull Mapping Consortium)	33
Plate 4.2	Frames and knees on *Pelican* (Philip Robertson)	34
Plate 4.3	Side-scan sonargraph of the *Pelican* (© Sound of Mull Mapping Consortium)	34
Plate 4.4	Stern frame and rudder assembly on the *Pelican* (Alison Fish)	34
Plate 4.5	Side-scan sonargraph of unidentified site Tobermory Bay (© Sound of Mull Mapping Consortium)	35
Plate 4.6	Internal structure of unidentified site Tobermory Bay (Alison Fish)	35
Plate 4.7	Composite image of a hulk on Calve Island (Alison Fish)	35
Plate 4.8	Side-scan sonargraph of the *Strathbeg* (© Sound of Mull Mapping Consortium)	35
Plate 4.9	Side-scan sonargraph of unidentified site, possibly the *Macduff* (© Sound of Mull Mapping Consortium)	35
Plate 4.10	Composite multibeam maps and images of the *Shuna* (© Sound of Mull Mapping Consortium)	36
Plate 4.11	Composite multibeam maps and images of the *Hispania* (© Sound of Mull Mapping Consortium)	37
Plate 4.12	Side-scan sonargraph of the *Shuna* (© Sound of Mull Mapping Consortium)	38
Plate 4.13	Side-scan sonargraph of starboard side of the *Hispania* (© Sound of Mull Mapping Consortium)	38
Plate 4.14	Shadow details of superstructure on the *Hispania* (© Sound of Mull Mapping Consortium)	38
Plate 4.15	Scour pit in the seabed, amidships of the *Hispania* (© Sound of Mull Mapping Consortium)	38
Plate 4.16	Composite multibeam maps and images of the *Rondo* (© Sound of Mull Mapping Consortium)	39

Plate 4.17	Internal deckhouse structure on the *Hispania* (© Simon Volpe)	40
Plate 4.18	Side-scan sonargraph of the *Rondo* (© Sound of Mull Mapping Consortium)	40
Plate 4.19	Ardtornish light and castle (Colin Martin)	41
Plate 4.20	The ring netter *Glencarradale*	41
Plate 4.21	Remains of the *Glencarradale* at the head of Loch Aline (Colin Martin)	41
Plate 4.22	The *Ballista* aground on Eilean Rubha an Ridire, around 1973 (000-000-110-804-R: © Colin J M Martin. Licensor www.scran.ac.uk)	41
Plate 4.23	Composite multibeam map and images of unidentified vessel, possibly the *Evelyn Rose* (© Sound of Mull Mapping Consortium)"	42
Plate 4.24	Side-scan sonargraph of the *Buitenzorg* (© Sound of Mull Mapping Consortium)	43
Plate 4.25	Composite multibeam map and images of the *Buitenzorg* (©Sound of Mull Mapping Consortium)	44
Plate 4.26	Multibeam view of Duart Point area, showing wreck site and possible areas of scour and accretion (© Sound of Mull Mapping Consortium)	45
Plate 5.1	The schooner *John Preston* (photographed by Owain Roberts with permission from the painting's owner Miss Mary Thomas, Amlwch Port)	45
Plate 5.2	Recording keelson structure at western end of the *John Preston* (Peter Pritchard)	45
Plate 5.3	Pump base adjacent to keelson (Steve Webster)	45
Plate 6.1	Dredging activity in Scallastle Bay, close to cannon site (© Sound of Mull Mapping Consortium)	63
Plate 6.2	Cannon under water (Philip Robertson)	64
Plate 6.3	Breeching loop close-up, the scale divisions are 5cm (Philip Robertson)	64
Plate 6.4	Lead apron; this object measures 26 cm by 26 cm (Edward Martin)	64
Plate 6.5	Lead apron close-up of possible inscription (Edward Martin)	64
Plate 7.1	Foredeck hold frames and missing plating on the starboard side of the *Thesis* (© Simon Volpe)	64
Plate 7.2	Side-scan sonargraph showing the *Thesis* and surrounding seabed (© Sound of Mull Mapping Consortium)	65
Plate 7.3	Remains of stern frame, lying on seabed close to vessel's starboard bow (Clive Field)	66
Plate 7.4	Reversing wheel in engine compartment (Philip Robertson)	66
Plate 7.5	Deadman's fingers (*Alcyonium digitatum*) on an exposed frame on the vessel's starboard bow (Philip Robertson)	66

Figures

Fig. 1.1	Location map of the Sound of Mull (Philip Robertson)	1
Fig. 1.2	Map of place names in the Sound of Mull (Philip Robertson)	2
Fig. 2.1	Map of historic sites (Philip Robertson)	4
Fig. 2.2	A puffer unloading at Quinish, Mull (000-000-464-618-R: © National Museums Scotland. Licensor www.scran.ac.uk)	7
Fig. 2.3	The *PS Carabinier* bought in 1893 by MacBrayne & Co. (000-000-601-298-R: © St Andrews University Library. Licensor www.scran.ac.uk)	8
Fig. 2.4	A Lerwick flying boat, moored in Oban Bay, around 1940 (000-000-128-988-R: © Imperial War Museum. Licensor www.scran.ac.uk)	8
Fig. 3.1	Extract of Captain Joseph Huddart's 'New chart of the West Coast of Scotland' (000-000-562-421-R: © National Library of Scotland. Licensor www.scran.ac.uk)	10

Fig. 4.1	Location map of sites in Tobermory Bay (Philip Robertson)	17
Fig. 4.2	MacCallum's coal hulks in Tobermory Bay c.1891 (Courtesy of Mull Museum, Tobermory)"	18
Fig. 4.3	Foredeck plan of the *Pelican* (Tim Walsh)	18
Fig. 4.4	Attributed as the *Anna Bhan*, unloading at Inch Kenneth (courtesy of Mull Museum, Tobermory)	19
Fig. 4.5	Location map of sites in northern sector (Philip Robertson)	21
Fig. 4.6	Angle of heel on the *Hispania* (© Sound of Mull Mapping Consortium)	23
Fig. 4.7	The *Rondo* aground on Dearg Sgeir	23
Fig. 4.8	Location map of sites in vicinity of Lochaline (Philip Robertson)	24
Fig. 4.9	Diver's sketch of the *Logan* (David Greig)	25
Fig. 4.10	Attributed as the puffer *Logan* beached at North Bay, Barra, during the 1940s (000-000-463-928-R: © National Museums Scotland. Licensor www.scran.ac.uk)	25
Fig. 4.11	The *Evelyn Rose* (courtesy of Richard Barton)	26
Fig. 4.12	Collapsed stone quay, Ardornish Castle (Vic Tomalin, Philip Robertson)	27
Fig. 4.13	Location map of sites around Duart Point and Eilean Rubha an Ridire (Philip Robertson)	29
Fig. 4.14	Large iron features on the site of HMS *Dartmouth* at the time of her excavation (adapted from Martin 1978: p.32 Fig.3)	30
Fig. 4.15	Large iron features on the site of HMS *Dartmouth* during the 1994 re-survey (Peter Diamond, Colin Martin, Philip Robertson)	31
Fig. 4.16	Iron features, search patterns and metal detector anomalies 2004 (Mark Beattie Edwards, Paula Martin, Philip Robertson)	31
Fig. 5.1	Location map for the *John Preston* site (Philip Robertson)	47
Fig. 5.2	The *John Preston* wide area site plan (Steve Webster, CFA Archaeology Ltd.)	48
Fig. 5.3	Hull assemblage of the *John Preston* (Steve Webster, CFA Archaeology Ltd.)	Fold out
Fig. 5.4	Elevation sections through hull structure of the *John Preston* (Antony Firth)	50
Fig. 5.5	The *John Preston* anchor windlass (Jonie and Richard Guest; CFA Archaeology Ltd.)	52
Fig. 5.6	Unidentified find from stern (Barry Kaye)	53
Fig. 5.7	Possible gudgeon at stern (Barry Kaye)	54
Fig. 5.8	Decklight from stern of the *John Preston*, drawn at 1:1 scale (Jo Cook)	55
Fig. 5.9	Location map, North Wales (Philip Robertson)	56
Fig. 5.10	Port Dinorwic around 1880 'Llongau wrth cei llechi a'r bont haearn… Y Felinheli', by John Thomas (by permission of Llyfrgell Genedlaethol Cymru/National Library of Wales)	56
Fig. 6.1	Location map for Scallastle Bay (Philip Robertson)	58
Fig. 6.2	Cannons site plan (Philip Robertson)	59
Fig. 6.4	Gun recording form (Jane Maddocks)	60
Fig. 6.5	Clay pipe drawn at 1:1 scale (Alo Parfitt)	62
Fig. 7.1	Location of the *Thesis* (Philip Robertson)	67
Fig. 7.2	Midship section (adapted from Lloyds Survey 3303, with permission from National Maritime Museum)	68
Fig. 7.3	Photograph of the *Theme*, renamed the *Glenarn* (© J and M Clarkson)	68
Fig. 7.4	Spread of debris on the seabed surrounding the *Thesis* (Barry Kaye, Philip Robertson)	72

Fig. 7.5	Angle of heel at deck level, and evidence of other deterioration (Barry Kaye, Philip Robertson)	73
Fig. 7.6	Plating survey and profile of port side (Barry Kaye, Gwynn Hodges, Philip Robertson)	74
Fig. 7.7	Plating survey and profile of starboard side (Barry Kaye, Vic Tomalin, Philip Robertson)	74
Fig. 7.8	General arrangement and tentative reconstruction (Philip Robertson)	75
Fig. 7.9	Deck plan, showing general arrangement (Barry Kaye, Philip Robertson)	78
Fig. 7.10	Foredeck collapse 2002–3 (Barry Kaye, Philip Robertson)	79
Fig. IV.1	Anchor nomenclature	107
Fig. IV.2	Hull nomenclature	108

Tables

Table 5.1	Ports visited and cargoes carried by the *John Preston* during a six-month period in 1863	47
Table 6.1	Gun recording measurements from the 1998 survey	61

Foreword

It is a most agreeable privilege to have been asked to write an introduction to this book. Though I have taken no part in the activities of SOMAP, I have followed its progress and successes since its inception with keen and close interest, for my work on the Duart Point wreck brings me to the Sound of Mull each summer, so naturally our paths frequently cross. While Philip Robertson has been the towering influence in SOMAP's development (I see no reason to spare his blushes), it is important to emphasise its wider antecedents. It is a child of the Nautical Archaeology Society's Training Programme, born of an initiative in 1994 by Chris Underwood and Martin Dean to organise an underwater archaeological field school in what is one of the UK's prime diving locations. It was an instant success. The excellent accommodation and technical facilities provided by the Lochaline Dive Centre, local charter boats geared to the needs of divers, teaching staff who combine archaeological expertise with diving skills and local knowledge, and a host of potential projects both underwater and on the foreshore, have proved a winning combination. The following year Philip took over the reins, and in 1996 he became the owner of the Dive Centre. SOMAP's future was assured.

From its beginnings SOMAP has been something special. Training has always been at its core, and all the projects have a teaching and skills-acquisition component, rooted in the NAS's well-established and internationally recognised progressive qualification ladder. But Philip's genius has been to subsume the training programme into a coherent research agenda, of which this monograph is the outcome. Participants know that while their detailed recording of (say) a decaying wooden fishing boat on the foreshore may gain them their NAS Part II qualification, it will also contribute to a wider study of the Sound of Mull as a maritime landscape, and the fruits of their work will ultimately be deposited in Scotland's sites and monuments records for access by other interested parties, now and in the future. Even the most hard-bitten diver finds this a far more rewarding outcome than a sorry relic rotting on the mantlepiece.

And SOMAP has developed a dynamic its instigators can hardly have anticipated. In the course of the first few seasons a 'hard core' of regulars emerged, coming year after year, and often pursuing increasingly specialised lines of enquiry which they have developed themselves. But far from forming a clique, this group (some of whose members have in the process acquired formidable archaeological skills which transcend 'amateur' and 'professional' distinctions) has been at pains to guide the tyros, teaching by example and unstintingly giving their encouragement and support. Though the NAS's formal instructional input will always be important, this self-generated research by amateurs is the ultimate measure of SOMAP's success, just as it is with archaeology on land.

Indeed, Philip Robertson is clearly troubled by the gulf which sometimes appears to exist between amateur and professional nautical archaeologists, prefering 'enthusiast' as a more positive term. This monograph, in addition to its value as a sound piece of research in its own right, shows how the gulf can be bridged to everyone's advantage. More than that, it demonstrates how much amateurs can do if provided with the right training, support, opportunities, and co-ordination. Let us hope that many others throughout the world will be inspired to follow this lead.

Colin Martin
28 October 2007

Acknowledgements

Firstly, thank you to the 200 or more enthusiasts (too many to name individually) who have contributed time, funds, and humour since 1994, in return for nothing but hard graft and a holiday (of sorts) in the Sound of Mull. Secondly, I am particularly grateful to Jane Maddocks (British Sub Aqua Club) and Steve Webster (Wessex Archaeology) who have contributed to individual chapters of this monograph and to Barry Kaye and Jo Cook (CookandKaye) as long-standing participants in SOMAP and as creators of the CD-ROM. Finally, I must acknowledge the ongoing support of Historic Scotland who provided grant aid for specific SOMAP projects and supported the writing-up phase. An additional contribution has enabled reproduction of the CD-ROM and colour pictures.

The following have provided particular assistance to the project and this monograph: Simon Adey-Davies, Olive Brown (Mull Museum), Richard Barton, Mark Beattie-Edwards (Nautical Archaeology Society), Jim Bennell (University of North Wales, Bangor), Peter Bennett (Kongsberg Simrad Ltd), Andrew Burke (Historic Scotland), Andrew Choong (National Maritime Museum), Deirdre Cameron (Historic Scotland), Gordon Campbell (Aspect Surveys), Mike Campbell, John Clarkson (Ships in Focus), David Cleasby, Tim Collyer (University of North Wales, Bangor), Ron Dalziel (Historic Scotland), Mary Davis ('Molly'), Geert Devogel, Peter Diamond, Calum Duncan (Marine Conservation Society), Martin Dean (University of St Andrews), Andrea Faux, Roy Fenton (Ships in Focus), David Ferguson (Lochaline Boat Charters), Antony Firth (Wessex Archaeology), Alison Fish, Noel Fojut (Historic Scotland), Bobby Forbes (SULA Diving), Neil Fortey (British Geological Survey), Sally Foster (Historic Scotland), George Forster, Neil Fraser (SCRAN), Paul Gallacher (Swift Charters), David Greig, John Grieve (Kinlochleven), Richard Grieve (Commercial Diving Services, Corpach), Richard Grieve (Salen, Mull), Jonie Guest, Richard Guest, Gwynn Hodges, Chubby Ives (Lochaline), Bob Jones (Gaelic Rose Charters), David Long (British Geological Survey), Jayne Lamont, Mark Lawrence (Lochaline Dive Centre), Annabel Lawrence (Lochaline Dive Centre), John Liddiard, Alan Livingstone (Lochaline Boat Charters), George Mair (Gem Marine), Colin Martin (Morvern Maritime Centre), Edward Martin, Paula Martin (Morvern Maritime Centre), Peter Martin, Rod Macdonald, Ian Maclean, the Maclean family (Duart Castle), Douglas McElvogue (Hampshire and Wight Trust for Maritime Archaeology), Peter Moir, Bob Mowat (RCAHMS), National Library of Wales, Ian Oxley (English Heritage), Alo Parfitt, Anne-Marie Pritchard, David Parham (University of Bournemouth), Peter Pritchard, Faith Raven (Ardtornish Estate), Macdonald Ratcliffe, RCAHMS, Mary Restell, Roy Restell, Jean Robinson (Lochaline Snack Bar), Chris Rowland (University of Dundee), Owain T.P. Roberts (Amlwch), Alexander Robertson, Angus Robertson, Catherine Robertson, Corinne Robertson, Jennifer Robertson, Rudi Roth, Andy Sproat, Commander Bob Stewart (Royal Navy), Tore Sannes (Cfloor A/S), Mary Thomas (Amlwch Port), Keith Thomson (Kongsberg Simrad Ltd), Iain Thornber (Knock, Morvern), Victoria Timberlake, Vic Tomalin, Chris Underwood (NAS), Simon Volpe, Tim Walsh, John Young. If I have omitted anyone from this list, this reflects badly only on me.

Philip Robertson
15 September 2007

Abbreviations

ADU	Archaeological Diving Unit (University of St Andrews).
IJNA	*International Journal of Nautical Archaeology.*
NSA	*The New Statistical Account of Scotland, 1845,* vol. 7, *Argyll.*
OSA	*The [Old] Statistical Account of Scotland 1791-99,* J. Sinclair (ed.), facsimile edn, I Grant and D Withrington (eds), Wakefield, 1983.
RCAHMS	Royal Commission on the Ancient and Historical Monuments of Scotland, John Sinclair House, 16 Bernard Terrace, Edinburgh EH8 9NX, www.rcahms.gov.uk.
SOMAP	Sound of Mull Archaeological Project
UKHO	United Kingdom Hydrographic Office

Location references

For ease of re-location, positions of sites situated above Mean Low Water are given in Ordnance Survey National Grid Reference (NGR) using OSGB36 datum. Except where otherwise advised, positions of sites situated below Mean Low Water are given in Latitude/Longitude to WGS 84 datum.

CD-ROM*

Accompanying this book is an interactive CD-ROM which reproduces the remote sensing images of the main sites identified in 2004, as well as additional material. The same copyright restrictions apply to the CD and to the images on it as to the printed material. The disk is for private purposes only and the images are not to be reproduced, sold or used for navigational purposes.

*Please note that the CD referred to above (and throughout the text) has now been replaced with a download available at www.barpublishing.com/additional-downloads.html

Chapter 1 – Introduction

Background to the Sound of Mull Archaeological Project (SOMAP)

The Sound of Mull, on Scotland's north-west coast (Fig. 1.1) has fascinated maritime archaeologists since the discovery in 1973 of the 5th Rate Royal Naval frigate HMS *Dartmouth* (sank 1690), and its investigation in the years that followed (Martin, 1998: 67–83). Between 1992 and 2004, investigations by the University of St Andrews on the Cromwellian vessel *Swan,* lost off Duart Point (Mull) in 1653, re-focused archaeological effort in the waters of the Sound (Martin, 1998: 46–66). At the time, few opportunities existed for public involvement in maritime archaeology and the *Swan* project established a focal point around which other initiatives could flourish.

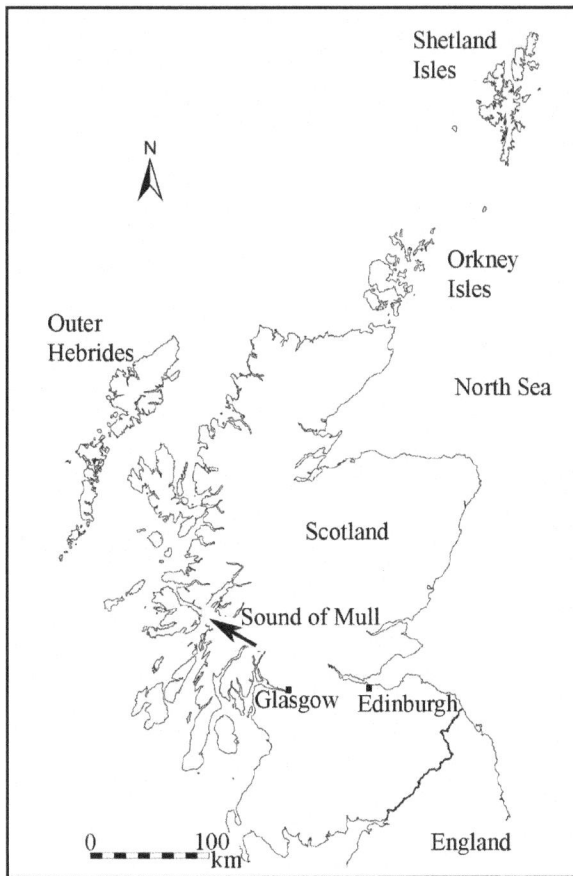

Fig. 1.1   Location map of the Sound of Mull (Philip Robertson)

Clear and sheltered waters make the Sound of Mull an ideal environment for training maritime archaeologists. In August 1994, Martin Dean of the Archaeological Diving Unit (University of St Andrews) and Chris Underwood (Nautical Archaeology Society) ran the inaugural Sound of Mull Archaeological Project (SOMAP) field school based at Lochaline, in Morvern, on the mainland side of the Sound (Plate 1.1). Its success persuaded the author to repeat the exercise in 1995 and at least one field school has taken place every year since. In 1996, the author took over the Lochaline Dive Centre and in 1997 became the Training Officer and director of NAS Scotland, a regional offshoot of the Nautical Archaeology Society (NAS), whose training programme has expanded worldwide since 1983. A strong link with an established and ideally situated dive centre provided NAS Scotland with a training base and a source of logistical support for SOMAP activities through the provision of air, diving equipment, classrooms and access to charter boats. The dive centre offered NAS Scotland a shop window for promoting more widely the importance of recording the underwater heritage and conserving it for future generations. With this in mind, the SOMAP project has provided a convenient umbrella for activities of a quasi-curatorial nature such as developing site interpretation, manning displays at local shows, conducting talks, and co-ordinating historic wreck visitor schemes.

The SOMAP project has benefited greatly from financial assistance from Historic Scotland for specific projects, such as remote-sensing work and initiatives to develop interpretation for the public, and from Historic Scotland's support for the general training activities run by NAS Scotland. There has been 'professional' involvement of individuals and organisations, but SOMAP would not have existed but for the energy of the 200 or more paying participants. We could call them amateur or avocational, but some are professional. Therefore, in the interests of providing a label that is neither pejorative nor paternalistic (Ransley, 2007; 228–9), we will describe them collectively as 'enthusiasts', because enthusiasm is the only characteristic common to all. With appropriate guidance and training where necessary, these enthusiasts, of all ages and levels of competency, from varied backgrounds and countries, each contributing a different set of skills, have provided a willing workforce. Many have returned year after year and some have used SOMAP as a springboard to success in their professional careers. Largely by trial and error and with many mistakes made along the way, SOMAP has developed methodologies to maximise archaeological outcomes while ensuring that participation remains enjoyable and safe.

Research has concentrated on sub-littoral remains connected mostly with post-medieval shipping. In this respect, the scope of the project is limited, but SOMAP's work should be seen as complementary to the work of other archaeologists such as Martin and Martin, who have considered the role of fish-traps (2003a), boathouses (2003b), historic shipwrecks (1998) and other components of the maritime landscapes of North Argyll.

Introduction

Investigations have identified a diverse collection of intact and scattered wreck sites, discarded cargoes, anchorage debris and collapsed harbour structures. Every attempt has been made to investigate the context of these sites and their role within the wider maritime cultural landscape, either as transitory participants in networks of maritime activity, as illustrations of contemporary technology, or as relics of a rural highland economy.

This monograph aims to describe SOMAP's work and to present achievements so far. Results of investigations are presented as preliminary evaluations and more detailed focal studies. Fieldwork has pinpointed several issues in relation to the area's resource management which are discussed in some detail.

The Sound of Mull

Detailed study has been restricted to the confines of the Sound of Mull, a channel 34 km long which separates the island of Mull from the isolated mainland peninsula of Morvern (Fig. 1.2). At its narrowest point (Ardnacross to Rhemore), the channel is 1.8 km wide, but around Salen Bay (Mull), it broadens to 3.5 km. The Sound's southern entrance (4.8 km wide) opens out between Duart and Inninmore Points onto the exposed waters of the Firth of Lorne. At its northern end, the channel between Rubha nan Gall and Auliston Point (3.9 km wide) opens out towards the exposed waters of the Inner Minch via the Ardnamurchan peninsula.

The channel's most diverse bedrock geology occurs at its southern end, close to where the Great Glen fault cuts across the Sound, reaching Mull at Duart Bay, before converging close to the Ross of Mull with the

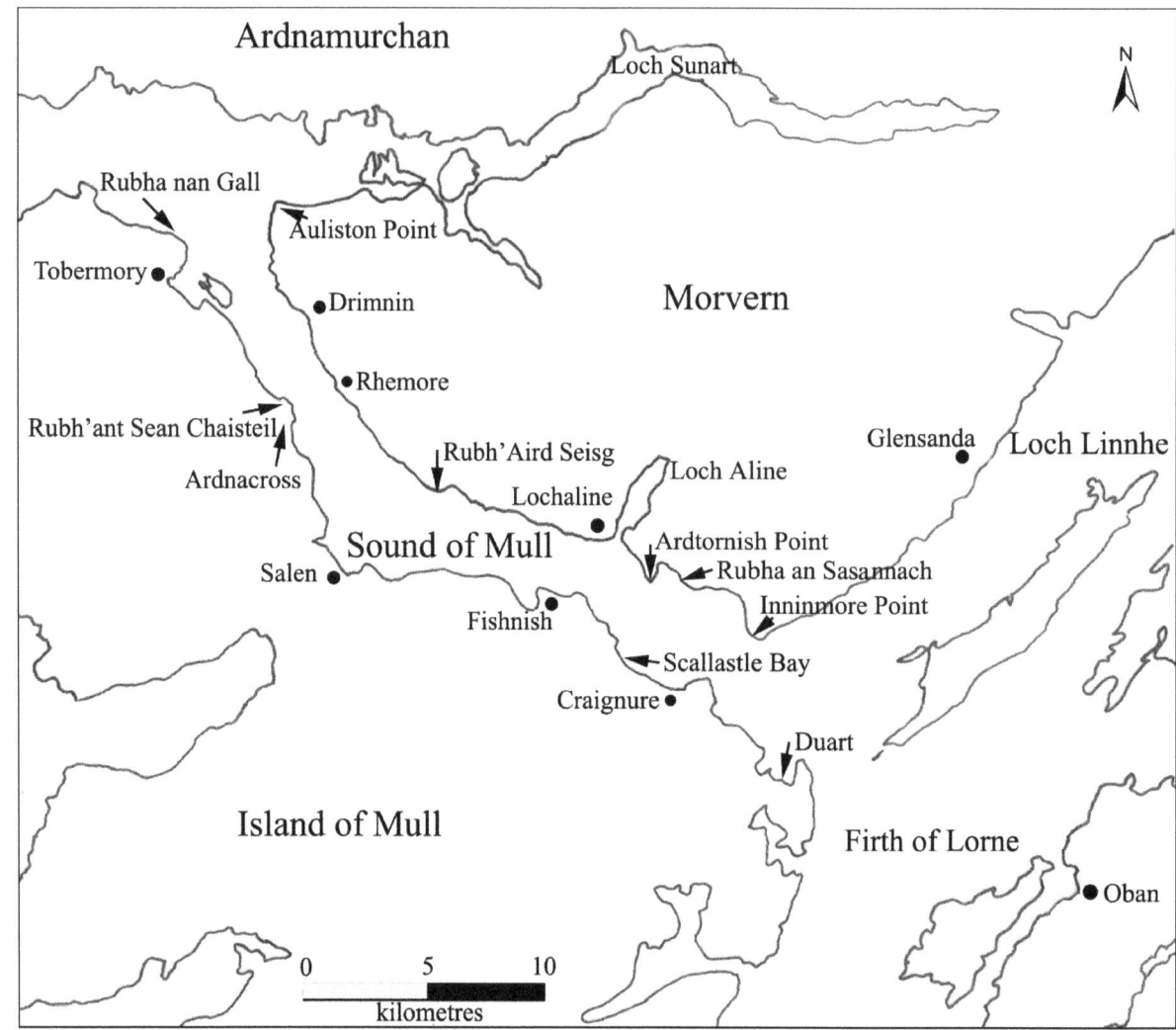

Fig. 1.2   Map of place names in the Sound of Mull (Philip Robertson)

Moine Thrust. At Ardtornish Point, the northern shore of Loch Aline, and Scallastle Bay, there are zones of Jurassic sedimentary lias. Close to Rubha an Sasennach, there is a narrow seam of carboniferous Westphalian Coal Measures. Inninmore Point has large deposits of metamorphic Moine quartz and igneous intrusive granites. A similar deposit of intrusive granites may be found in the vicinity of Duart (Mull). Otherwise, the bedrock of the coastal fringe is composed almost entirely of Tertiary volcanic lavas formed between 60 and 50 million years ago (Stevenson, 2005: 5). These lava-beds are most spectacular in the sheer cliffs south of Tobermory (Mull) and Lochaline (Morvern) and in the hills that once formed the giant caldera of the Mull Central Volcano (Stevenson, 2005: 10).

Although Tertiary volcanic activity dominates the coastal fringe, it is thought that the bedrock of the seabed of the Sound mostly comprises rocks of the Moine sequence (Fyfe *et al.*, 2003: 23). Like the numerous sea-lochs of the west coast of Scotland, this fjord-like channel was created by erosion and glaciation early on in a cycle of glacial periods (separated by warmer interglacial periods) that began some 2.6 million years ago (Stevenson, 2005: 22). Glacial activity created a deep trench eroding away hard Tertiary volcanic deposits before cutting into the softer rocks of the Moine series. The result is a channel with impressive pinnacles, cliffs, and sub-sea channels, with depths ranging from 0 to 150 m. The last ice-age in Mull ended around 11,500 years ago (Stevenson, 2005: 25), since when the effects of 'isostatic readjustment', the loss of weight of the ice causing a rebound of the landmass and relative drop in sea level, may be seen in raised beach deposits at Fishnish, Scallastle, Torosay and Duart (Mull). Those on north-western Mull reach some 30 m above sea-level, reflecting sea-levels around 30,000 years ago, prior to the last widespread glaciation (Stevenson, 2005: 27). This means that the potential for seabed remains of prehistoric settlement is limited in much of Argyll

A variety of factors are relevant to the geomorphological equation today. The British Geological Survey has analysed 49 grab-samples recovered from the seabed between 1969 and 1981 (pers. comm. David Long). These suggest that the Sound of Mull is reasonably sediment-rich. Most of the sediments relate to glacial activity, intermixed with bioturbation (material of biological origin) and run-off from the land. The Sound is adjacent to two large sea-loch systems and numerous smaller rivers, which supply some run-off sediment, particularly at times of high rainfall. While Loch Linnhe drains mostly into the Firth of Lorne, the ebb tide at the mouth of Loch Sunart may drain water and sediment at times of peak rainfall into the northern end of the Sound of Mull. A limited onshore fetch and the wind-shadow created by the hills of Mull and Morvern make the Sound of Mull a relatively-sheltered coastal environment. However, at times, short, sharp seas can occur when wind blows against tide. Tidal currents run at up to two knots in places and are most notable around Ardtornish Point, Duart Point, Rubh'ant Sean Chaisteil, and through Glas Eileanan.

Today the Sound of Mull remains an isolated coastal area, bounded by small communities on the Morvern and Mull shores. In the 2001 census the usual resident population of Mull, Iona and Ulva was 1841. Much of the population lives in Tobermory, the only town on the island, and its capital. The main community on the Morvern shore is Lochaline, a village of some 250 inhabitants.

The sea remains important to the rural economies of Mull and Morvern. There are salmon fish-farm sites at Lochaline, Fishnish, Scallastle Bay, Tobermory Bay and in the bay north of Rubha Aird Seisg. The flat seabed areas are fished commercially by nephrops (langoustines etc.,) - trawl and scallop-dredging boats from the local harbours at Oban and Tobermory, and by boats from far afield. Large commercial ships continue to use the channel. Some of these are vessels in transit to British and European ports. Others are servicing local industries such as the super-quarry at Glensanda (Fyfe *et al.*, 2003: 76), and the sand-mine (Upper Cretaceous sandstone) at Lochaline (Barnes, 2004: 14). Ferries continue to provide a lifeline to island communities with services operating between Oban and Craignure, Oban and the Inner and Outer Hebrides, Fishnish and Lochaline, and Drimnin and Tobermory. Timber too is taken away to market by sea from piers at Lochaline and Torosay. Recreational users favour the Sound's sheltered waters. Sailing, diving, and sea-angling are all popular and contribute significantly to the local economy.

Chapter 2 – History of the Sound of Mull

Prehistory (Mesolithic, Neolithic, Bronze Age, Iron Age)

Until recent times the easiest way to travel in this remote coastal landscape was by sea. As a result, many of the earliest settlements occurred along coastal margins. Evidence of the periodic island migrations that occurred during the Mesolithic period, and a diet based largely on marine produce (shellfish and finfish), has been found at nearby Risga island (Loch Sunart), Rhum, Oronsay and Oban (Finlayson, 1998). Bronze-Age cairns, including several close to Rubha Dearg on the Morvern shore (NM 664 444) and Ardnacross on the Mull shore (NM 550 501) suggest that this seaway was also important 4000 years ago. During the Iron Age too, the Sound of Mull provided a sheltered seaway and control of the seaways was supported by coastal forts or duns, built on promontories on the Morvern shore (Fig. 2.1) at Mungasdale (NM 560 530), Fiunary (NM 614 468), Caisteal Nan Con (NM 583 486), on the Mull shore at Salen (NM 576 436), and a broch at Ardnacross on the Mull shore (NM 551 498).

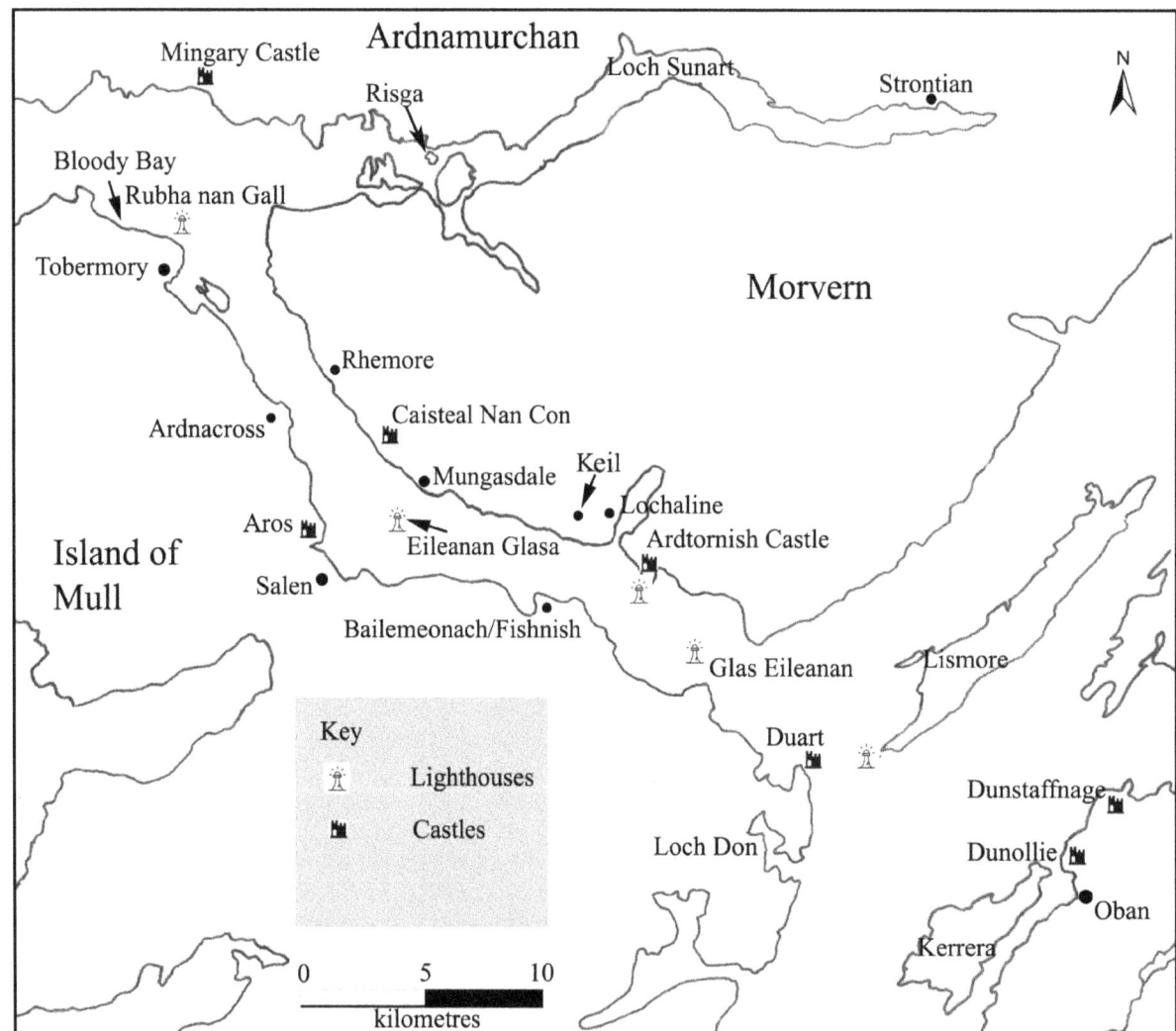

Fig. 2.1   Map of historic sites (Philip Robertson)

Early Medieval Period (c.500–c.1200 AD)

Around AD 500, the tribes of Gaels from Antrim (Ireland), known as the Dál Riata, established the kingdom of Dalriada in Argyll (Foster, 2004: 13) gradually displacing the Pictish tribes. Columba came by sea from Ireland to Argyll in 563 and within a few years he had established an important early Christian monastery and power centre at Iona (Foster, 1996: 80). Other early Christian sites may be seen throughout the islands of western Argyll (Foster, 1996: 79–89) and legend has it that the church at Keil (Morvern) dates to around this period (Thornber, 2002: x-xi). This is unlikely, as almost all early Christian sites are at sea level and only later were churches built in more prominent sites higher up and slightly inland, as at Keil. However, there is an earlier Christian site on the Morvern shore at Killundine (NM 579 498). Documentary sources confirm that the Dál Riata, like the Picts, could muster large navies and were renowned sea-raiders (Foster, 2004: 102) and Lavery (2001:14) believes that the Mull axis was important because it was at the centre of routes to the Hebrides, mainland Scotland and back to Ireland. The establishment of a coastal fort at Dunollie (Oban) during the early historic period (Foster, 2004: 46) perhaps reflects this (Fig. 2.1).

Viking raids on Iona had taken place as early as 795 and by the 10th century the Norse had footholds in the mainland of western Scotland by virtue of their sea power (Friel, 2003: 40). However, they did not venture far inland in Argyll and left little behind but place-names to illustrate the 'sphere of their influence' (Nicolaisen, 2001: 124). Part-Norse origins may be seen in Scallastle (*dalr* = valley); many others incorporate later Gaelic and English additions. For example, Ardtornish Point is made up of Norse (*nes* = headland), Gaelic *(Ard* = rock or headland*)* and English (*Point*), saying the same thing in three languages (Nicolaisen, 2001: 72).

Later Medieval Period (*c.*1200–1599)

Norse supremacy declined with the rise of the Lords of the Isles, Hebridean descendants of Somerled, *c.*1263. The Sound of Mull, strategically placed to provide access to the north and south of the kingdom, was one of a number of power bases for the Lordship's independent confederacy (Martin and Martin, 2003a: 41), enforced from a network of coastal castles (Fig.2.1) built during the 13th century at Mingary on the Ardnamurchan shore (NM 503 631), Aros (NM 563 449), Ardtornish (NM 692 426) and Duart (NM 749 353). These castles were strategically positioned at intervals along the coast in line of sight, so that beacon fires could be readily seen, and warnings communicated throughout Lorne and Morvern (Williams, 1984: 212). They overlooked bays and anchorages to afford protection for the large fleets of oared galleys or *birlinn* which protected the area from outside intervention. However, frequent disputes broke out between the clans. Perhaps the most famous battle took place in 1481 with great loss of life at 'Bloody Bay', north-west of Tobermory (Fig. 2.1), between the galleys loyal to John, fourth Lord of the Isles, and his son Angus Og (Rixon, 1998: 87).

In 1493, after an unsuccessful and ill-advised rebellion, John, Lord of the Isles, was deprived of his possession by the Scottish Parliament. King James IV followed this up with two naval expeditions to the area, the first in 1493 to Dunstaffnage Castle (Oban) and Mingary Castle (Ardnamurchan) and the second in 1495, through the Sound of Mull to Mingary Castle (Taylor, 1980: 10). In 1498, the title 'Lord of the Isles' was forfeited to King James IV (Lavery, 2001: 18) and the Macleans of Duart established control over the area.

A developing Scottish Navy and expanding trade by sea required pilotage knowledge for safe navigation of the treacherous waters off Scotland (Taylor, 1980: 10). To the Scottish pilot Alexander Lindsay is attributed compilation of a rutter of the Scottish Seas at the command of King James V, prior to his circumnavigation of Scotland in 1540. Taylor (*passim*) believes that the king's route passed through the Sound of Mull. The rutter certainly includes a detailed description of several major navigational marks in the area: 'If ye ly in the Sound of Mule at the castell Arroys ye sall have good ryd. At x or xiiij fadomes. Iff ye lye at the castell of Dewar ye sall find xxviij fadomes. There is a good rode for all wyndis in the Calyow of the Mull, in the Sound of Wllway, and in the Lough Spelle, also amongst the ylees of Caruera, Cewill, Lowyng and Swinnay' (Taylor, 1980: 49).

In 1588, the shelter afforded by Tobermory Bay (Fig. 2.1) was known to the captain of the Spanish Armada vessel *San Juan de Sicilia* when he sought permission from the Maclean of Duart to shelter there and replenish his ship (Martin and Parker, 1988: 244). In return, the Maclean co-opted the Spanish troops on board to aid his skirmishes with rivals at Mingary, Coll, Islay and Kintyre. The loss of this vessel in Tobermory Bay achieved wide renown by virtue of rumours of gold treasure aboard. Its initial salvage around 1677 by the Earl of Argyll (McLeay, 1986) and the Maclean of Duart's looting of the merchant vessel *Providence of Dumbartane,* stranded on Mull in 1627 (Lavery, 2001: 24), represent the origins of a long-standing local salvage tradition.

Post-medieval period (1600–1945)

Maclean of Duart's castle stronghold high above the south-east entrance to the Sound of Mull (Plate 2.1) was easy to defend against attack by small arms. However, the advent of larger sailing ships and ship-borne artillery provided a new threat to these coastal fortifications (Martin and Martin, 2003b: 92). In 1645, ships under the command of Alastair MacColla besieged Donald Campbell at Mingary Castle (Plate 2.2) before joining forces with the Marquis of Montrose against the Covenanters (Stevenson, 1980: 111–14, 124–5). In 1653 Oliver Cromwell dispatched a squadron of six ships to the Western Isles to stamp

History of the Sound of Mull

out Royalist support, including an attack on Duart Castle (Martin, 1998: 46–7). General Hugh Mackay's expeditionary force to the Western Isles to secure allegiance to the throne of William and Mary (Martin, 1998: 68–70) targeted Duart again in 1690 because Maclean of Duart was a Jacobite sympathiser.

By the end of the 17th century the Maclean of Duart's influence had declined and the Campbell family, headed by the Earls, later Dukes, of Argyll, fought its way into control of the Duart estates, ultimately bringing a measure of emancipation and prosperity to the area (Gaskell, 1980: 1, 4). So too did the Act of Union of 1707, which removed trading monopolies which favoured the Royal Burghs at the expense of more efficient taxation systems (Hunter, 2004: 11). A burgeoning smuggling trade in west Argyll and Lochaber resulted in the establishment of a customs post at the garrison in Fort William, with officers active throughout the seaways of the area. In July 1732, for example, excise officers seized at Tobermory cargoes of illegally imported meal and other general goods from Ireland, aboard the brigantine *Betty* (registered in Londonderry) and destined for Strontian Lead Mine aboard the mining company's own vessel *Strontian* (Hunter, 2004: 32–3).

Attempts by the second Duke of Argyll in 1737 to reform agricultural tenancies with the aim of securing loyalty brought some prosperity to the area. However, within a few days of Bonny Prince Charlie's landing at Glenfinnan in July 1745, many of the people of Mull and Morvern had allied themselves with the Prince's army and not with the loyalist Argyll militia (Maclean-Bristol, 1998). During 1745 the Royal Navy was active in the Sound of Mull, collecting intelligence, keeping open supply routes to Fort William, harassing the inhabitants and preventing assistance from reaching the rebels (Fergusson, 1951). A letter sent by Archibald Campbell to the Duke of Argyll details his request 'to the Commanders of the Ships of War in the Coast of Mull to give them all the interruption in their power of disabling the Boats' (Letter, 13 October 1745, Campbell Papers MS3733/11). In February 1746, acting under orders from the Duke of Cumberland, the naval sloops *Terror* and *Princess Anne* based at Tobermory under the command of Captain Robert Duff, combined with General Campbell's militia based at Mingary Castle to burn houses, farmland and woodland, and to destroy boats around Morvern and Loch Sunart (Letter from Captain Duff to Major Gen. Campbell, 11 March 1746, Campbell Papers MS3734/185; Fergusson, 1951: 118–19).

After the Jacobite Rebellion, the population of Mull and Morvern increased in common with other areas of the west highlands (Gaskell, 1980: 6) and there was a commensurate increase in trade, prosperity, and associated local infrastructure. Aros (Plate 2.3) remained a principal embarkation point on Mull (Currie, 2000:189–90) during the late 18th century, but coastal communities were establishing ferry routes to transport cattle and other staple produce to and from the major market places. A ferry from Fishnish (Plate 2.4), near the market place at Bailemeonach (NM 6600 4227), to an old pier (NM 6822 4541) inside the narrows at the entrance to Loch Aline was in use by at least 1787 (Douglass, 1988: 21). This became important for droving cattle from the market at Salen on Mull to market in Strontian. The route was also probably used by cattle drovers from Morvern to take their beasts to Kerrera via Mull's major cattle port at Grass Point at the mouth of Loch Don (Haldane, 1995: 86). By at least 1794, a crossing from Ardnacross on Mull to Rhemore (an inlet situated at NM 568 507) was established at the narrowest point in the Sound of Mull, and another operated to Ardnamurchan from Dorlin at the mouth of Loch Sunart (*OSA:* viii, 368). McKenzie Senior's chart of the Sound of Mull also suggests that a ferry crossing was in place across the Loch Aline narrows by the date of publication (1778). Despite improving local connections, the uncertainty of communication with the low country remained: 'Though a vessel, called a packet, runs at times between the Clyde and the Sound of Mull, it has been only set agoing and continued by private adventurers for their own interest, and is subjected to no rules calculated for the public good; no dependence can be had either on the time of its sailing, or the rate of freight'. (*OSA*: viii, 374–5).

Of the fisheries, Donald Monro describes Loch Buie (Fig. 2.1) and Loch na Keil (Mull) as being 'ane gud tak of hering and uther fishingis' (Monro, 2002: 314). Macleod states that 'herrings are found sometimes in great abundance, of good size and quality, in the months of August and November' in Loch Sunart (*OSA*: viii, 367). Fish-traps were probably in use from the medieval period and early maps suggest that some had fallen into disrepair by the mid 19th century (pers. comm. Paula Martin). In Morvern, there were 'no fewer than 100 small boats in the parish kept for the purposes of fishing and carrying seaware as manure to their lands' and 'likewise boats of greater tonnage for following the herring industry at a distance (*OSA*: viii, 368). Yet, it appears that the industry had little organisational structure until the British Fisheries Society's attempts to develop Tobermory as a fishing harbour around 1789 (Currie, 2000: 190 and chapter 4). The industry's development was hindered by a draconian Salt Tax, and the consequent need for a bonded salt warehouse.

In addition to the 100 or so smaller boats, Macleod (Thornber, 2002: 22) mentions that landowners and tacksmen of Morvern owned 12 or 14 'barges' of a larger size for transporting themselves to neighbouring islands. These vessels were stored in specially constructed boathouses and seem to have been open decked, oared vessels of between 18 and

27ft in length overall, sometimes with a simple sailing rig as well (Martin and Martin, 2003b: 108). The *OSA* (viii, 368) also states that in Morvern there was 'one vessel of about 20 tons burden, employed in the coasting trade', and the Parish of Kilninian (Mull, which included Tobermory) is said to have had 'not above 3 or 4 boats of a large size, which carry coastwise for freight' (*OSA*: viii, 328). But what of the industry that larger vessels such as this were servicing? The sandstone quarries of 'Lochalin and Ardtornish' were said to produce stone of the very best quality and appearance, used in the 19th century for the construction of the Crinan Canal locks (*NSA*: 170). One of the sites may be seen at Inninmore sandstone quarries (NM 725 418) and Admiralty chart 2155 (surveyed 1851, published 1852) suggests that this may have had an associated quay (no longer visible on the ground). Limestone was quarried from the Morvern shore as recently as 1933–6 (Gaskell, 1980: 171) and short-lived attempts were made to develop open-cast coal mining near Lochaline during the 18th century: 'a few tons of good quality found; but, not being prosecuted with vigour, it has not succeeded. This is the more to be regretted, as the mine lies close by the shore of this good and commodious harbour' (*OSA*: viii, 375).

Oak, ash and birch woods bordering Loch Sunart, Loch Aline and the Mull shore are said to have benefited local proprietors who felled them for use by the Lorn Furnace Company and others for charcoal (*OSA*: viii, 375). Further afield, the lime kilns of Lismore, the slate quarries of Ballachulish and Easdale and the granite quarries of the Ross of Mull probably supplied local markets by ship. As alluded to by Ayton and Daniell (1978: vol iii, 35), kelp-burning was practiced in Mull. Torosay parish yielded an annual quantity of 90–100 tons (*OSA*: xx, 341). Douglass (2003: 36) has identified two kelp kilns at Scarisdale Point (Fishnish, NM 519 378), but no confirmed kelp kilns have yet been identified on the Morvern shore (Martin and Martin, 2003a: 40) where the kelp industry may not have been as influential (Gaskell, 1980: 8).

The early 19th century saw a period of unrest in the Highlands. Economic recession after the end of the Napoleonic wars led to a depression lasting from approximately 1815 to 1850 (Gaskell, 1980: 25–6). Kelp and cattle values dropped and the collapse around 1830 of the herring fishery throughout the Western Isles (*NSA*: 173) meant that Tobermory never attained prominence as a fishing port. The sale of properties in Morvern and Mull by the spendthrift sixth Duke of Argyll in 1819 set in train mass changes in land use as the new landowners sought to make their purchases profitable. Eviction of tenants had begun in the late 18th century, but the pace of change increased after the Argyll sales when landowners turned to large-scale sheep farming (Gaskell, 1980: 26). This in turn resulted in poverty, crop famine (notably the potato famine of 1846) and mass depopulation of Morvern and Mull, with census returns for Morvern showing 2083 residents in 1801 and only 819 by 1881 (Gaskell, 1980: 123). Some emigrated on ships bound for the New World, others

Fig. 2.2   A puffer unloading at Quinish, Mull (000-000-464-618-R: © National Museums Scotland. Licensor www.scran.ac.uk)

moved to the lowlands in search of employment. Numerous deserted settlements on the Mull (Douglass, 2003) and Morvern (Martin and Martin, 2003a) shores resulted.

The advent of steamships brought increased levels of merchant traffic through the Sound of Mull after 1818, when the sight of the first steamer to pass through brought 'great surprise' to the old inhabitants of Morvern (*NSA*: 189). The opening of the Crinan (*c*.1801) and Caledonian (1822) canals improved connections with the central belt and the east coast (Lindsay, 1968: 127–8), while steamships brought the benefits of regular communication and supply of staple goods such as coal (Fig. 2.2). In May 1822, the paddle steamer *Highlander* started a regular service between Glasgow and Tobermory, calling at Lochaline as one of the intermediate ports. In 1827 the paddle steamer *Maid of Morven* started on the Glasgow–Tobermory and Glasgow–Fort William run in alternate weeks (Duckworth and Langmuir, 1987: 4). New piers at the entrance to Loch Aline (NM 6796 4462: Fig. 1.2) and at Craignure (NM 721 369) were built by 1848 to cope with this new traffic, which increased further with the completion of the railway line to Oban *c*.1880 (Thomas, 1984: 30). Shortly afterwards, David MacBrayne inaugurated his Sound of Mull ferry and mail service, and his first ship, the paddle-steamer *Pioneer*, sailed daily from Tobermory to Oban, calling at Salen (Plate 2.5), Lochaline and Craignure (Fig. 2.3)

Fig. 2.3   The PS Carabinier *was bought in 1893 by MacBrayne & Co. The* Carabinier *was stationed at Tobermory and used on the Oban-Sound of Mull to Tobermory-Loch Sunart service. She was sold to J J King & Sons of Garston, for breaking up at Troon in 1908. (000-000-601-298-R: © St Andrews University Library. Licensor www.scran.ac.uk)*

An increase in shipping brought about an increase in shipwreck incidents. Movements to reduce the excessive number of wrecks led to the construction of a chain of lighthouses around the coast of the UK. By 1833 the southern entrance to the Sound of Mull was marked by a lighthouse at the south end of Lismore, built at least in part using 'freestone' from the 'quarries of Lochalin and Ardtornis' (*NSA*: 170–1). The completion in 1857 of a lighthouse at Rubha nan Gall (NM 5077 5704) at the suggestion of David Stevenson (engineer to the Northern Lighthouse Board between 1853 and 1878) soon secured safer passage at night around the channel's northern end (Plate 2.6). A string of secondary lighthouses followed, partly to stimulate development of the highlands and island fishing fleet (Munro, 1979: 200). In addition to these 'official' marks there are 'private' markers such as the pair of concrete pillars for leading lights set up on the west shore of Loch Aline by Valentine Smith for bringing his steam yacht *Dobhran* in at night (Gaskell, 1980: 172).

The Sound of Mull and its environs saw intensive maritime activity during World War II. From 1940 to 1945, Tobermory was used as a base for training the crews of anti-submarine vessels. Exercises were carried out aboard HMS *Western Isles* and a number of smaller vessels under the overall command of Commodore Sir Gilbert Stevenson, the 'Terror of Tobermory'. By the end of the war around 200,000 men had received training in Tobermory on 1132 work-up sessions for 911 different vessels (Baker, 1999: 155). Around the same time, RAF Oban was a crucial flying-boat base for Sunderlands and Catalinas (Fig. 2.4). These aircraft formed part of Coastal Command whose job it was to escort the merchant fleet. The deep but sheltered Oban Roads were used as a convoy rendezvous point for vessels heading directly westwards out into the Atlantic, or northwards to Russia. The relative safety of this meeting-point is confirmed by the fact that Oban came under aerial bombardment only once. Damage from two Heinkel 111e bombers sank the merchant vessel SS *Breda* in Ardmucknish Bay, Oban, soon after 23 December 1940 (Moir and Crawford, 1994: 128).

Fig. 2.4   A Lerwick general reconnaissance flying boat of 209 squadron, moored in Oban Bay, around 1940 (000-000-128-988-R: © Imperial War Museum. Licensor www.scran.ac.uk)

Chapter 3 – Work Undertaken by SOMAP

A decade of work since 1994 has involved participants in a wide variety of background research, fieldwork and site-management tasks.

Background research

The project has reviewed a wide range of written and oral historical sources. The earliest written pilotage instructions for the Sound of Mull are found in Alexander Lindsay's *Rutter of the Scottish Seas*, c.1540 (Taylor, 1980). Around 1549, Sir Donald Monro transcribed his personal observations of the western isles, including Mull, Calve Island and the smaller islands of the Sound (Monro, 2002). Skye-born Martin Martin's *Descriptions of the Western Isles of Scotland* (2002) depicts Mull probably c.1695 and certainly well before the 1745 rebellion, 'the beginning of the end of ancient Scotland' (Levi, 1984: 11). These earlier accounts inspired James Boswell and Dr Samuel Johnson to tour the Highlands and Western Isles in 1773 (Johnson, 1984; Boswell, 1984), by which time processes of change in the Highlands were already gathering speed. Mainland Morvern is mentioned less than Mull in these earlier works, but Norman Macleod, minister of Morvern (1745–1824) offers authoritative views of its condition at the end of the 18th century in his contribution to the *Statistical Account of Scotland* (vol. x, Argyll (mainland), 1791–99) and in *Remniscences of a Highland Parish* (first edition 1867, modern edition by Thornber, 2002). For the 19th century, both Morvern and Mull feature in the extensive writings of Sir Walter Scott (Scott, 1998), and in the descriptions and lithographs of Ayton and Daniell (1978), based on voyages around Britain in 1813–14.

Early nautical charts of the area are vague and impressionistic. Nicolas de Nicolay's 1583 chart of Scotland is the earliest known printed chart (Munro, 1979: 20), but was largely an interpretation of Alexander Lindsay's *Rutter*. Blaeu's *Atlas* of 1654, and several 17th- and early 18th-century general charts of the West Coast of Scotland (e.g. Adair, 1703; Mount and Page, 1715; Knapton et al., 1728) provide little useful information about the Sound of Mull. Aldridge (1992: 78) cites Captain Gregory of the sloop *Happy* who, on his return to Belfast Lough in December 1715, requested continued use of a pilot for the Minch, considering the Sound of Mull 'the most dangerous in the world and it will take years to be acquainted with it'. In 1746 Major General Campbell's correspondence with Captain Duff recommends Captain John Fergussone at Tobermory as being 'perfectly acquainted in the Sound of Mull & other sounds round the Western Isles, and may be usefull to you in your Cruizes as a Pilot' (Letter, 8 January 1746, Campbell Papers MS3733/73).

Significant improvements came in 1775, with publication of Murdoch McKenzie Senior's chart of the Sound of Mull for the Admiralty. McKenzie included depth soundings close to shore and encoded descriptions of seabed morphology. He also identified the principal rock hazards in their correct locations, while indicating a possible route for vessels to avoid the rock skerries of Dubh Sgeir, Glas Eileanan, and Eilean Rubha an Ridire. To aid pilotage, he included drawn elevations, showing features such as hills, coastal settlements and castles which can aid the navigator. Other 18th- and early 19th-century examples (e.g. Huddart et al, 1794) are similar in appearance. Huddart et al. confirm that the 'track for sailing from the west coast of Britain for Norway' involved a passage through the deep, sheltered channels of the Sound of Mull (Fig. 3.1). An alternative route around the west side of Mull was exposed to the Atlantic's prevailing south-westerly and westerly winds, where shallows, currents and rocky outcrops were particularly hazardous for mariners (Munro, 1979: 17). Improvements in charting occurred in 1851 when the Hydrographic Office surveyed the Sound to exacting standards (UKHO, 1852).

Disputes over land-ownership between various Macleans and Campbells during the 17th century are detailed in estate papers at Inveraray Castle and elsewhere. Both Morvern and Mull were at the centre of the Jacobite Rebellion in 1745, as discussed by Fergusson (1951) who summarises, amongst other sources, extensive accounts in the Campbell Papers of naval movements around the Sound of Mull during 1745–46. Estate papers, including 19th-century records for Morvern (held at Ardtornish Estate) have been extensively investigated by other researchers (e.g., Gaskell, 1980).

Extensive lists of shipwrecks are provided by Larn and Larn (1995), and Whittaker (1998), and maritime records are now incorporated within the database compiled and managed by the Royal Commission on the Ancient and Historical Monuments of Scotland (RCAHMS). Contemporary records are patchy for the 17th century and gradually more reliable for the 18th and 19th centuries. The first reports of a ship loss received by Lloyd's of London were entered in Loss and Casualty Books. However, there were often subsequent reports, containing greater detail or recording efforts at salvage; and these, like the first report, were all published in *Lloyd's List* from 1827. From the 1850s, local shipwrecks were reported in the *Oban Times and Argyllshire Advertiser*. To aid the study of wreck sites located on the foreshore at Calve Island (Mull), the RAF's 1:10,000 scale vertical stereoscopic aerial photographs gathered during the 1940s (in the collections of RCAHMS) were compared with Ordnance Survey aerial photographs

Work Undertaken by SOMAP

Fig. 3.1 Extract of Captain Joseph Huddart's 'New chart of the West Coast of Scotland from The Mull of Galloway to Dunan Point in Sky. Including the Western Islands of Ila, Jura, Mull, Tire-iy, Coll, Rumm & c. with The opposite coast of Ireland and the North Channel' (000-000-562-421-R: © National Library of Scotland. Licensor www.scran.ac.uk)

taken during the 1950s (at scales between 1:7500 and 1:27,000). Wrecks and associated features must not be seen in isolation. Background research has involved a brief review of the RCAHMS survey of Argyll (RCAHMS, 1980) which details the main prehistoric and early historic sites along the coastal fringe, as well as more recent surveys by Douglass (1988) of 19th-century monuments on Mull, and by Martin and Martin of aspects of the maritime landscape of Morvern and Mull (2003a; 2003b). Underwater, the Hydrographic Office surveys from the mid-19th century onwards have identified some of the known wreck sites, but most have been located by sport divers, who have visited the area in increasing numbers since the 1960s. The only previous archaeological fieldwork under water had taken place on two 17th-century wrecks—HMS *Dartmouth* (1690) and the Duart Point Wreck (1653) (Martin, 1998).

The Lochaline-based scallop-diver George Forster has provided positions of several sites he has located during dives around the scallop banks of Scallastle Bay and Inninmore Point. Sea-angler Davy Holt has offered information on seabed obstructions, knowledge gained during pioneering work to establish a skate-tagging scheme in association with Glasgow Museums. Charter boat operators, salvage contractors, visiting and local divers have also added valuable information on underwater sites and how they have evolved over time.

Fieldwork

SOMAP has completed preliminary evaluations of most known underwater sites, including intact wrecks, anchorage-debris, the collapsed remains of a pier in Ardtornish Bay and a crannog in Loch Tearnait, a hill loch three miles inland from Lochaline (pers. comm. Simon Adey-Davies). The crannog survey is omitted from this monograph as it is not maritime. These preliminary assessments established the extent, character, condition, date and origin of each site, providing baseline maps, accurate locations, and seabed bathymetry, and recording physical evidence of obvious impacts caused by human activity.

Detailed recording has been completed on the wrecks of the 19th-century merchant steamship *Thesis* (1999–2005), the slate-carrying schooner *John Preston* (1994–1999), and a scatter of cast-iron guns in Scallastle Bay (1995–1999). These sites were chosen partly because of logistical suitability, but also because they are significant examples of particular types of shipwreck site.

Remote sensing

The challenges of recording large areas of seabed and large shipwrecks militated against an approach based only on diver survey. Four geophysical expeditions have been made possible by virtue of the rapid technological advances in remote sensing and by the willingness of both the public and private sector to assist SOMAP's research.

In 1995 the Royal Navy survey vessel HMS *Berkeley*, under Commander Bob Stewart, carried out a sonar search of Scallastle Bay and Ardtornish Bay. In 1999 a side-scan sonar and proton-magnetometer survey was undertaken in association with the School of Ocean Sciences, University of Wales, Bangor. This used a dual-high-frequency tow-fish (100 and 325 kHz), providing a 10° transducer beam for maximum range and optimum operational capacity in the expected water-depths. Differential Geographical Positioning System (DGPS) enabled positioning accurate to ±10 m (Collyer, 2000). The sonar survey recorded large areas of Scallastle and Ardtornish Bays, as well as the Duart Point wreck and those of the *John Preston*, *Buitenzorg*, *Logan*, and *Hispania*. During the same year, the Archaeological Diving Unit, based at the University of St Andrews, carried out field-trials on new side-scan equipment on the *John Preston* and *Hispania*.

The most ambitious expedition occurred during June 2004 under the umbrella of the Sound of Mull Mapping Consortium — Aspect Surveys Ltd, Historic Scotland, the Centre for Digital Imaging (Duncan of Jordanstone College of Art and Design, University of Dundee), Morvern Maritime Centre, and Lochaline Dive Centre (Robertson, 2005). This survey, carried out on board the dive charter vessel *Gaelic Rose* (Plate 3.1), covered approximately 25.7 km^2 of seabed in areas of high archaeological potential, recording most of the known wreck sites. The survey rig included a high-resolution Kongsberg Maritime EM3002 shallow-water multibeam system set to operate at a frequency of 293 KHz and dual-frequency Klein 3000 side-scan sonar (100 kHz and 500 kHz). Sonar-integrated Real Time Kinematic (RTK) position-systems on the vessel were set-up to receive DGPS RTK corrections from an onshore RTK base-station (Plate 3.2). The base-station antenna co-ordinates were positioned using static GPS methods with accuracy of ±100 mm, and levelled from ordnance datum benchmarks adjusted to chart datum using Admiralty Tide tables (NP 2001–04). Real-time tidal levels were provided using a Valeport 740 digital tide-gauge mounted on the west pier at Lochaline, and accurate to ±10 mm. DGPS corrections with sub-metric accuracy were also input to the multibeam positioning-system for use during periods when RTK reference-station signals were unavailable (for example in the vicinity of Tobermory)

Work Undertaken by SOMAP

Diver-based fieldwork

For diving surveys SOMAP has relied on the participation for short periods of fluctuating numbers of volunteers with varied levels of experience. At the beginning of each field school, experienced tutors ran NAS Introductory and Part 1 courses for participants without prior archaeological experience and training in specific Part 3 modules was provided where more advanced project work required it. NAS students were also able to accredit their hours of practical experience within their training log-books. The task of safely mobilising this workforce on complex tasks necessitated the instigation of a rigid system of pre-dive planning (Plate 3.3), a preference for low-tech approaches to archaeological recording (see Dean *et al.*, 1992), and equipment which is proven and easy to use.

Two levels of recording were practised under water. For preliminary assessments, divers used the NAS Diving With A Purpose A5 dive slate complemented by stills and video photography. The focal-study surveys started with the establishment of a primary network of datum points, on either the seabed or the wreck site. Once established, offset or trilateration survey methods were used to measure in secondary points of interest (Plate 3.4). Dive-computers were used to record depths relative to a tidal bench-mark on the seabed, which can be measured in to Chart Datum at any stage. Planning frames were used extensively on the *John Preston* and to record details of construction on the *Thesis*. Where detailed recording of complex 3D objects was required, measured drawings have generally been complemented by still and video photography.

Early SOMAP projects relied heavily on computer-aided survey programmes such as Web for Windows (Rule, 1989) and Site Surveyor (Holt, 2003). However, it became clear that prolonged attempts to improve accuracy often delayed writing up and interpretation of results. With experience, it became clear that software applications performed best as an aid to establishing a control network of primary datum points. From then on students were encouraged to return to traditional survey techniques, to achieve accuracy sufficient to establish meaningful relationships between artefacts on the seabed and to draw up their results by hand. The use of pre-formatted recording sheets was eschewed in favour of loosely formatted SOMAP-specific survey record sheets which incorporated basic dive and archaeological information. A separate form was designed for detailed object recording to which drawings, sketches and photographs (including digital images) could be appended as required.

When research considerations recommended it and logistical considerations allowed, limited excavation was carried out. Two small trial trenches on the *John Preston* were excavated and subsequently backfilled; one of these produced several finds which were recovered, recorded on shore and reburied on the seabed. Two vulnerable objects were recovered from the Scallastle Bay site and conserved by a SOMAP volunteer who happened to be an experienced conservator with access to laboratory facilities. These finds are now available for public viewing, on request, at Lochaline Dive Centre.

Adopting an interdisciplinary approach to investigate burial environments, Barry Kaye and Jo Cook developed a sediment-measuring system using perspex stakes with mild steel rods (Plate 3.5). They tested this approach on the *Dartmouth* and *John Preston* sites in 1999 (Cook and Kaye, 2000) before instigating metallurgical and biological assessments on the *Thesis* and the *Pelican* in 2002–03. This work was augmented in 2004 by further qualitative biological mapping of the SS *Thesis* by MCS (Marine Conservation Society) Seasearch.

Resource management

Few divers have the time or inclination to participate in recording projects; many more want to be able to visit and appreciate what historic wreck sites under water have to offer. Non-divers too often express interest at what lies beneath the waves and SOMAP has instigated several projects with all these groups in mind.

Historic Wreck Visitor Schemes

The Duart Point historic wreck site (Mull) is designated under the Protection of Wrecks Act 1973 and a 'visitor' licence from Historic Scotland is now required to dive as a tourist on this wreck. In 1994 no 'visitor' licence existed, with access to designated wrecks limited to those actively investigating them. However, organisers of the inaugural field school co-ordinated an open day for its participants, with permission from Historic Scotland and with the full support of the wreck's licensee Dr Colin Martin, who, with a team of professional diving archaeologists from the University of St Andrews, was engaged in preliminary rescue excavations.

The success of this open day prompted SOMAP organisers to propose a widening of the visitor scheme so that recreational divers could witness fieldwork on the site in 1995 (Robertson, 2003). Since 1994, approximately 1000 visitors have dived on a specially designed visitor trail and visited the wreck

Sound of Mull Archaeological Project

exhibition in Duart Castle (Plate 3.6). In 1996, a second visitor scheme was established on the historic wreck of HMS *Dartmouth* (Eilean Rubha an Ridire, Morvern) and this has attracted some 400 visitors to date. Situated as it is in an isolated corner of the Sound of Mull close to the unprotected wreck of the SS *Ballista*, the *Dartmouth* is vulnerable to unlicensed diving; the establishment of a visitor scheme has provided a legal means of access for visitors to the area, as well as a means of carrying out periodic monitoring work. The success of the two Sound of Mull visitor schemes perhaps helped to bring about reform of licensing arrangements under the Protection of Wrecks Act 1973, and any one can now apply for a 'visitor' licence to visit a designated wreck site.

Other initiatives

The Duart Point wreck and the *Dartmouth* are the only designated historic underwater sites within the boundaries of SOMAP's study area. The *Thesis* and *John Preston* have been 'adopted' under the NAS Adopt a Wreck scheme. This aims to provide a voluntary management framework of benefit to the wreck site and its many visitors but without any statutory framework. Survey data gathered during recording projects has been used to underpin interpretation initiatives aimed at both divers and non-divers. Projects included production of specially designed leaflets and animated information on a website (Plate 3.7), promoting a conservation ethos and independent discovery. Copies of the animations for *John Preston* and *Thesis* are included in the CD acompanying this publication. Talks about the work have also been presented to organisations around Argyll and further afield and a boat excursion to the sites was run in association with the Morvern Heritage Society

The SOMAP archive

Some SOMAP archive material has already been deposited with RCAHMS. On publication of this monograph, copies of all existing working material will be deposited with RCAHMS and a copy of the monograph will be supplied to Historic Scotland, the West of Scotland Archaeology Service, and the Highland Council Archaeology Service.

Plate 1.1   Lochaline 'old pier', and Lochaline stores (Philip Robertson)

Plate 2.1   Duart Castle (000-000-110-630-R: © Colin J M Martin. Licensor www.scran.ac.uk)

Plate 2.2 Mingary Castle, Ardnamurchan (Philip Robertson)

Plate 2.3   A possible harbour below Aros castle, Mull (Philip Robertson)

Plate 2.4   Bailemeonach pier, Mull (Philip Robertson)

Plate 2.5   Remains of a steamer pier at Salen, Mull (Philip Robertson)

Plate 2.6   Rubha nan Gall lighthouse, Mull (Philip Robertson)

Plate 3.1   Multibeam sonar leg and position system set up on MV Gaelic Rose *(Philip Robertson)*

Plate 3.2   Setting up the survey base-station close to the west pier, Lochaline. (Philip Robertson)

Plate 3.3   Pre-dive planning (Philip Robertson)

Plate 3.4   Offset survey on the Thesis *(Philip Robertson)*

Plate 3.6   Visitors at the Duart Point wreck interpretation board prior to their dive on the visitor trail (Philip Robertson)

Plate 3.5   Sediment monitoring stakes were used on the John Preston *and the* Thesis *(Philip Robertson)*

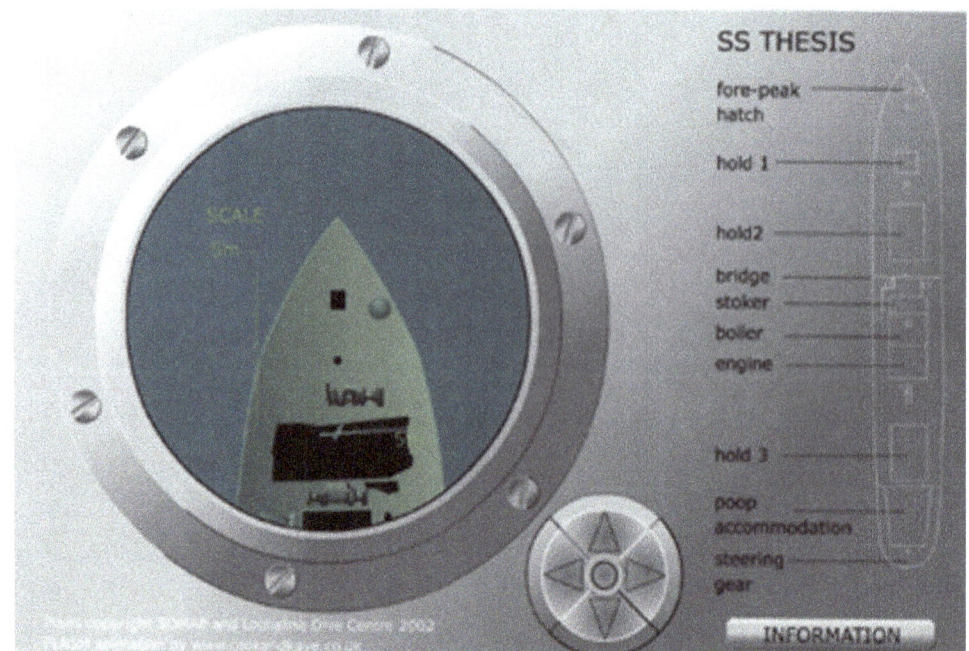

Plate 3.7   Online interpretation of the Thesis *(Barry Kaye)*

Chapter 4 – Smaller Projects

Tobermory and Calve Island

As early as the 16th century Sir Donald Monro had commented that Tobermory Bay, sheltered from the sea by Calve Island, was 'with ane sufficient raid [road] for shippis…'(Monro, 2002: 318). In October 1773, Johnson and Boswell described an already established port: 'there are sometimes sixty or seventy sail here; today there were twelve or fourteen vessels. To see such a thing was the nearest thing to seeing a town. The vessels were from different places; Clyde, Campbelltown, Newcastle, &c. One was returning to Lancaster from Hamburgh' (Boswell, 1984: 349).

As part of a nationwide plan, the British Fisheries Society decided around 1789 to develop a proper harbour at Tobermory. A custom house and post office were established in 1791 (Daniell, 2006), in which year the custom-house recorded 47 vessels and boats cleared for the herring fishery (*OSA* xx, 330–31). Many of the early houses for fishermen were built on the hill overlooking Tobermory Bay. Currie (2000: 190) cites Walter Scott (1998), who, following his visit in 1814, concluded that the fishing harbour should have been built on Calve Island, with a causeway linking the island to Mull, so that the fishermen could be nearer to the sea.

Major development of the seafront did not occur until the 1820s, at about the same time as Ayton and Daniell described the harbour as possessing 'a fine commodious pier of masonry that affords good shelter for boats … it lies directly in the track of shipping which pass from the western parts of Britain to the northern countries of Europe. It also has the advantage of an easy navigable communication with the fishing lochs in one direction and with the Firth of Clyde, as well as with Liverpool and many considerable ports in the other' (1978: 70).

Huddart, Laurie and Whittle's chart (1794) includes a mark in Tobermory Bay denoting 'where one ship from the Spanish Armada perished in 1588'. The loss of this vessel (discussed in chapter 3) provides us with the first of many records of wrecking incidents in the vicinity of this established harbour. During the 19th century, notable incidents included the loss 'near Tobermory' on 5 October 1860 of two coal-carrying smacks, the *Elizabeth* (RCAHMS reference NM55NW 8029) and the *Ardnamurchan Packet* (NM55NW 8029), with the loss of two lives. On occasion, damaged vessels limped into Tobermory seeking repair.

Boswell felt that Calve Island 'is too low, otherwise this would be a secure port; but the island not being a sufficient protection, some storms blow very hard here. Not long ago fifteen vessels were blown from their moorings' (1984: 349). Perhaps as a result of the proximity of assistance nearby, most of the recorded incidents did not result in a total loss. The Stornoway-registered sloop *Telegram* (RCAHMS reference NM55SW 8015), for example, carrying coal and general cargo, ran ashore on Calve Island on 17 November 1870 'full of water, cargo discharging in a damaged state'. In many cases, vessels like this were patched up and soon returned to service.

SOMAP has carried out preliminary surveys on the following wreck sites which reflect the development of Tobermory as a local maritime hub (sites numbered in Fig. 4.1 as per the numbering system below).

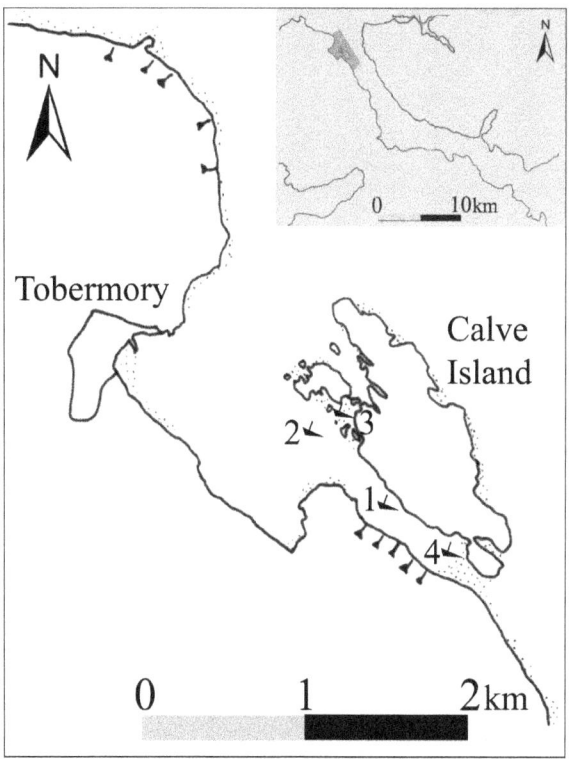

Fig. 4.1   Location map of sites in Tobermory Bay (Philip Robertson)

1   The Pelican: Calve Island, Doirlinn A'Chailbhe (RCAHMS ref. NM55SW 8009)

Built in 1850 by E. Pike of Ireland as an iron screw-driven steamship, the *Pelican* served for many years with the Cork Steampacket Company and then for David Macbrayne on his Scottish west-coast ferry routes. The vessel is recorded by *Lloyd's Register of Shipping* (1888–9) as being 651 gross registered tons (grt) with an LOA of 205.6ft (62.6m), a beam of 28.3ft (8.6m) and a depth of 15.8ft (4.8m). She was equipped with a two cylinder steam engine (built by J. Dickinson of Sunderland) that generated 140hp. Given the relatively low power output of this engine it was probably used as an auxiliary to sail power.

After service for David Macbrayne, the *Pelican* was then stripped of her engines for use as a coal-hulk and ended her days at Portree, then Tobermory.

Smaller Projects

Fig. 4.2 MacCallum's coal hulks in Tobermory Bay c.1891 – see vessel second from right (Courtesy of Mull Museum, Tobermory)

Photographs of similar coal hulks moored or beached in Tobermory harbour suggest this practice was common, storing coal supplied by steamship for sale to the local community, but also for onward sale to passing ships (Fig. 4.2). *Pelican* broke her moorings in Tobermory Bay before she was driven aground on Calve Island in a storm on 5 December 1895.

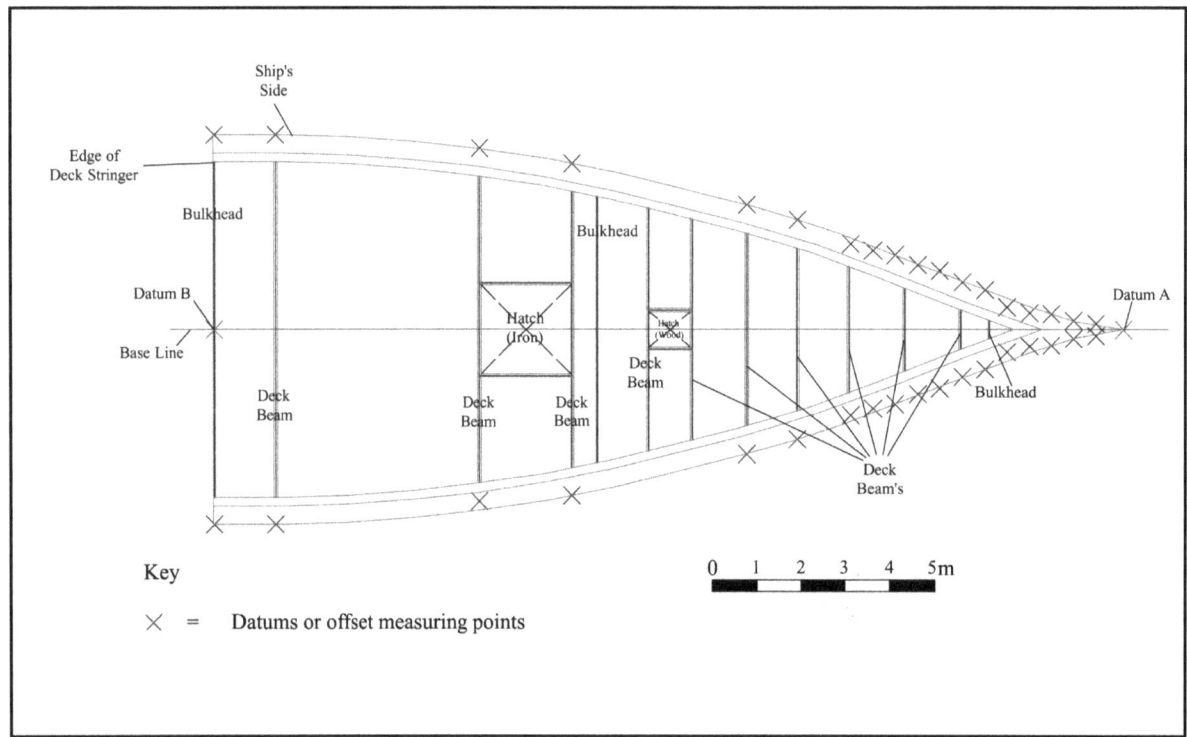

Fig. 4.3 Foredeck plan of the Pelican *(Tim Walsh)*

Sound of Mull Archaeological Project

The centre of the wreck was charted by remote sensing at N56° 36.8993', W6° 2.4930'. The highest points of the ship's bow lie in 10–12 m below chart datum and the stern in 18–20 m (Plate 4.1). The seabed depth at the stern on the vessel's starboard side is 22–24 m below chart datum and at the bow 16–18 m. This site is not subject to significant current.

Remains of the *Pelican* consist of a semi-intact hull structure within a tightly-confined debris field. Additional objects apparent astern of the vessel on the multibeam sonar trace (Plate 4.1) were not identified on the seabed and are therefore interpreted as erroneous sonar 'ensonifications'. The *Pelican* has a clipper-shaped bow (Fig 4.3) and an iron hull with plates overlapping in the clinker fashion, by contrast to the 'in and out' plating system used in later iron-built vessels. The iron frames appear lightly constructed and the spacing between them irregular. The influence of timber shipbuilding may be seen in the use of light iron stringers, visible between the top and second decks and used to strengthen the hull. There seem to be three distinct sections to this site (Walsh, 2003: 4). The forward-area deck frames are intact for 15 m and the remains of a foredeck hatch and forward cargo hatch may still be seen (Fig. 4.3) within an intact hull. Aft of this, the side frames, stringers, supporting knees and beams remain mostly intact, but the deck beams have all but collapsed (Plate 4.2). However, in places there is evidence for a second deck 2.05 m below the top deck, where single angle iron beams are supported on lightly-constructed iron knees. At the ship's stern there is a confused area of twisted metal and debris presumably from the collapsed superstructure (Plate 4.3). Despite the tangle of metal, a heavily constructed sternpost and remains of the rudder are impressive (Plate 4.4). Otherwise, with the exception of some capstans, almost all her machinery has been removed, presumably to make more space for coal storage (no coal is obviously visible).

The light framing-system and hull-plating design illustrate early approaches to the construction of iron vessels at a time when only 10% of the new tonnage added to the British register was of iron. Lloyd's introduced rules for the construction of iron vessels in 1855 and by 1870 iron vessels represented 70% of newly-built tonnage. So, at the time the *Pelican* was built, only seven years after the launch of the famous SS *Great Britain* and two-thirds her length, the methods of construction used in the *Pelican* were by no means standard (McCarthy, 2000: 8).

Fig. 4.4   Attributed as the Anna Bhan, *unloading at Inch Kenneth (courtesy of Mull Museum, Tobermory)*

Smaller Projects

2 Unknown: Calve Island, Tobermory Bay (RCAHMS reference NM55SW 8017)

Remote sensing in 2003 located a previously unrecorded wreck at N56° 37.1102′, W6° 3.0416′, 220 m WSW of a small bay at the north-western end of Calve Island (Fig. 4.1). SOMAP divers recorded the wreck in 2005. The vessel is 20.1 m long and 4.2 m wide. She lies upright on the seabed with a slight list to port and her bows pointing towards the east (Plate 4.5). The vessel has an iron hull and is double-ended with no sign of an engine or rudder. She is open-decked and has a single mast post towards her bow. Her hold is filled with fine silt to within 50 cm of the side coaming (Plate 4.6). At her bow and stern, the vessel's top was 2.4 m and 1.3 m above the seabed respectively.

In construction and design, this wreck resembles a vessel similar to a smack or a barge-like lighter such as a gabbart, though iron-built. A photograph said to be of the Tobermory smack *Anna Bhan* shows a vessel of a similar type (but with a different stern design) unloading livestock at Inch Kenneth (Fig. 4.4). The *Anna Bhan* was reported to be lost close to Calve Island, although several bibliographic sources appear to confuse the identity of this vessel with the *Pelican*. It has not been possible to identify this newly-located site but her barge-like appearance is reminiscent of the small sailing vessels used frequently to carry coal, animals, or general goods between isolated west coast communities, prior to the advent of steam coasters.

3 Two unknown vessels: Calve Island

The scattered remains of a fishing-boat at NM 5174 5493 (broken up by 1972, as evidenced by aerial photographs) may be the vessel *Elizabeth*, reported as being blown up in July 1961 (RCAHMS reference NM55SW 8007). In the same bay, the keelson and keel, sternpost, diesel engine and some steering-gear of a small fishing-boat may still be seen at about NM 5193 5480 (Plate 4.7). A *terminus post quem* of 1972 is postulated for this second vessel because she does not appear in aerial photographs of that date (RCAHMS reference NM55SW 8011).

4 Strathbeg: Cnap a Chailbhe (RCAHMS ref. NM55SW 8004)

The wreck of MFV *Strathbeg* was charted by side-scan sonar at N56° 36.7450′ W6° 2.1064′, lying upright in 8–10 m on a flat, silty seabed and blocking the shallow channel between Mull and Calve Island close to the islet of Cnap a Chailbhe (Fig. 4.1), with her bows pointing northwards. The *Strathbeg* foundered at her moorings in Calve Sound on 3 May 1984. Admiralty Chart 2390 suggests that the vessel's masts were exposed at low water at the time of the chart's amendment in 1991. The *Strathbeg* is 21.4 m long, wooden with metal fittings (see picture in Whittaker, 1998: 292). Her wheelhouse remains. Gaps appear between the planking and the starboard side appears to be in better condition than the port side (Plate 4.8).

The Morvern shore north of Fiunary and northern approaches to the Sound of Mull

Murdoch McKenzie Senior (1775) denotes a scattered group of rocks off the Mull shore east of Ardmore Point. 'New Rock' and 'the Red Rocks' represent the principal hazard for vessels entering or leaving the northern end of the Sound of Mull. By the time of publication of the Admiralty Chart 2155 (surveyed 1851, published 1852), a 'New Buoy' marks New Rock and treacherous reef-systems, denoted by McKenzie Senior as lying off the Auliston (Morvern) shore, are named 'Little Stirk' and 'Big Stirk' (Fig. 4.5). A reef-system around Fiunary Point forced ships to keep towards the centre of the Sound when navigating in either direction. Many of the reported losses appear to have occurred on the shore around Drimnin. Typical of these is the smack *Kitty* (NM55SW 8001, carrying coal and one passenger on 3 October 1860), which was driven by a westerly hurricane onto a lee shore and became a total loss.

5 Unknown, possibly Macduff: Ardmore Point, Mull (RCAHMS ref. NM45NE 8004)

The previously unrecorded site of a semi-intact wreck was found and charted by remote sensing at N56° 39.6124′, W6° 5.2809′, 4 km NNW of the entrance to Tobermory harbour and 2 km from the New Rocks reef. Seabed depths on the site are 53–55 m below chart datum and this wreck appears from side-scan sonar images to be approximately 20 m long and 6–7 m wide, lying upright on the seabed (Plate 4.9). Due to sonar 'noise' in the side-scan images (caused by sea swell), it is not possible to decipher more from them. However, unconfirmed reports suggest that this may be the wreck of the Glasgow-registered steamship *Macduff* which foundered on 20 July 1908 with a cargo of salt, in transit through the Sound of Mull.

6 Shuna: Rubha Aird Seisg (RCAHMS ref. NM54NE 8004)

The SS *Shuna* is the best preserved of the large intact merchant steamships lost in transit through the Sound of Mull. Owned by the Scandinavian Shipping Company and managed by Messrs Glen & Co., Glasgow, the *Shuna* was on passage from Glasgow to Gothenburg with a cargo of coal and iron. She struck on Green Island (Eileanan Glasa: NM 595 450) and was forced to beach on the Morvern shore before sinking on 8 May 1913 (Fig. 4.5). The wreck of the

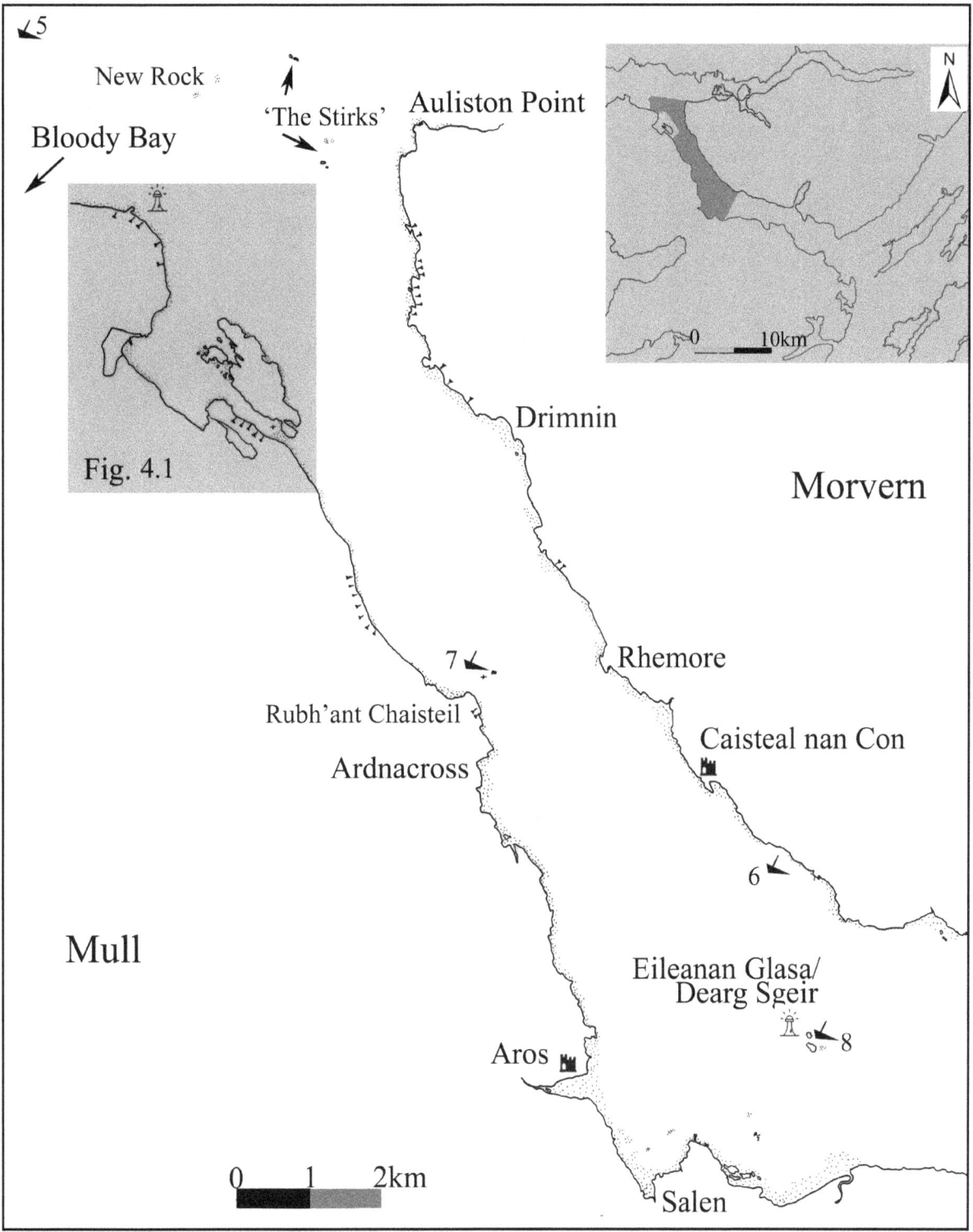

Fig. 4.5   Location map of sites in northern sector (Philip Robertson)

Shuna was charted by remote sensing in 2004 at N56° 33.380′, W5° 54.840′. The highest points of the raised forecastle and bridge-deck lie at 20–21 m below chart datum (Plate 4.10). The seabed depth at the stern on the starboard side is 30–31 m below chart datum and on the port side 28 m. This wreck is subject to flood and ebb currents which typically run in a NW–SE direction, but never at speeds of greater than 0.5 knots. The site is diveable at all states of the tide. The bow of the *Shuna* is oriented ESE and the vessel lies upright on a featureless, sloping gravel seabed (Plate 4.10). There are signs of a tightly confined and limited debris field at the bow. It was possible to define one object (*c*.2.3 m long) positioned *c*.23 m off the starboard bow. Three objects more than 2 m long are located within 10 m of the stern. Nephrops-trawl or scallop-dredging marks are visible within 50 m of the wreck. Although tidal regimes do not prevent diving at any time, some scouring of sediments is apparent on the vessel's port side, forming pits up to 1

Smaller Projects

m deeper than the surrounding seabed (it is just possible that this phenomenon is actually due to data errors). There are signs of sediment accretion at the bow.

The sonar has recorded length measurements of 67.5 and 69.3 m and both datasets clearly demonstrate a steamship with engine amidships (Plate 4.10). Much of the bridge-deck structure and companionways remain intact with the exception of the roof which has mostly rotted through. The funnel has gone from above the boiler cavity and the triple-expansion engine cavity lies exposed just to the stern of steel footings that probably mark the original location of a wooden deck house that has disintegrated (Plate 4.12). This superstructure is off-set to port to leave room for an outhouse on the starboard side of the deck (Liddiard, 2003).

The Mull shore: Calve Island to Pennygown

The pilot Alexander Lindsay (c.1540, see also chapter 3) remarked on the availability of good anchorage ground off Aros castle and Aros attained some significance as an embarkation port for Mull during the later 18th century (Currie, 2000: 189–90). Certainly, Aros ('Arras') is denoted as anchorages in a chart of the Sound of Mull by Mackenzie Senior (1775). He also identified the principal navigational hazards: Eileanan Glasa (Green Island) and Dearg Sgeir are two closely grouped islands which lie between a deep navigation channel to the north and shallow water towards the Mull shore at Salen (Fig. 4.5). An unmanned or 'minor light' was built in 1907 on Dearg Sgeir (RCAHMS ref. NM54NE 19). Towards Tobermory, a reef off Rubh'ant Chaisteil protrudes 400 m from the Mull shore, creating awkward tidal eddies.

SOMAP has carried out preliminary surveys on the two most notable shipping losses in this area, both cargo-vessels in transit through the Sound of Mull.

7   Hispania: *Rubh'ant Chaisteil (RCAHMS ref. NM55SE 8005)*

The wreck of the Swedish general-cargo steamship SS *Hispania* was charted by remote sensing at N56° 34.9260', W5° 59.22W', 500 m off Rubh'ant Chaisteil (Fig. 4.5). At the vessel's bow (which points to the Mull shore) the seabed depth is 24–26 m below chart datum. The top of the superstructure amidships was charted at 14–16 m below chart datum (Plate 4.11). The seabed at this point consists of gravel and sand with rocky outcrops. The vessel sits on a shelf, close to the edge of a drop-off into the glacial trough to a depth in excess of 90 m.

The *Hispania* was built in 1912 and wrecked on 18 December 1954 after leaving Liverpool with a cargo of steel, asbestos, rubber and fishing line, bound for Sweden. She navigated through the Sound of Mull to

The *Shuna* has an impressive raised forecastle (2–3 m off the deck) equipped with anchor winches and the like (Plate 4.10). Four cargo-holds (two each fore and aft of the bridge-deck) have high hatch-coamings which, like the stanchion plating and bulwarks, remain mostly intact. Twin winches and a mast were used to handle cargo from the two sets of holds and can be found between each. The winch and masts appear semi-intact. Much of the coal cargo remains within the holds, but all non-ferrous items were recovered shortly after her discovery during the 1980s. Both the counter-stern and rudder remain intact with the propeller still in place (the propeller appears to have a radius of c.4.3 m). A spare propeller may be seen on the flush stern deck, where many mooring fittings remain.

escape bad weather, but hit the reef off Rubh'ant Chaisteil and sank soon afterwards (*Oban Times*, 25 December 1954). The propeller was salvaged during the 1950s (pers. comm. Pete Lassie) and the wreck's popularity with sport divers has resulted in the removal of all non-ferrous artefacts.

The *Hispania*'s five holds are all visible on the side-scan trace, as are her forecastle and poop (Plate 4.13). The poop accommodation block is collapsing badly now, but in 1999 only the roof had rotted away (Liddiard, 1999). On the side-scan trace, the floor frames are visible within the holds, suggesting that little cargo remains. The superstructure amidships has lost its funnel, but the engine-room roof frame appears to remain substantially intact although the plating has mostly disappeared, as elsewhere (Plate 4.17). A mast or kingpost between holds 1 and 2 is partially collapsed, with fresh damage visible during 2001. Liddiard (1999) described it as intact in 1999. Other features identifiable on the seabed and side-scan traces include the counter-stern and rudder (Plate 4.14). SOMAP divers have commented that auxiliary steering gear (aft), a spare propeller (secured to the forward side of the poop accommodation block) and an anchor lying on the seabed off the starboard bow all remain *in situ*.

In November 1999, a scallop-dredger caught its gear in the superstructure, possibly causing minor scrape damage to the hull and laying one of the masts over on its side (Plate 4.13). Additional signs of damage viewed by SOMAP during June 2001 included newly corroding impact scrapes on the port side about 7 m from the bow (measuring about 2 m across) and on the starboard side of the deckhouse aft of the engine. A multibeam sonar cross-section through the bridge structure (Fig. 4.6) records a list to starboard of 30° degrees in 2003. Periodic monitoring since 2000 and discussions with visiting divers suggest that there has been an increase in the vessel's list to starboard over five years. It is possible that this is being caused at least in part by a scour-pit which appears to be opening up amidships on the vessel's starboard side (Plate 4.15). The mid-point of the scour-pit is located at 316552.650E, 6274856.705N (UTM30N) and the seabed depth is 24.82 m below chart datum, 0.70 m deeper than the adjacent seabed. This position converts using TatukGIS calculator (ver.1.0.2.19) to N56° 34.554', W5° 59.130'. It is likely that a stronger ebb tide and eddies created on the flood tide are interacting with the wreck and a fringing bedrock reef (which extends up to 10 m away from the vessel) to create scour. By contrast, on the port side of the vessel and at either end, there is some evidence for accumulation of sediment.

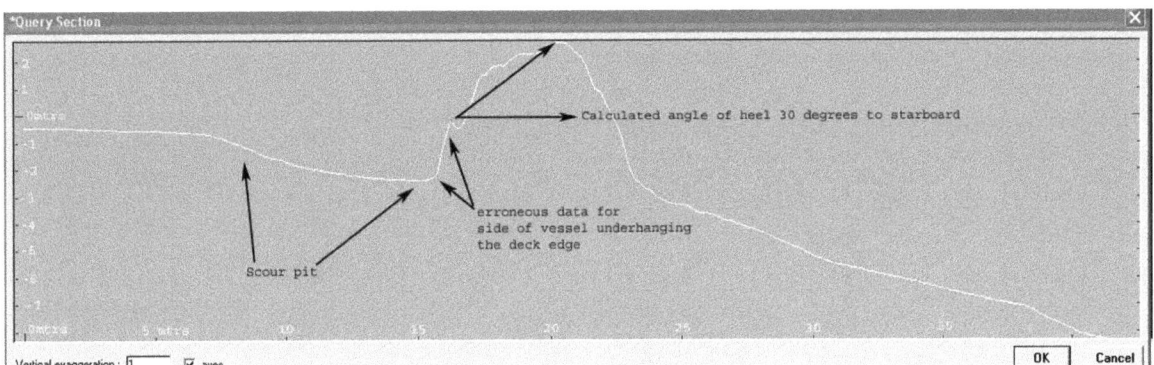

Fig. 4.6   Angle of heel on the Hispania *(© Sound of Mull Mapping Consortium)*

8   SS *Rondo: Dearg Sgeir, Eileanan Glasa (RCAHMS ref. NM54NE 8001)*

The wreck of the SS *Rondo* is located off Dearg Sgeir at N56° 32.275', W5° 54.6667'. Precariously poised on a steep slope, her stern sits on bedrock at a depth of 4–6 m below chart datum and her bow lies at the foot of the slope at a depth of 48–50 m below chart datum (Plate 4.16). Tides at this point reach up to 2 knots at springs on the flood. However, the site is generally diveable from 1½ hours before high water and through the ebb tide, although current may be felt during the ebb, particularly at depth.

Fig. 4.7   The Rondo *aground on Dearg Sgeir*

The history of the *Rondo* has been described in diver-guides (e.g. Macdonald, 1993: 35–48; Moir and Crawford, 1994: 188–90). In brief, this general (dry) cargo steamship of 3500 tons deadweight tonnage (2363 gross tonnage) was built in 1917 in Tampa, Florida (in then neutral America) under the name *War Wonder I* and to a standard design. *Rondo* was lost during the night of 25 January 1935, having broken her anchor cable while sheltering in Aros Bay. The ship was in ballast at the time and much of her gear was removed before she sank. Figure 4.7 shows the vessel aground, depicting a 'three island' ship of typical form for the period, of relatively full section and with a raised forecastle, a large superstructure amidships housing a triple-expansion engine and poop accommodation at the stern. Two masts and derricks are situated forward and aft respectively, apparently to serve four holds. The stem is straight or nearly so and the vessel has a counter-stern.

The slope consists of exposed bedrock steps, most prominent on the vessel's port side; on the starboard side the hull may be trapping sediment carried by the flood tide. The overall gradient of the slope is estimated to be 30° and at its foot (at 40 m below chart datum), the seabed consists of coarse gravel and pebbles (Liddiard, 2002) and bedrock outcrops. The remote-sensing data suggests that the bow has become embedded in this sediment, which may have accumulated around the outside of the bow (particularly on the port bow), perhaps up to 3 m deeper than the surrounding seabed. This accumulation of sediment may contain buried archaeological material. Wreckage at the bow may be exposed by as much as 1–2 m proud of the seabed. Within the hull, there is some evidence for scouring and the plating and inner frames are exposed in places to a depth greater than surrounding seabed. There may be one item of debris (approximately 4 m long) lying *c*.10 m from the vessel's starboard bow that requires checking by divers. Another anomaly can be identified on the side-scan sonar trace (Plate 4.18) approx 110 m from the bow of the *Rondo* at a bearing of 69° (target 0022) at N56° 32.3264', W5° 54.6259'.

Smaller Projects

It is likely that this is geological, but it should be checked on the seabed.

Amidships, up to 2 m of the side of the lower hull remains. Here external plating above the turn of the bilge appears to be intact, but twisted inwards and frames are visible, exposed in places on starboard side towards the stern. Within the hull structure, the remains of what may be a deck support protrude up to 1.5 m off the ground amidships. In the shallows, the sternpost remains semi-intact and 7 m of stern tube remains (the propeller has long since disappeared).

The side-scan sonar images suggest that shellfish-trawling occurs close into Dearg Sgeir, with the closest dredge-marks within 200 m of the wreck. Yet the position of the *Rondo*, so close in to the foot of the Dearg Sgeir cliff, must reduce the threat of impacts to the wreck. Souvenir-hunting by visiting divers has also taken its toll, but the rapid deterioration evident on this wreck can also be explained by its precarious position on a steep slope within a dynamic tidal environment.

Fiunary, Rubha Dearg, Loch Aline, Ardtornish Point

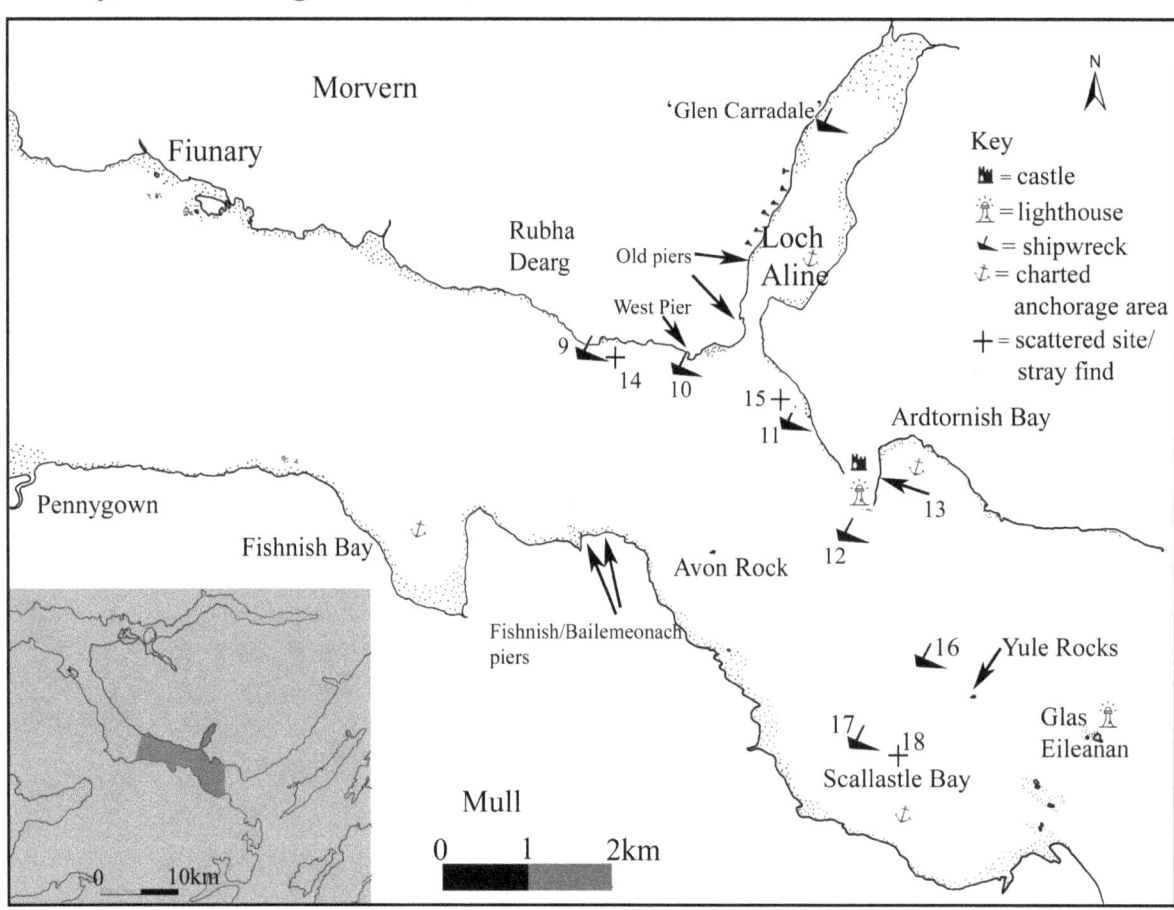

Fig. 4.8   Location map of sites in vicinity of Lochaline (Philip Robertson)

McKenzie Senior (1775) denotes Artornish (Ardtornish) Bay and Loch Alin (Aline) as providing good anchorage ground (the history of Loch Aline and Ardtornish are discussed in chapter 3). The principle navigation hazards are Fiunary Rocks and Ardtornish Point (Fig. 4.8; Plate 4.19), where a light was constructed c.1927, soon after a trawler ran aground in full daylight (Raven, 2003: 24).

Notable losses include the collision off Loch Aline of the wooden schooner *Kalafish* with SS *Albicore* on 22 August 1885 (RCAHMS ref. NM64SE 8009) and the stranding near Ardtornish on 28 February 2002 of the 'full-rigged ship' *Ann(ie)hetta*, (RCAHMS ref. NM64SE 8010), en route from Lewis to Liverpool. *Lloyd's List* (no. 4951, London, Tuesday February 28 1815) suggests that part of the materials from the ship were saved.

Smylie (2001: 39–40) has recorded the remains of the Campbeltown ring netter *Glen Carradale* which lies rotting at the head of Loch Aline (Plates 4.20; 4.21). SOMAP has carried out recording on the following sites:

9   The John Preston: Rubha Dearg (RCAHMS ref. NM64SE 8005)

Work on this wreck site is described in chapter 5.

10 The Logan: Lochaline West Pier (RCAHMS ref. NM64SE 8006)

Remote-sensing surveys in 2003 charted a small wreck at N56° 31.854′, W5° 47.220′, off the West Pier (Lochaline). The highest points of the ship's superstructure towards the stern (possibly the deckhouse) lie in 105.89 m below chart datum. At the ship's bow, the seabed depth is 109 m below chart datum. Judging from multibeam sonar images, the wreck mound has a maximum width of 8.6 m and a maximum length of 19.19 m.

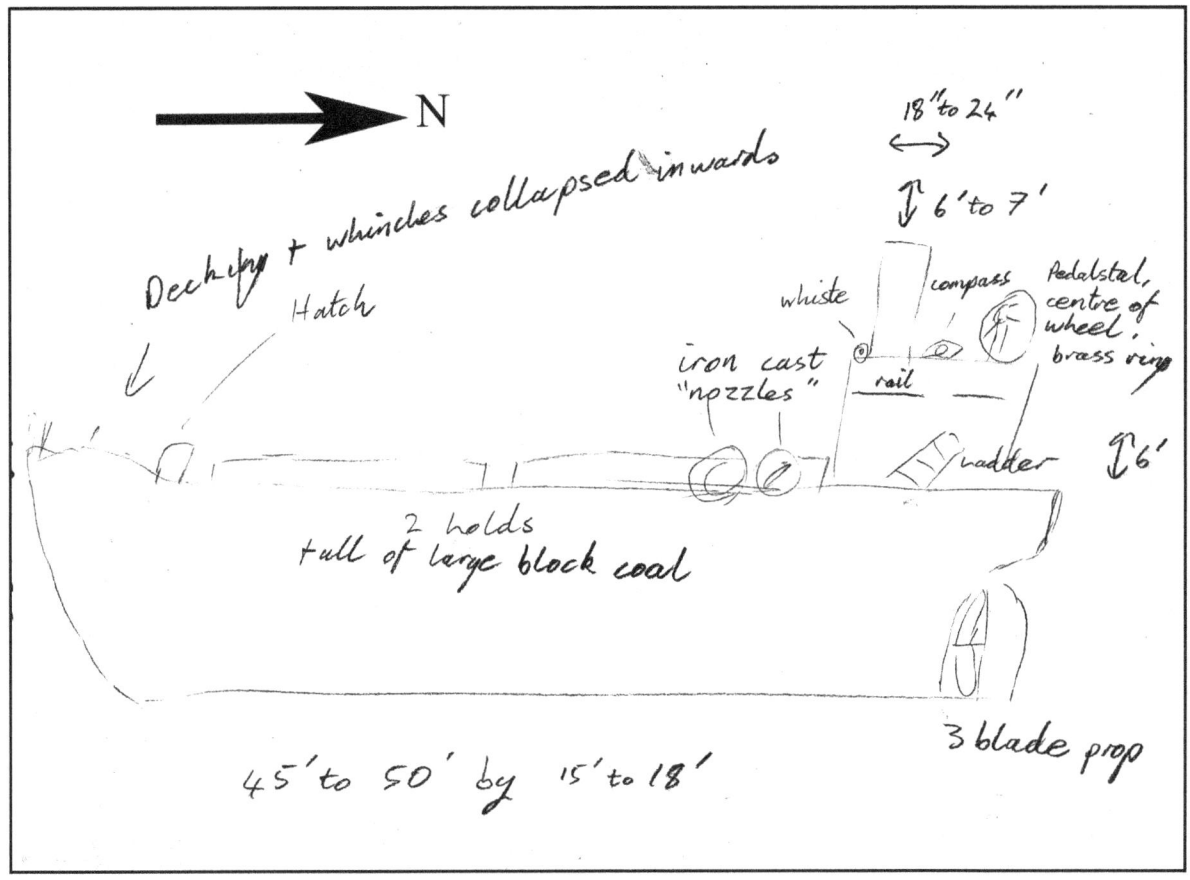

Fig. 4.9   Diver's sketch of the Logan (David Greig)

Despite extreme depths, divers have verified that this is the wreck of the Puffer *Logan*, of 98 tons, lost on 15 December 1961 en route from Troon to Skye with a cargo of coal. David Greig (pers. comm.) has drawn a puffer with coal cargo in twin holds, lying intact and upright on the seabed, with her stern pointing towards the north (Fig. 4.9). Figure 4.10 shows a puffer attributed as the *Logan* unloading on the beach at North Bay, Barra.

11   Unknown: Ardtornish Point (not recorded by RCAHMS)

Remote sensing by side-scan and magnetometer in 1999 identified the wreck of a small vessel on a slope between Ardtornish Point and the entrance to Loch Aline, at position N56° 31.57′, W5° 47.436′. Measurements off the side-scan trace suggest a length of 7.8 m and a height off the seabed of *c*.1 m (Collyer, 2000: 20). Reports suggest that this is the wreck of a small fishing boat dumped in recent times (pers. comm. Bob Jones).

12   The Evelyn Rose (possibly): Ardtornish Point (RCAHMS ref. NM64SE 8004)

Remote-sensing surveys in 2003 located a previously unrecorded wreck 330 m south of Ardtornish Point at N56° 30.910′, W5° 45.340′ on a sloping seabed at depths of between 115 and 130 m below chart datum.

Fig. 4.10   Attributed as the puffer Logan *beached at North Bay, Barra, during the 1940s (000-000-463-928-R: © National Museums Scotland. Licensor www.scran.ac.uk)*

Smaller Projects

Ebb tides of up to 3 knots pass Ardtornish Point; down currents have been observed on the flood tide at the tip of the point.

The anomaly consists of a linear mound (Plate 4.23), approximately 40 long and 8 m wide. At the north-eastern end of this mound, the seabed depth is 115 m below chart datum; at the south-western end, 125–130 m below chart datum. At its highest point (towards the north-eastern end), this feature stands $c.4$ m off the seabed. A linear feature, possibly 5–10m long and resembling a small mast, appears to be resting on the seabed, but remains attached to the mound on its eastern side. It is likely that this mound represents a wreck rather than a geological feature. This hypothesis is strengthened by the presence of a curved track (Plate 4.23), approximately 330 m long between the mound (115 m below chart datum) and the foot of the underwater cliff off Ardtornish Point (45 m below chart datum). This track appears to be of similar width to the mound, but it is not possible to define how deep it is. There is also an item of debris at a depth of 97 m below chart datum, at E330584.166, N6266949.789 (Projection UTM30 N and WGS84 datum). This position converts using TatukGIS calculator (ver.1.0.2.19) to lat/long: N56° 30. 590', W5° 45.131' (Plate 4.23). This feature appears to be $c.5$ m wide and is protruding $c.0.5$ m off the seabed. While this could be of geological origin, its position, some 10–15 m from the indented track, points to this being debris from a wreck which hit Ardtornish Point before sliding down a steep slope to rest some 330 m offshore.

The size of the 'wreck' corresponds closely with documented measurements for the 327-ton steam trawler *Evelyn Rose*, commanded by skipper W. Dawson of Fleetwood (Fig. 4.11). She was registered in Grimsby and operated from Fleetwood, owned by the Cevic Steam Fishing Co. of Fleetwood. (*Oban Times*, 8 January 1955). She sailed from Fleetwood on 30 December 1954, bound for the Faeroe fishing grounds, but was lost on 31 December 1954 after hitting Ardtornish Point, 'only 15 yards or a little more from the (Ardtornish) Light itself..' (Merchant Shipping Act, 1894, *report of court, No.S.433: s.t. Evelyn Rose O.N. 143857*). Ten of her 12-man crew died in the incident.

Fig. 4.11   The Evelyn Rose *(courtesy of Richard Barton)*

Precise identification will probably require survey by Remote Operated Vehicle (ROV). Any subsequent ROV dive should also attempt to investigate the seabed morphology between the wreck and Ardtornish Point, to aid understanding of the wrecking process.

13   Stone quay: Ardtornish Bay (NM693 428)

The remains of an old stone quay were identified while walking along the rocky western shore of Ardtornish Bay, adjacent to Ardtornish Castle. The pier does not appear on Admiralty chart 2155 (surveyed 1851) so must post-date this. It is not recorded by RCAHMS.

On the landward side, a rough track (covered by moss and earth) supported by a stone retaining wall, leads from Ardtornish Steading (built $c.1800$), down to the quay. Two phases of activity are apparent. The older remains (Phase one: Fig. 4.12) consist of the track, retaining wall and seven squared blocks visible around low water and laid edge-to-edge (length of remaining quay is 4.65 m) onto basalt bedrock. These blocks appear to be sandstone and two drilling holes were seen in one of them. Diving surveys confirmed that the remains of the facing stones and rubble infill of the quay now cover the rocky slope below mean low water springs. A second phase of construction (Phase two: Fig. 4.12) post-dates the collapse of the earlier pier and is evident in the form of rough mortar/cement steps leading down to the rock edge and several ferrous mooring bolts/rings.

It seems likely that the early phase is associated with expansion work around 1846 to Ardtornish Steading (NM6920 4326), the demolition in 1907 of Old Ardtornish House (NM 693 433), a late 18th-century mansion house built by the factors of the Earl of Argyll (Raven, 2003: 23–3) or with 19th- and early 20th- century restoration activity at the castle.

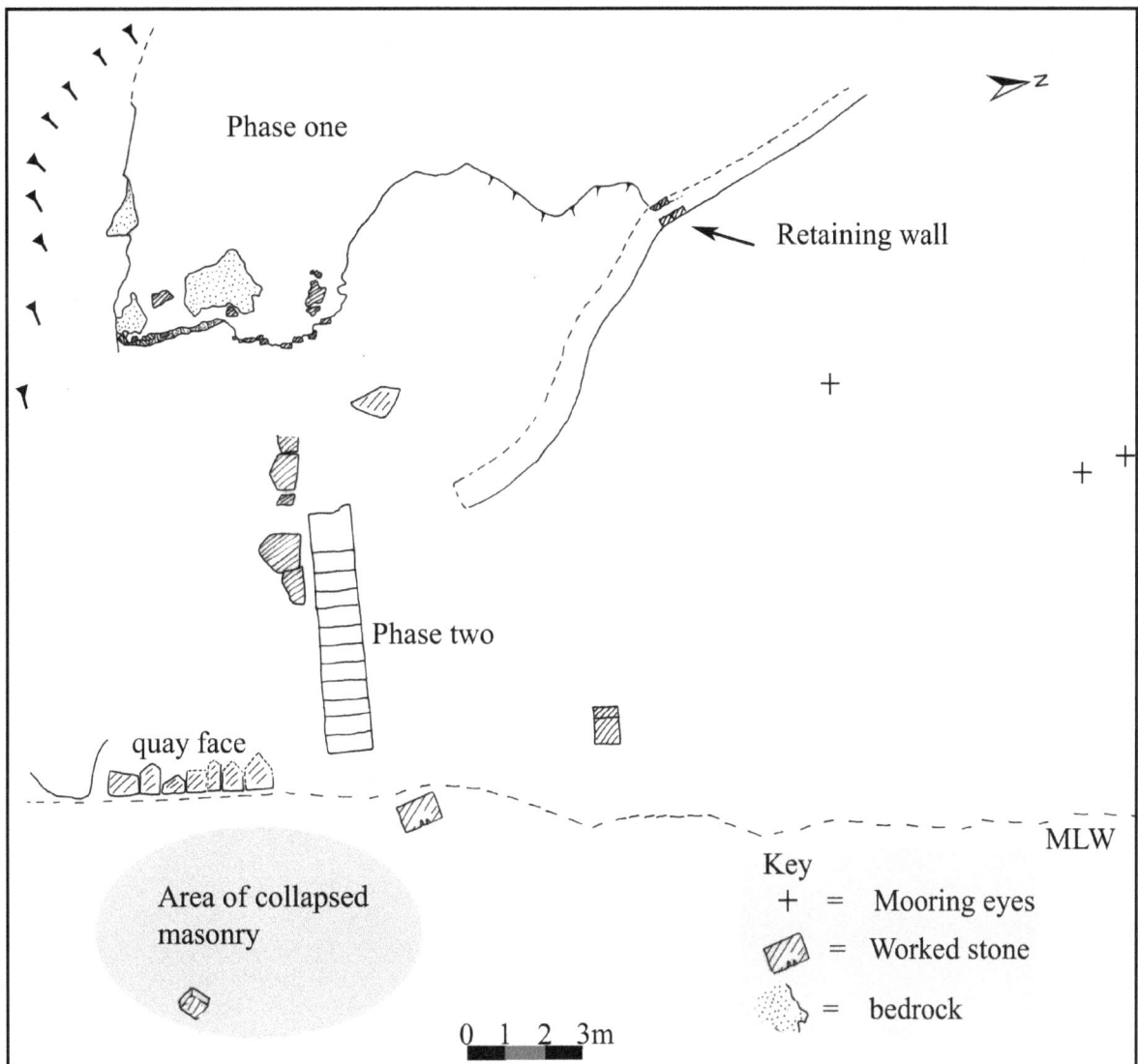

Fig. 4.12   Collapsed stone quay, Ardtornish Castle (Vic Tomalin, Philip Robertson)

14; 15   Scattered finds

In 1995 divers reported to SOMAP the recovery of a round, single-hole stone from steep ground between Rubha Dearg and Lochaline (approximate location on an Ordnance Survey map is NM 665 444). It was described it as a 'granary stone' (quern). Around 2000, a scallop-dredger from the Isle of Man discovered a brass deck light while dredging in 20–30 m of water between Ardtornish Point and the entrance to Loch Aline (approximate location on an Ordnance Survey map is NM 684 438).

Fishnish to Scallastle Bay and Grey Island (Glas Eileanan)

Both Coranihenach (Fishnish) and Scalistal (Scallastle Bay) are marked as anchorages by McKenzie Senior (1788). This annotation is retained on later charts where alternative names for Scalistal include Macallasters Bay (Huddart et al., 1794) and Scallasdale Bay (Admiralty Chart 2155: surveyed 1851). Notable navigation hazards at the southern entrance to Scallastle Bay include Yule Rocks, which are marked by a black buoy on Admiralty chart 2155, and Glas Eileanan (Grey Island), on which one of Scotland's first unmanned or 'minor lights' was built in 1890 (Munro, 1979: 200).

Smaller Projects

Mystery surrounded the possible loss of a Cessna 150 aircraft (RCAHMS ref. NM64SW 8002) in the Sound of Mull near Fishnish. The aircraft took off from Glenforsa airfield on Christmas Eve 1975, but never arrived (*Aberdeen Press and Journal*, 27 April 1976).

Captain Pottinger of HMS *Dartmouth* had favoured anchorage in Scallastle Bay prior to a planned attack on Duart Castle, but the *Dartmouth*'s anchor cable broke and she stranded on Eilean Rubha an Ridire on 9 October 1690 (Martin, 1978: 31). Then, in March 1746, Captain Duff wrote to Major General Campbell 'from onboard the *Terror* in Scalistal Bay', to explain that the men of Morvern had gone to join the Young Pretender (Campbell papers MS 3733/108).

Anchor-dragging incidents resulted in the stranding or loss of several vessels. For instance, the Belfast-registered Brigantine *Hero*, on her way from Cumberland to Riga with a cargo of pig iron, 'dragged anchor in Scalasdale bay on morning of 15th [September 1878], during a hurricane from SW, struck Scalasdale island, Sound of Mull and sank: hull visible at low water: crew saved...' (*Lloyd's List* no. 20,093: London, 19 September 1878). A later incomplete record cited by RCAHMS (NM54NE 8002) suggests that, by 29 October, divers were engaged in recovery of her cargo. The loss of an Avro Shackleton bomber (RCAHMS ref. NM64SE 8003) has also been noted. During fieldwork, SOMAP has recorded the following sites.

16 The Buitenzorg: Glas Eileanan (RCAHMS ref. NM64SE 8002)

Remote sensing located a large wreck at N56° 30.2618', W5° 44.4068', upright on a gradually-sloping seabed of sand and mud, with the bow pointing in a northerly direction. Seabed depths at the vessel's stern vary from 81–83 m below chart datum and exceed 90 m at the bow. Depths of the ship's structure vary from 76m below chart datum (amidships) to 79 m (on some of the topmost deck structures) and 80–85m below chart datum in some of the hold areas (Plate 4.24).

This site has been identified by salvage teams and recreational divers as the wreck of SS *Buitenzorg*. Documentary sources provide conflicting accounts of her loss and the purpose of her voyage. Given her final position and the nature of her cargo (rubber, tea and metal) it is most likely that she was en route from Calcutta to Dundee. The *Buitenzorg* stranded on a reef on 14 January 1941 (Whittaker, 1998: 295) with some suggestions that the crew had scuttled their vessel for fear of the U-boat threat that awaited them on their journey around the Pentland Firth to Dundee.

The RCAHMS database suggests that the *Buitenzorg* was salvaged using remote grabs and divers sometime between 1977 and 1983. The remote-sensing data provides some evidence of salvage impacts to the contents of the forward hold, where use of grabs has ripped a large hole (3-5 m wide) out of the port side of the vessel (Plate 4.25). This hole may also extend to the starboard side at the same point, as documentary sources indicate a breach in the starboard side (see RCAHMS reference NM64SE 8002). There is some evidence for distortion of the bow forward of this impact damage, but it is uncertain what might have caused this.

However, the *Buitenzorg* remains largely intact. At deck level there is a substantial raised forecastle and poop, four or five holds with associated winches and intact masts, cranes or davits. The midship bridge and engine superstructure appear semi-intact. There is evidence of wreck debris up to 40 m from the starboard side of the vessel, but no evidence for debris to port. The starboard debris includes one large object 5.3 m long and 1.5 m off the seabed. A possible piece of debris was also identified 45 m off the port bow. Both the side-scan and multibeam sonar traces indicate a degree of seabed scouring of up to 2 m deep around the stern of the vessel, with tentative evidence for some accretion of sediments towards the bow.

17 The Jane Shearer (possibly): Scallastle Bay (RCAHMS ref. NM63NE 8004)

A scallop-diver reported his discovery of a compass binnacle and piles of coal lying in a depth of 18–20 m in Scallastle Bay. He guessed that this was the remains of the brigantine or schooner *Jane Shearer*, lost 28 December 1879 in Scallastle Bay. This Greenock registered vessel was built in 1865 by J and R Swan, Kelvindock and owned by Ninian and Thomas Shearer, Gourock. She foundered at anchor during a storm while in transit with a cargo of coal from Liverpool to Arisaig (pers. comm., Iain Maclean). In 2000, SOMAP divers identified large amounts of coal (blocks between 4 cm^2 and 20 cm^2), an anchor and a possible wood fragment. The position of this site was recorded by standard boat mounted GPS at position N56° 29.637', W05° 44.881'.

18 Unknown: Scallastle Bay (RCAHMS ref. NM63NE 8005)

Work on this site is described in chapter 6.

Inninmore Point and Eilean Rubha an Ridire

Inninmore Point and the rocks now known as Eilean Rubha an Ridire mark the Morvern shore at the south-east entrance to the Sound of Mull (Fig. 4.13). McKenzie Senior (1775) and Huddart *et al.* (1794) use the name Ardinrider to refer to the point and island group; Admiralty Chart 2155 (surveyed 1851) uses the names Inninmore Point and Ridire Island.

In addition to those sites identified below, notable losses include the schooner *Onyx* (NM45NE 8006) of

Sound of Mull Archaeological Project

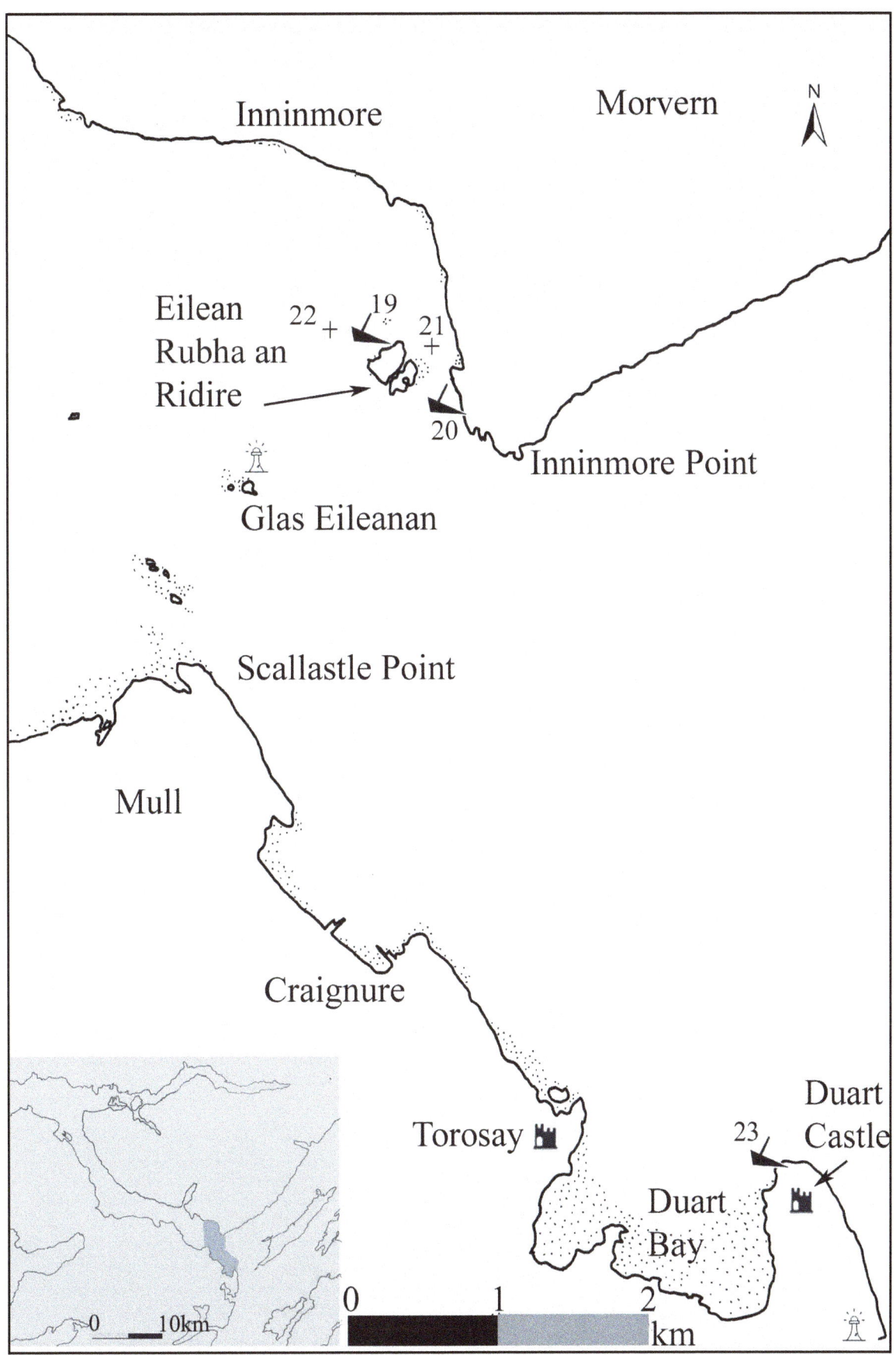

Fig. 4.13   Location map of sites around Duart Point and Eilean Rubha an Ridire (Philip Robertson)

Smaller Projects

Porthmadog. En route from Beauly to the Mumbles with potatoes, on 20 February 1861, 'she has sunk off Point Ardineurder, with mast heads above water at low water spring tides' (*Lloyd's List* no. 14,637, London, 4 March 1861). The north-west side of Eilean Rubha an Ridire may have claimed at least three other wrecks (*River Tay* NM74SW 8008; *Aleksander* NM74SW 8007; *Ballista* NM74SW 8003), supposedly lying on top of one another. The *Ballista* at least, remains visible at low water, but her hull structure is now well broken up (Plate 4.22 shows the wreck in 1973). SOMAP has carried out recording on the following sites.

19 HMS Dartmouth, Eilean Rubha an Ridire (RCAHMS ref. NM74SW 8002)

The fifth-rate frigate HMS *Dartmouth* was wrecked on the island of Eilean Rubha an Ridire in a storm on 9 October 1690 (Martin, 1998: 67). Divers from the University of Bristol discovered the wreck of the vessel in August 1973, while exploring the nearby wreck of the *Ballista* (see Plate 4.22). They applied for it to be designated under the Protection of Wrecks Act 1973. Documentary research confirmed the vessel's identity soon afterwards (Martin, 1998: 70–71). Three seasons of excavation followed, providing a valuable insight into the navy of Samuel Pepys (Martin, 1998: 71–77).

In 1979, after excavations were complete, the Government's Advisory Committee on Historic Wreck Sites recommended that the designation of the *Dartmouth* be revoked and it remained so until 1992, when reports of the removal of guns and anchors from the site prompted a swift re-designation. These reports also led SOMAP to undertake a re-survey of the guns and anchors for comparison with the original site-plan (Fig. 4.14). This survey (Diamond, 1994) yielded a new site plan (Fig. 4.15). Comparisons failed to account for and locate two anchors and two cannon (cannons numbered 18 and 19 on Fig. 4.14) and suggested that further, targeted searches were required.

In October 2003, Wessex Archaeology assessed the site as part of their contract in support of the Protection of Wrecks Act 1973. The team did not locate the missing items and concluded either that they had been removed or were buried in sediment and/or partially obscured by thick kelp growth (Wessex Archaeology, 2004: 5). Wessex Archaeology also raised concerns regarding exposed timbers in the vicinity of the remaining main anchor.

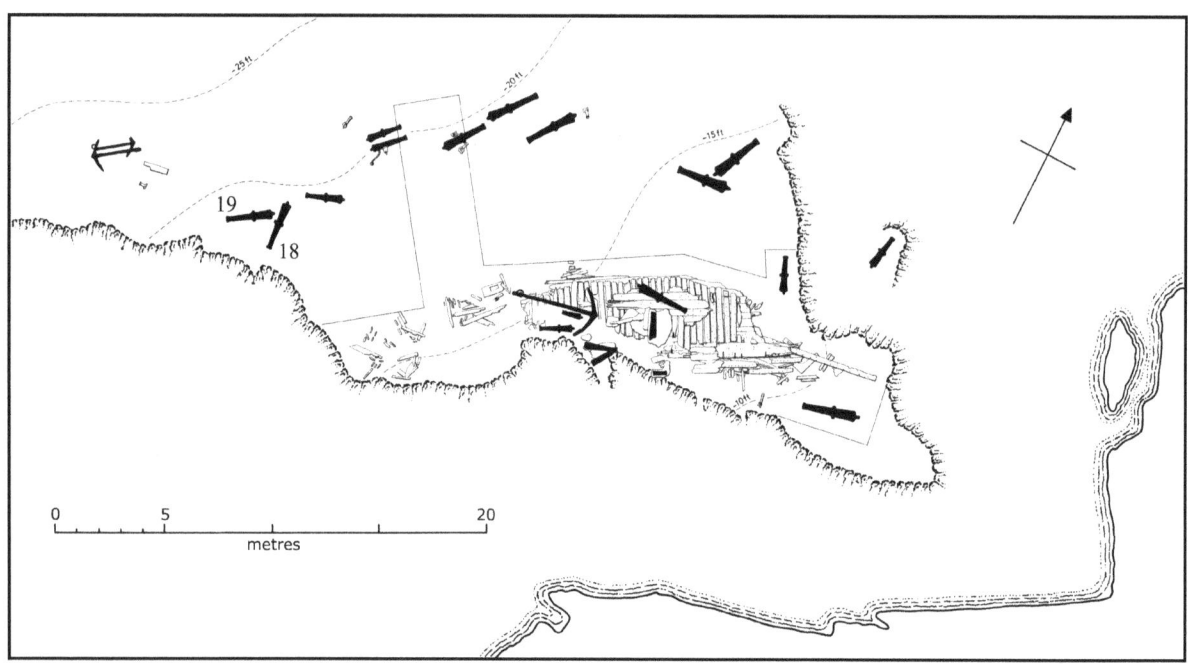

Fig. 4.14   Large iron features on the site of HMS Dartmouth *at the time of her excavation (adapted from Martin 1978: p. 32 Fig. 3)*

In response, SOMAP volunteers in 2004 covered 1 m² of exposed timbers with sandbags and carried out a metal-detector search and some probing of buried magnetic anomalies in an attempt to locate the missing artefacts (Robertson, 2004). No large anomalies were identified although 11 smaller anomalies were found, including a cluster close to where one of the missing guns had lain (Fig. 4.16). In 2005, the author identified an anchor on display at Tobermory Museum and attributed to the *Dartmouth*. This discovery confirmed that recoveries had been made at some stage in the past following the end of the excavations. In conclusion, the cluster of smaller anomalies identified in 2004 may be fragments of corroded iron from one of the removed guns.

Sound of Mull Archaeological Project

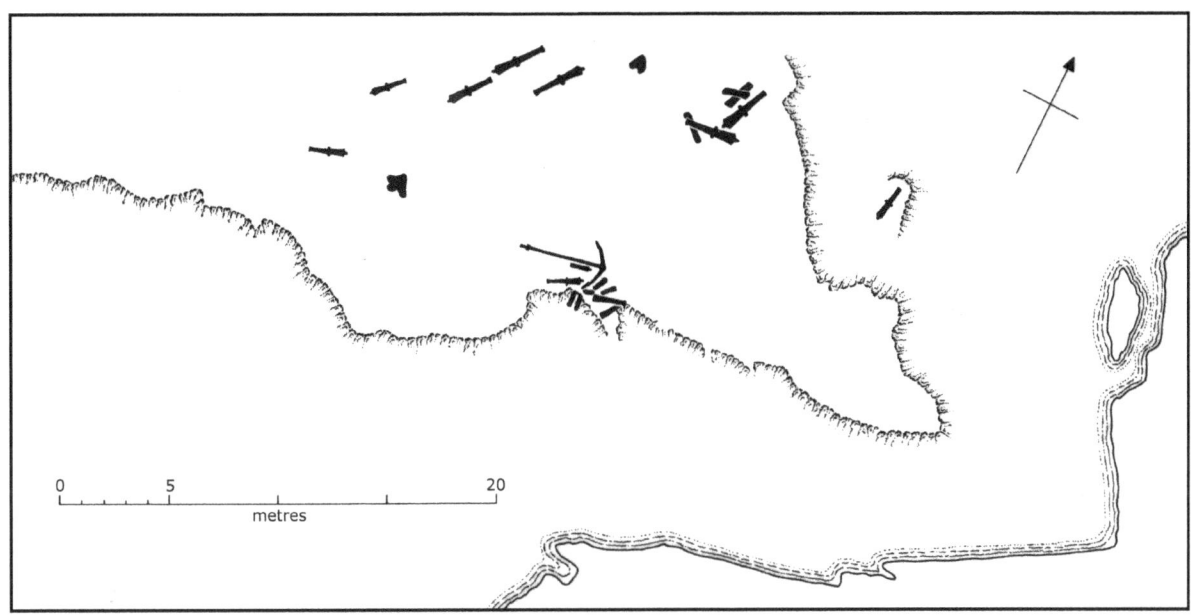

Fig. 4.15   Large iron features on the site of HMS Dartmouth *during the 1994 re-survey (Peter Diamond, Colin Martin, Philip Robertson)*

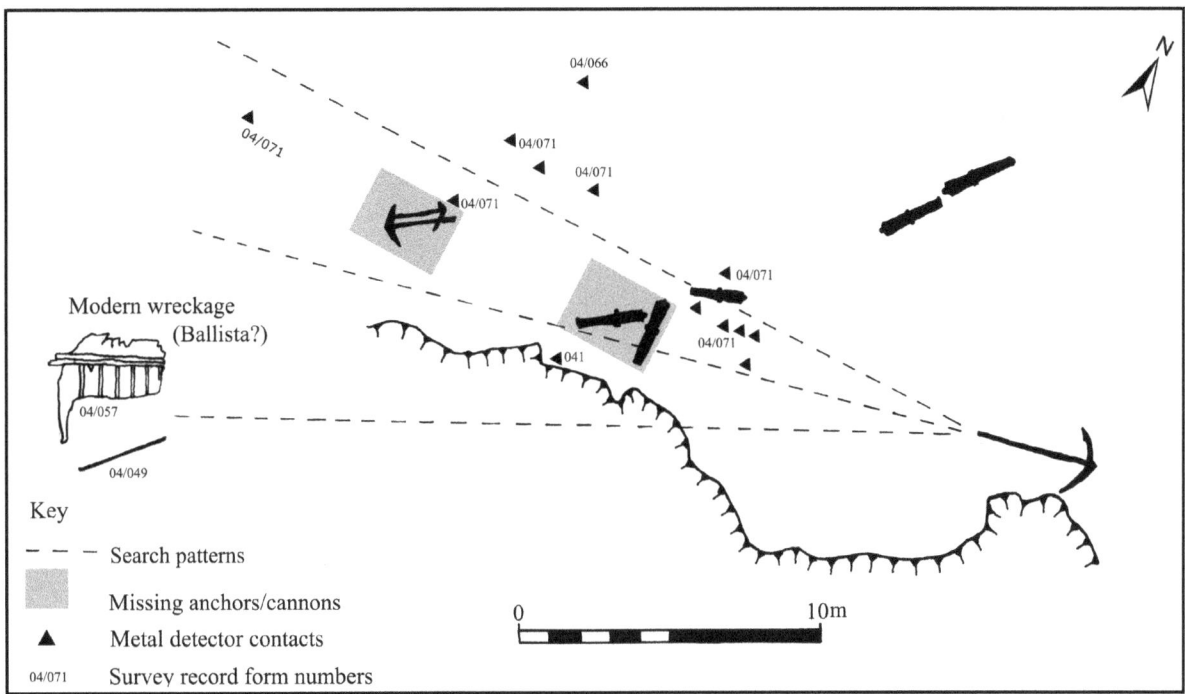

Fig. 4.16   Iron features, search patterns and metal detector anomalies 2004 (Mark Beattie Edwards, Paula Martin, Philip Robertson)

20   The Thesis: Rubha an Ridire (RCAHMS ref. NM74SW 8001)

Work on this site is discussed in chapter 7.

21; 22   Scattered finds: Eilean Rubha an Ridire

Around 2002, a scallop-diver reported the discovery of several large, holed stones in the narrows between Eilean Rubha an Ridire and Inninmore Point (approximate location on an OS map: NM727 428). Cursory diver searches of the area were unsuccessful, but it is thought that these objects are still on the seabed and that they may be associated with 19th-century quarrying activity on the Morvern shore nearby, where marks can be seen where millstones have been cut from the rock.

Smaller Projects

Duart and Craignure

The imposing structure of Duart Castle guards the Mull shore at the south-eastern entrance to the Sound of Mull. McKenzie Senior (1775) denotes anchorages in the bay at Duart. However, Craignure, the modern harbour and ferry terminal in the next bay up the Sound, is not named on charts until the Admiralty chart 2155 (surveyed 1851), perhaps signifying that it did not attain any significance as a harbour until the mid-19th century.

The loss of the *Swan,* the *Martha and Margrett* of Ipswich and the *Speedwell* of Lynn 'within earshot of the [Duart] castle' brought a fateful end to a Parliamentarian naval mission with six ships in 1653 to stamp out Royalist support which existed in pockets throughout the Western Isles (Martin, 1998). Frequent strandings occurred in Duart Bay during the 19th century, including two on 27 February 1860 (Smack *Liberty* NM73NW 8014; Schooner *Thomas Graham* NM73NW 8013). Documentary records suggest that these vessels were either re-floated or stripped, as no traces remain. SOMAP surveys have concentrated on cursory attempts to locate the two other wrecks from the 1653 incident and on wider environmental mapping of the Duart sector of the Sound.

23 The Duart Point wreck (possibly the Swan) *(RCAHMS ref. NM73NW 8005)*

Royal Navy diver John Dadd first identified the wreck of a small warship in February 1979 (Martin, 1998: 48). After it was independently found by members of the Dumfries and Galloway Sub-Aqua Club, the wreck was designated in 1991 under the Protection of Wrecks Act 1973 and a rescue excavation by the University of St Andrews began soon after, concluding in 2003.

SOMAP's searches for the *Martha and Margrett* of Ipswich and the *Speedwell of Lynn* have proved unsuccessful, but the bathymetric maps illustrate the complex geomorphology of the seabed off Duart Point (Plate 4.26). Sediments have accreted at the western and eastern sides of Duart Point. Between the two areas of accretion, the seabed appears to be stable or possibly experiencing some erosion, with depths typically 1 m greater than in adjacent areas. The wreck of the *Swan* lies on the boundary between these two distinct zones where some accretion may help to explain why the excavations have revealed such a good degree of preservation, particularly of hull structure and organic artefacts

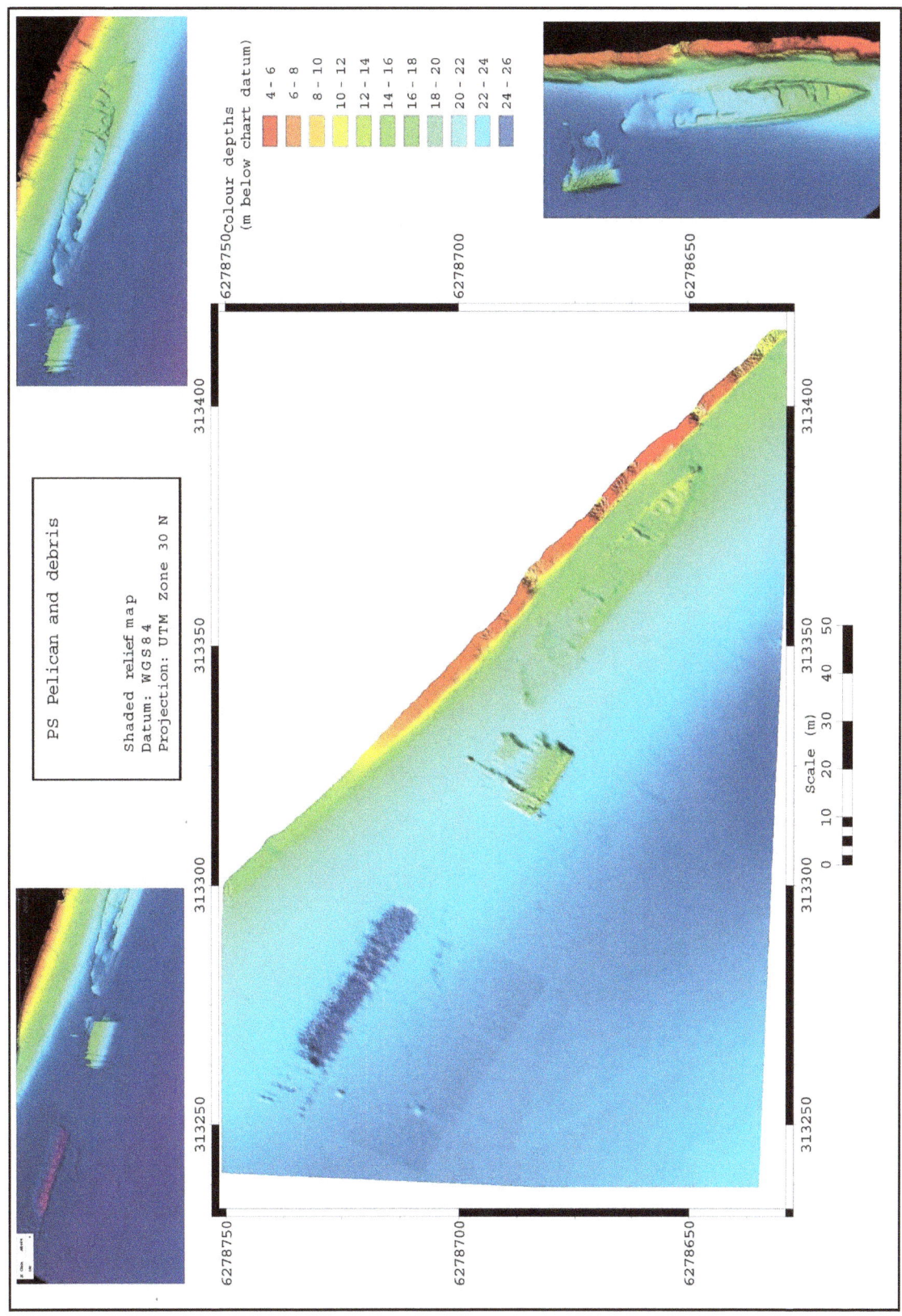

Plate 4.1   Multibeam sonar composite images of the Pelican (© *Sound of Mull Mapping Consortium*)

Plate 4.2   Frames and knees on the Pelican
(Philip Robertson)

Plate 4.3 (below left)   Side-scan sonargraph of the Pelican *(© Sound of Mull Mapping Consortium)*

Plate 4.4   Stern frame and rudder assembly on the Pelican *(Alison Fish)*

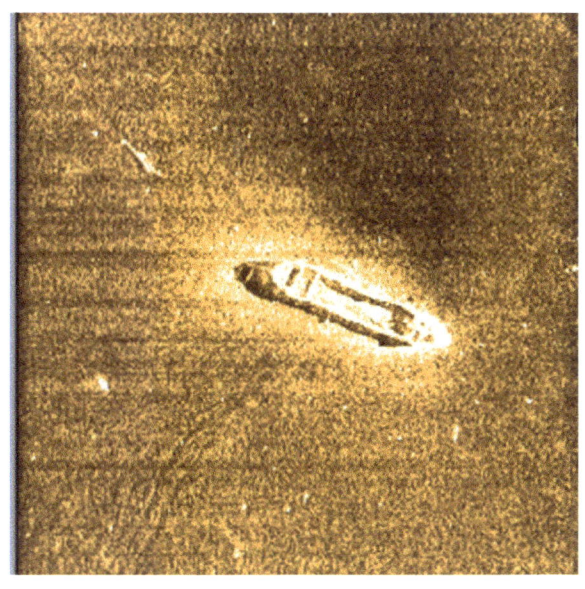

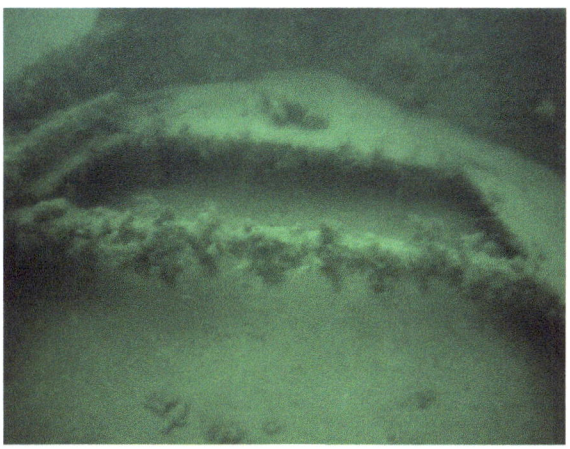

Plate 4.6   Internal structure of unidentified site Tobermory Bay (Alison Fish)

Plate 4.5   Side-scan sonargraph of unidentified site Tobermory Bay (© Sound of Mull Mapping Consortium)

Plate 4.7   Composite image of a hulk on Calve Island (Alison Fish)

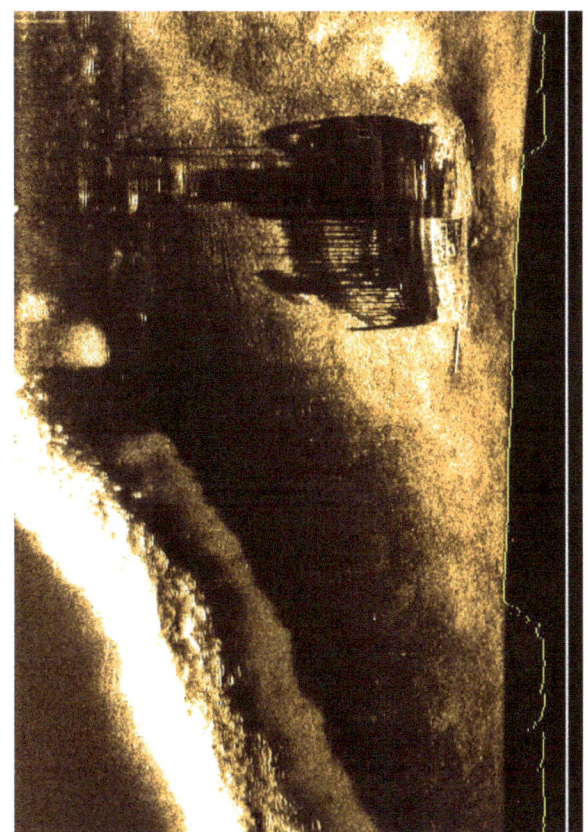

Plate 4.8 (left)   Side-scan sonargraph of the Strathbeg (© Sound of Mull Mapping Consortium)

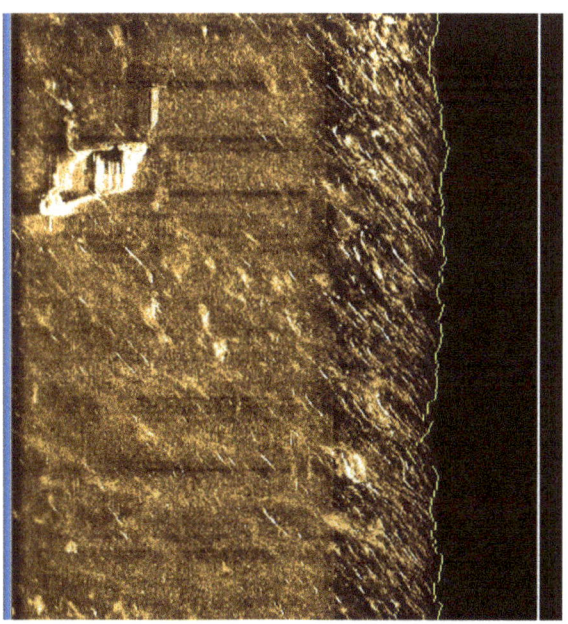

Plate 4.9   Side-scan sonargraph of unidentified site, possibly the Macduff (© Sound of Mull Mapping Consortium)

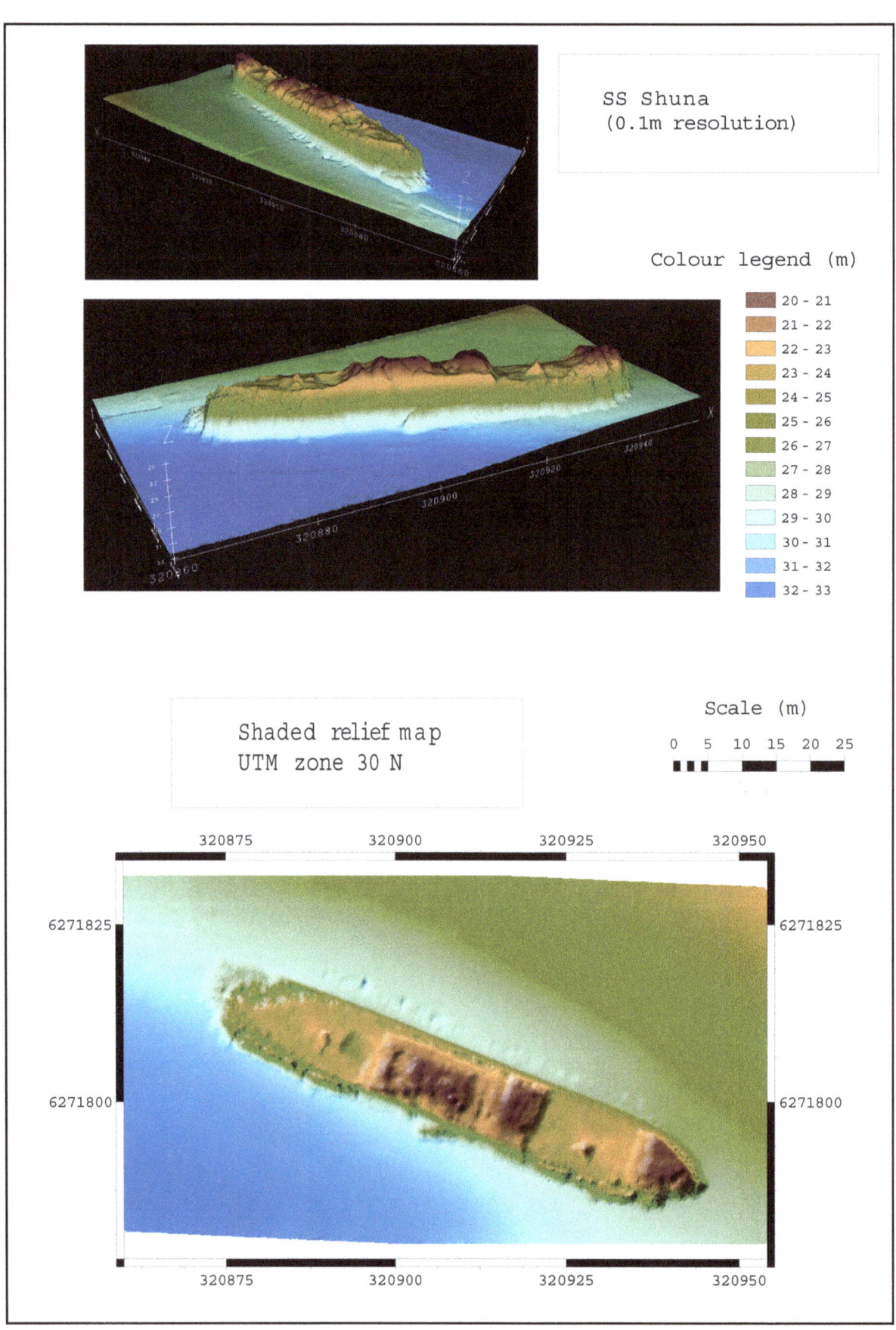

Plate 4.10   Composite multibeam maps and images of the Shuna *(© Sound of Mull Mapping Consortium)*

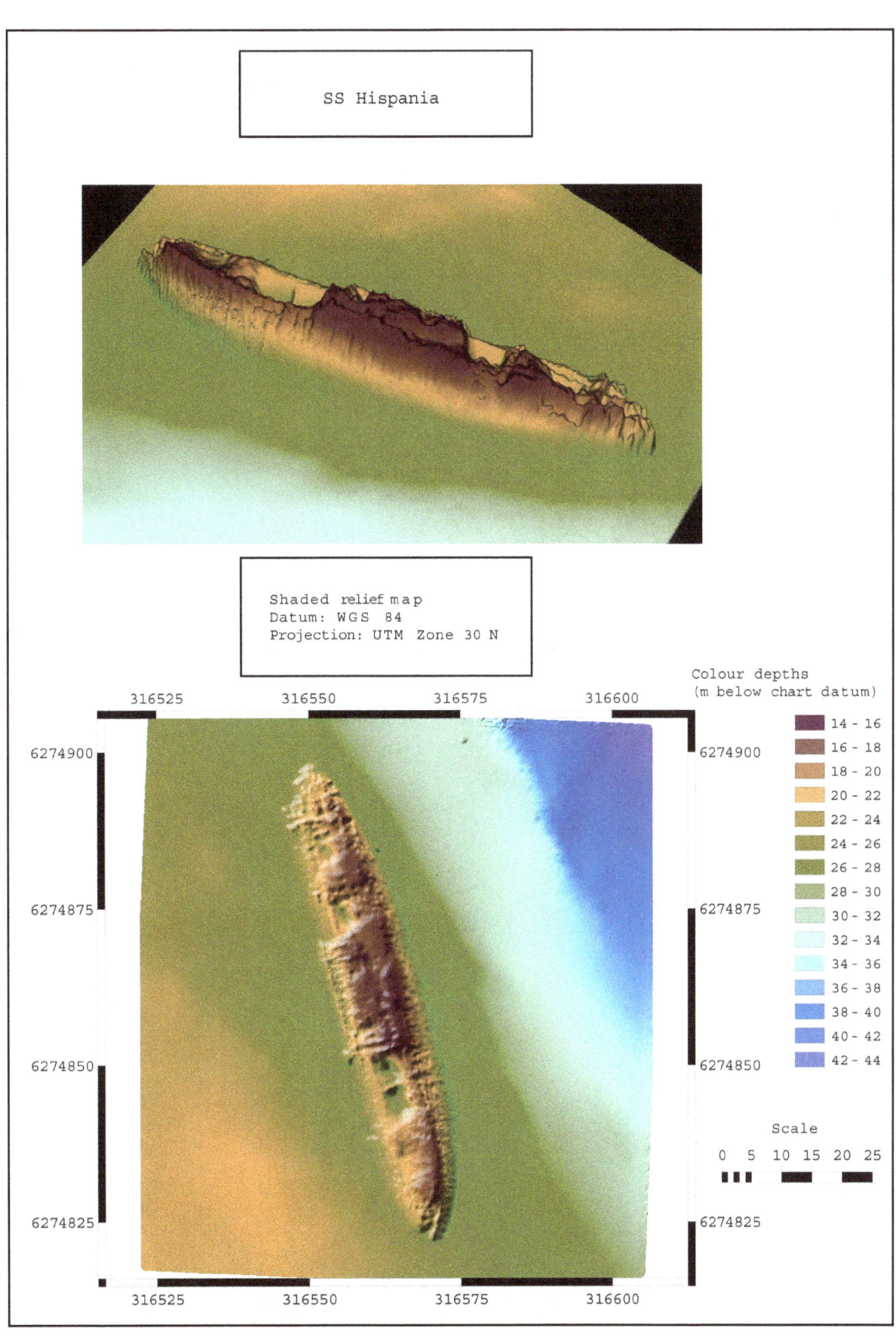

Plate 4.11   Composite multibeam maps and images of the Hispania *(© Sound of Mull Mapping Consortium)*

Plate 4.12 Side-scan sonargraph of the Shuna
(© Sound of Mull Mapping Consortium)

Plate 4.13 (right) Side-scan sonargraph of starboard side of the Hispania *(© Sound of Mull Mapping Consortium*

Plate 4.14 Shadow details of superstructure on the Hispania *(© Sound of Mull Mapping Consortium)*

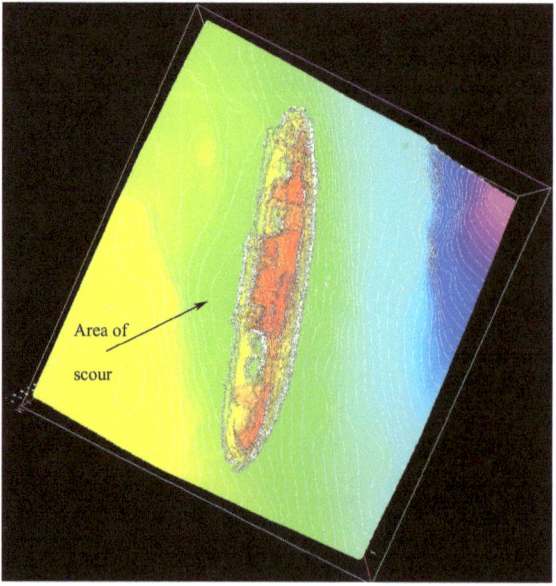

Plate 4.15 Scour pit in the seabed, amidships of the Hispania *(© Sound of Mull Mapping Consortium)*

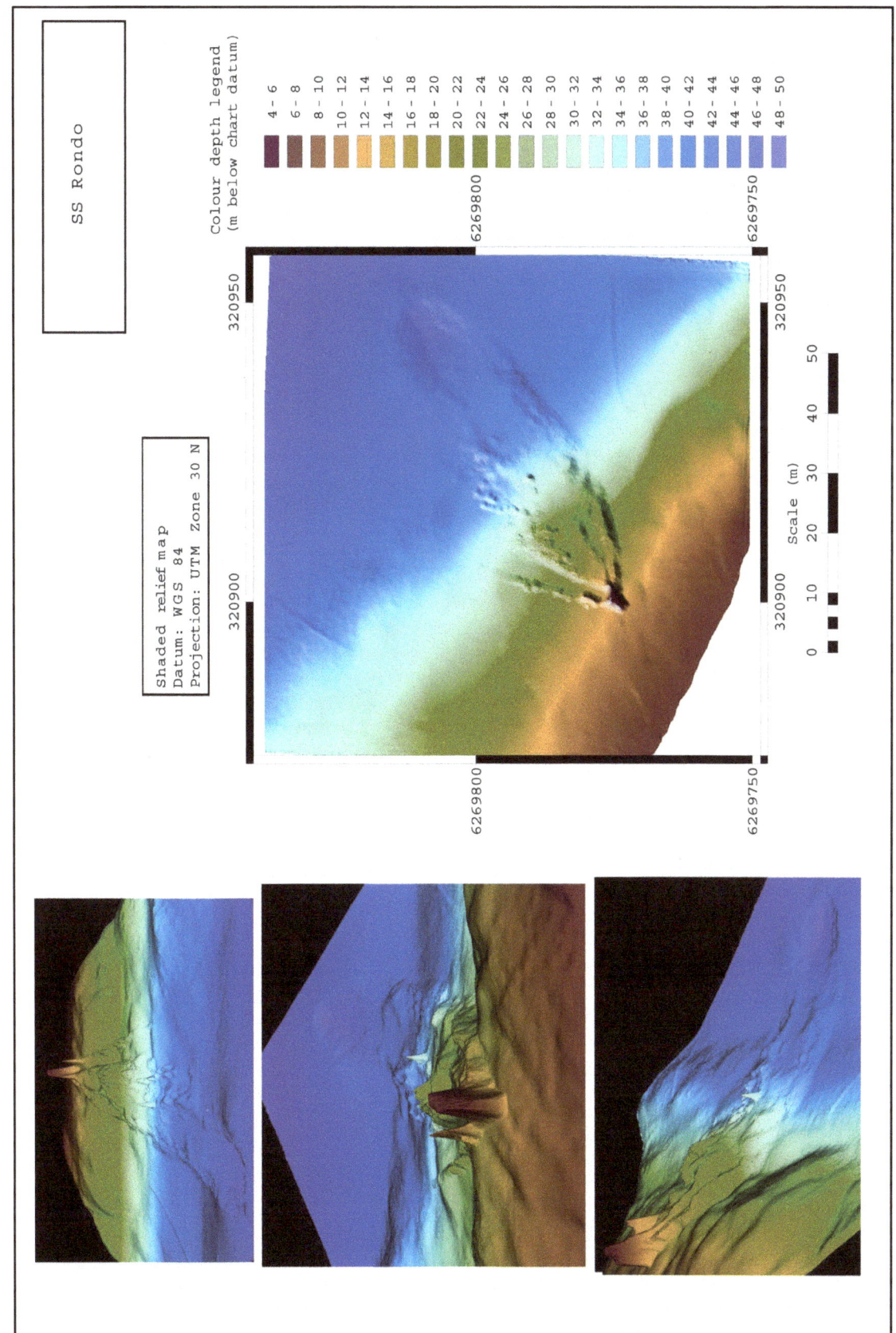

Plate 4.16   Composite multibeam maps and images of the Rondo (© Sound of Mull Mapping Consortium)

Plate 4.17   Internal deckhouse structure on the Hispania *(© Simon Volpe)*

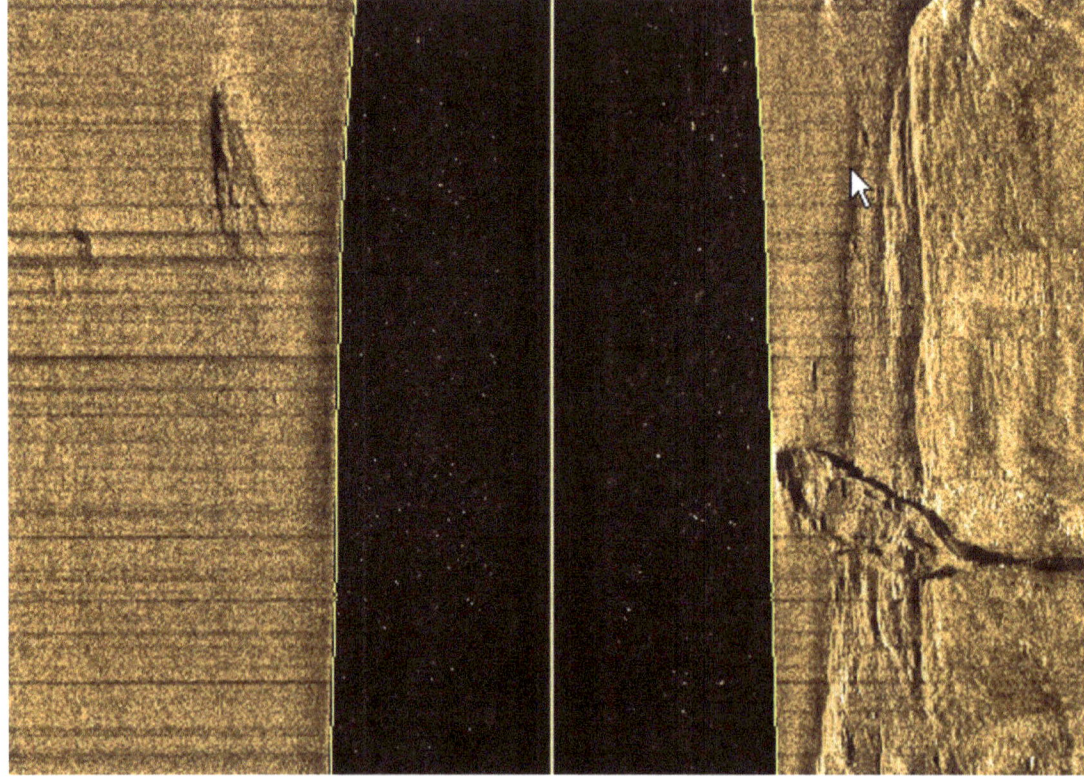

Plate 4.18   Side-scan sonargraph of the Rondo *(© Sound of Mull Mapping Consortium)*

Plate 4.19   Ardtornish light and castle (Colin Martin)

Plate 4.20   The ring netter Glencarradale

Plate 4.22   The Ballista *aground on Eilean Rubha an Ridire, around 1973 (000-000-110-804-R: © Colin J M Martin. Licensor www.scran.ac.uk)*

Plate 4.21   Remains of the Glencarradale *at the head of Loch Aline (Colin Martin)*

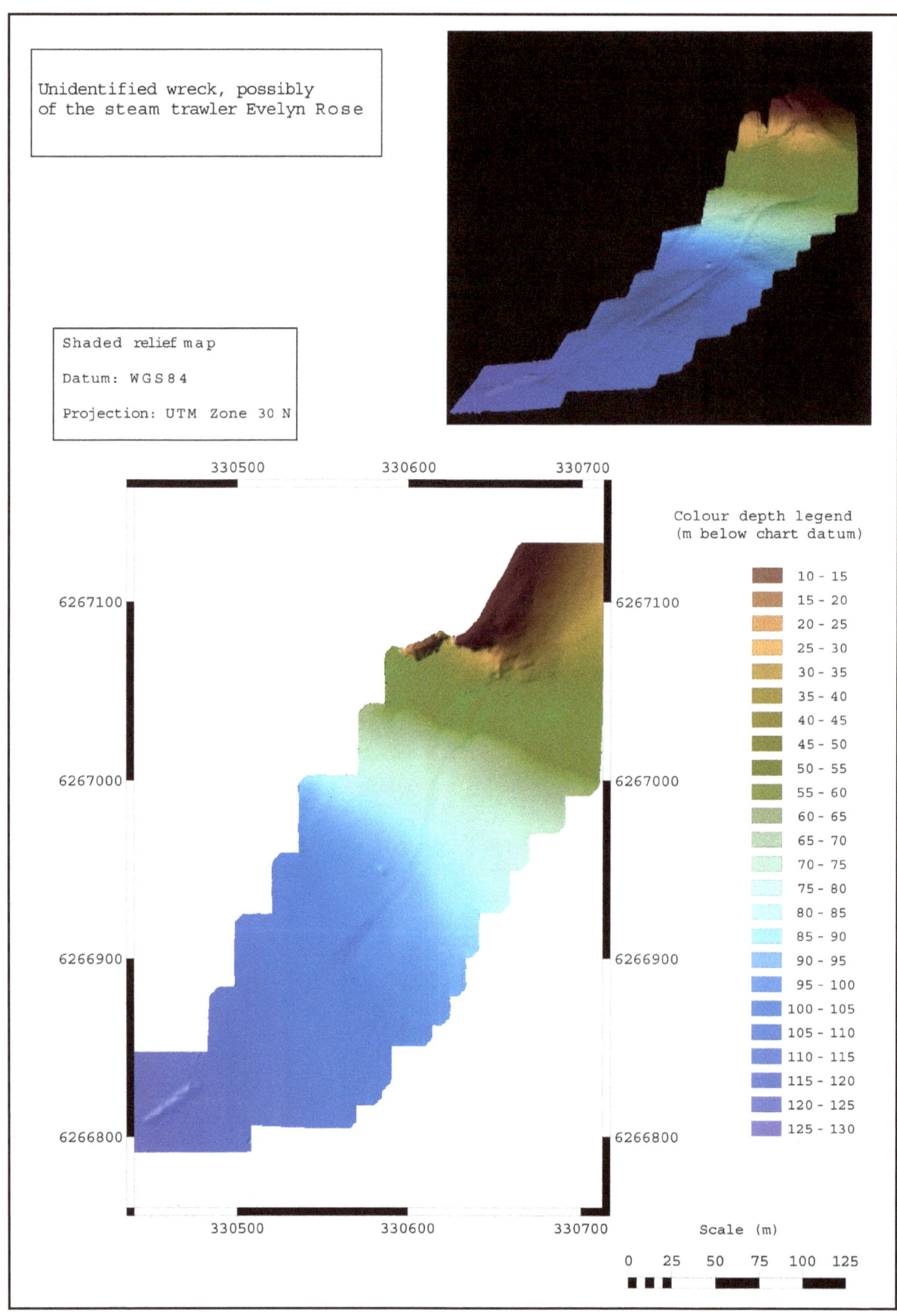

Fig. 4.23   Composite multibeam map and images of unidentified vessel, possibly the Evelyn Rose *(© Sound of Mull Mapping Consortium)*

Plate 4.24 Side-scan sonargraph of the Buitenzorg (© Sound of Mull Mapping Consortium)

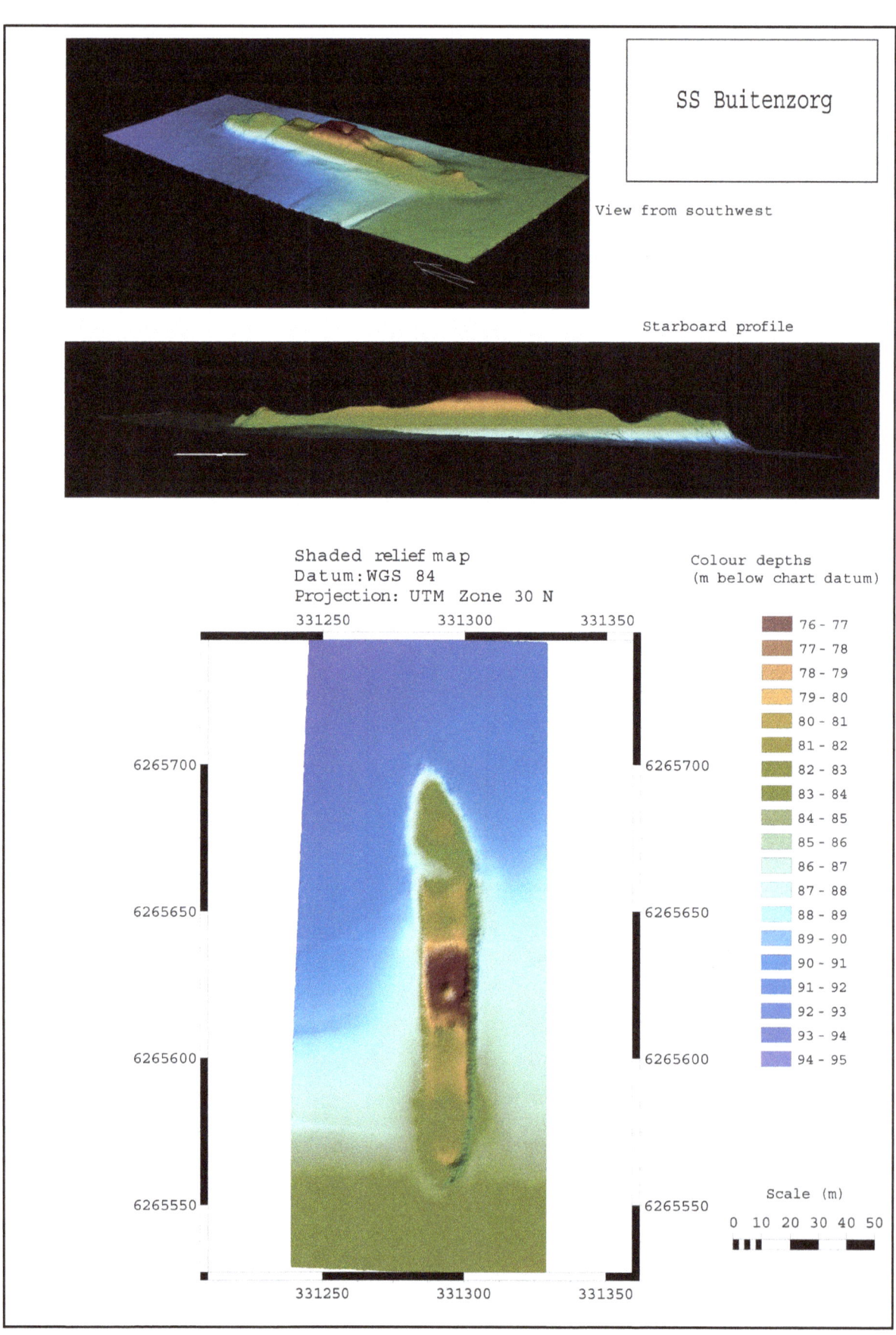

Plate 4.25   Side-scan sonargraph of the Buitenzorg *(© Sound of Mull Mapping Consortium)*

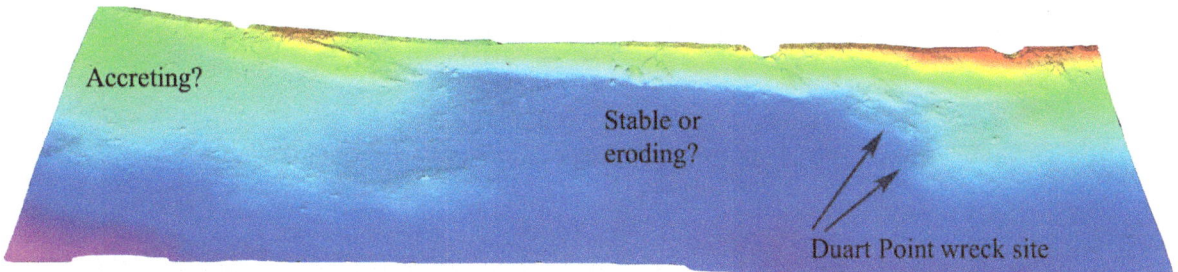

Plate 4.26   Multibeam view of Duart Point area, showing wreck site and possible areas of scour and accretion (© Sound of Mull Mapping Consortium)

Plate 5.1   The schooner John Preston *(photographed by Owain Roberts with permission from the painting's owner Miss Mary Thomas, Amlwch Port)*

Plate 5.2   Recording keelson structure at western end of the John Preston *(Peter Pritchard)*

Plate 5.3   Pump base adjacent to keelson (Steve Webster)

Chapter 5 – The *John Preston*, Rubha Dearg
(RCAHMS ref. NM64SE 8005)
Steve Webster with contributions by Owain Roberts

Background

Some time during the late 1970s, divers discovered a 'slate wreck' off Rubha Dearg, west of Lochaline, on the north shore of the Sound of Mull (Plate 5.1). In 1986, John and Richard Grieve (Commercial Diving Services, Corpach) recovered approximately 250,000 Welsh slates from the site, employing youths from Lochaline to wash the cargo at Lochaline's Old Pier before its sale (pers. comm. John and Richard Grieve).

A consignment of approximately 11,000 slates was bought to re-roof the mansion house at nearby Glensanda and many Lochaline households benefited too (pers. comm. Iain Thornber). A subsequent but unconfirmed and smaller salvage operation may have taken place in 1997, when further exposure of hull timbers coincided with the appearance of piles of slate on Craignure pier, Mull.

Yet, despite salvage and souvenir hunting by divers, the wreck remains a popular tourist attraction. When the inaugural SOMAP field school took place in 1994, the 'slate wreck' was identified as a perfect training site for teaching the techniques of underwater survey and the wreck was 'adopted' by Lochaline Dive Centre under the Nautical Archaeology Society's Adopt a Wreck scheme. Over six years, SOMAP divers undertook a thorough seabed survey of visible remains (Faux, 1994; Pritchard, 1994; Guest and Guest, 2000). This focal study involves a description of SOMAP's work, with a discussion of the ship and the role of schooners in the Welsh slate trade. Historical research undertaken by the monograph authors has been supplemented by investigation of printed primary sources by Owain Roberts.

Documentary history

No plans of the ship have been found, but her evolution has been traced through consecutive editions of *Lloyd's Register* (1863–78) and through *Caernarfon Port Registers*. The *John Preston* (official number 4119) was built in 1855 under special survey at Port Dinorwic (a small dock system at Y Felinheli), North Wales, by Rees Jones, a respected builder of large ships and barques for the Atlantic trade rather than for local owners (pers. comm., Owain Roberts). She was of wooden construction with iron bolt fastenings and is recorded as being schooner-rigged, with a square stern, carvel planking, a standing bowsprit and with 'a man's bust' at her head (*Caernarfon Port Register* XRS 16, No. 12 – dated 19 April 1855). Her dimensions are recorded (*Lloyd's Register*, 1863–4) as L.O.A. 73 ft 3 in (22.3 m); breadth 19 ft 5 in (5.94 m); depth 11 ft 7 in (3.56m); net tonnage 126 tons. She was registered at Caernarfon and her first survey was in Port Dinorwic in 1855 where she was rated A1. In October 1865, her initial nine-year survey expired and, following minor repairs, she was resurveyed and rated A1 for a further six years. In 1872, in spite of further repairs, she was downgraded to AE1 (for the conveyance of dry or perishable goods on shorter voyages) following a survey conducted in Porthmadog. In 1875, following a special survey she was upgraded to A1 and her tonnage changed to 115 tons. This suggests a major rebuild/refit. Then, in 1878 a new deck was fitted and, following a survey in Harwich, she was rated A1 for a further six years. A painting in the ownership of Miss Mary Thomas shows the *John Preston* as a two-masted schooner, with seven distinctive painted gun-ports or scuppers, not often seen on coasters (Plate 5.1). This painting shows a topgallant schooner rig, although she is officially described as having a top-sail rig. Roberts (pers. comm.) believes that a photograph in Lloyd (1989: opposite p. 178) of an unidentified top-sail schooner 'nearing completion' may actually be the *John Preston* during an annual re-fit.

Abstracts from *Caernarfon Port Registers* (Folio 277: Archive reference number XRS21-T2) transcribed by Roberts, suggest that, as was common for small coasters, the *John Preston* changed masters and owners several times. The majority shareholder in 1855 was John Preston of Leeds, with 24 64th shares (*Caernarfon Port Registers* archive reference number XRS16). Over the years, Welsh ownership develops, but from 1872 approximately one third of the shares were in the ownership of William and then John Anderson, slate and stone merchant of Macduff (Banffshire). At the time of her loss, the remaining 42 64th shares were in the ownership of Edward Williams, as captain and managing owner.

Purpose and trade

Table 5.1 transcribes details ports visited and cargoes carried by the *John Preston* during a six month period (*Crew Agreement List D No. 67* dated 10 July 1863*)*.

This picture of British coastal trading in slate, iron and coal with occasional cross-channel and North Sea voyages is typical perhaps of the year-in-year-out trading pattern for the ship. During the last six month's of the vessel's life, she voyaged between Port Dinorwic, Lancaster or Glasgow and harbours in North East Scotland. No details of the cargo carried during this period are provided (*Crew Agreement List D* dated 22 December 1882).

Departure date	Departure/arrival port	Cargo
10 July	Leith to Kirkcaldy	Ballast
22 July	Kirkcaldy to Cardiff	184 tons of iron
10 August	Cardiff to Port Dinorwic	Ballast
20 August	Port Dinorwic to Leith	180 tons of slates
24 September	Bo'ness to Dieppe	172 tons of coal
9 October	Dieppe to Caernarfon	Ballast
12 November	Port Dinorwic to Leith	182 tons of slates
11 December	Kennetpans to Newcastle	104 tons iron stones
18 December	Newcastle to Dublin	83/4 Keels of coals

Table 5.1

Circumstances of loss

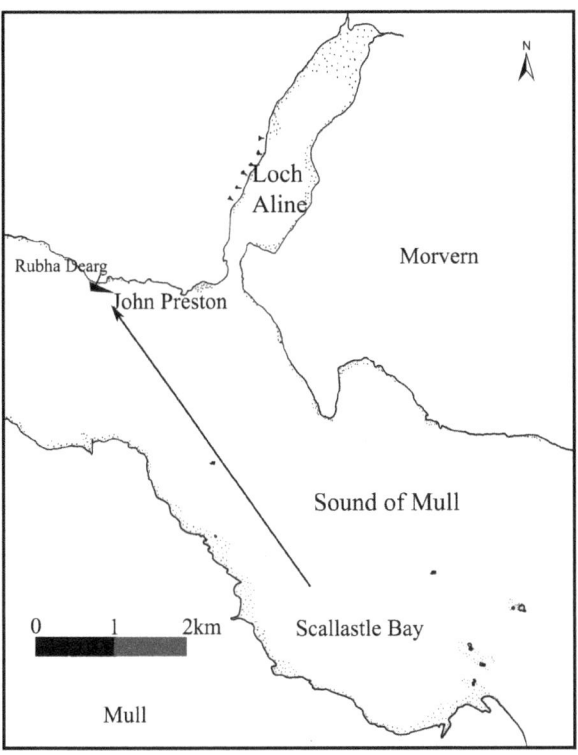

Edward Williams is recorded as staying 'at home during the winter' of 1882. Under her new captain, W. Jones, documentary sources record:

> 2 December 1882, JOHN PRESTON, 27 yrs old, of Caernarfon, wooden schooner, 116 tons, 5 crew, Master W. Jones, Owner E. Williams, Port Dinorwic, departed Port Dinorwic for Fraserburgh [Aberdeenshire], carrying slates, wind SW10, stranded, total loss, near Lochaline, Sound of Mull, Argyllshire (from RCAHMS database).

The Times newspaper column on the 'latest shipping intelligence' (9 December 1882) quotes Lloyd's sources, stating that the *John Preston* had been blown from her moorings in Scallastle Bay and that, once she had sunk, her topmasts were visible above the waves (Fig. 5.1). Her master and four crewmen were saved in the vessel's boat.

Fig. 5.1 (left)   Location map for the John Preston *site (Philip Robertson)*

Geographical location and site description

The remains of the *John Preston* lie in 14–21 m of water on a sloping rocky shelf at Rubha Dearg, a rocky promontory 1 km north-west of Lochaline. The wreck lies on a ledge measuring approximately 27 by 11 m (Fig. 5.2). This ledge is sediment-rich, with small boulders overlying a sand, shell and gravel matrix.

It is possible to identify the lower part of the hull including the central structural timbers and the frames on one side of the vessel. Surrounding the wreck are a scattered collection of iron fittings, including iron knees, an anchor winch, ship's galley stove and rigging equipment (Fig. 5.2). The degree of preservation, of both iron objects and organics, varies across the site. The rider keelson (the uppermost

The *John Preston*

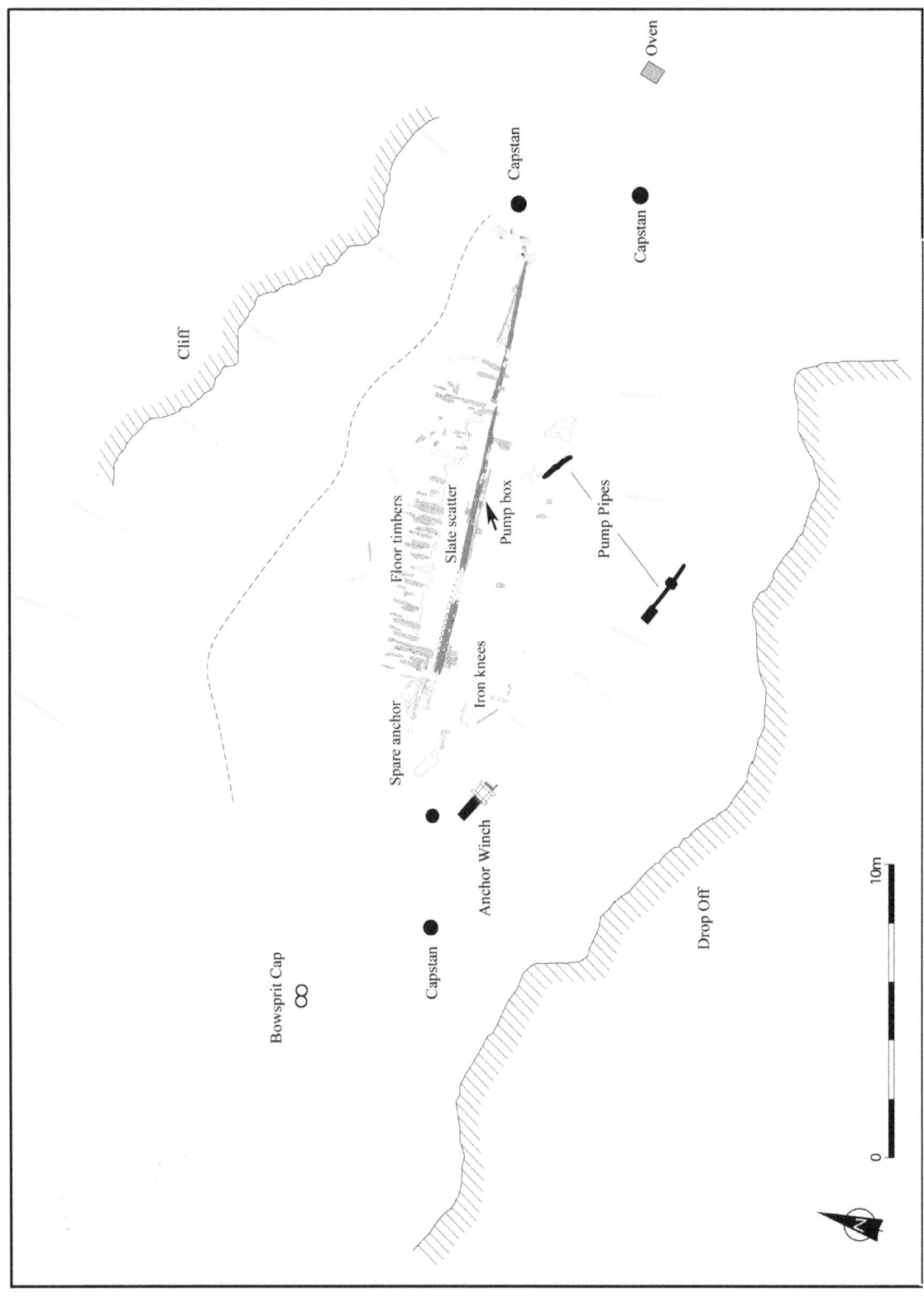

Fig. 5.2   The John Preston wide area site plan (Steve Webster, CFA Archaeology Ltd.)

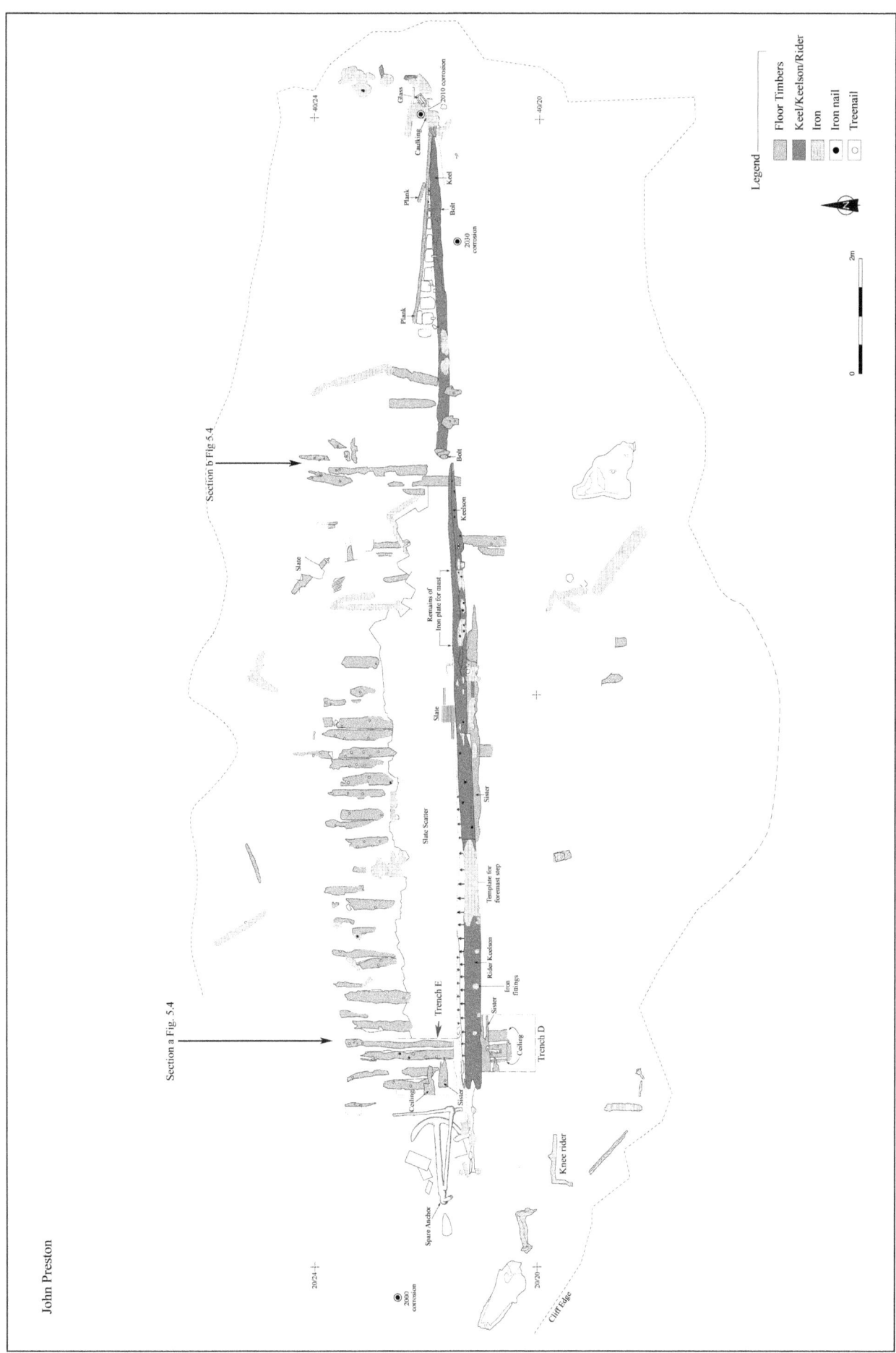

Fig. 5.3   Hull assemblage of the John Preston (Steve Webster, CFA Archaeology Ltd.)

Please note that a full-size version of this figure is available online, at www.barpublishing.com/additional-downloads.html.

surviving central timber) is the best-preserved timber, whereas the starboard floor-timbers exhibit heavy worm action and surface erosion in places but survive in good condition in others. This may be explained by the partial coverage of these timbers by the slate cargo prior to salvage. Similarly, the degree of corrosion of the iron objects appears to vary from area to area within the wreck, with the better-preserved objects generally located in the area around the keelson. Non-ferrous metals were poorly represented, but when found, were well preserved.

Work undertaken

Many mistakes have been made and lessons learned since recording began on the *John Preston* in 1994. The initial strategy revolved around constructing a site 'web' of measurements, by measuring between datum points fixed to individual objects within the site. Datums consisted of plastic tags fixed by string (in the case of iron objects) or nails (in the case of the wooden features). Attempts were made to take four straight-line measurements and a relative depth measurement for each datum, though this was not possible in all cases. By these means, coherent networks of measurements were generated during the course of each season. However, it proved to be impossible to unite measurements taken in different years to produce an overall site-plan. Lost and moving datum-tags, erroneous measurements, topographic obstructions and poor post-dive recording were all contributory factors. Attempts were made to address these problems by repeating measurements and adding new datums to shorten the measurement distances. However, the problems associated with tags and objects moving were insurmountable.

By 1997 it was becoming clear that fresh areas of hull were being exposed. This, combined with verifiable damage to certain areas of the site, prompted a change of strategy. In 1999, a major hull-recording programme was undertaken in an effort to record the exposed areas before the condition of the wreck deteriorated further. Instead of using multiple datum points, the team adopted a grid-based recording system using a small number of fixed control-points.

The grid set up in 1999 was 20 m E-W by 4 m N-S. It was marked at each corner with wooden pegs driven in to the seabed. The accuracy of the grid and its corner points was checked using Web for Windows (Rule, 1989). Within this grid, 1-m wide tape measure corridors were fixed in place and planning frames were used to draw all seabed features at a scale of 1:20.

Given observations on the deterioration of the hull, the project team decided to undertake some limited excavation to aid understanding of the stratigraphy of the deposits overlying the ship and the construction of the vessel. Three trial-trenches of approximately 1m square were dug by hand to a depth of approximately 60 cm. All stratigraphy was recorded and planning-frames were used to record the buried hull features. The trenches were then back-filled and stabilised with sandbags.

Several site-monitoring techniques were deployed to enhance understanding of the seabed environment and its impact on archaeology. The wreck was surveyed in 2000 and 2003 by remote sensing (as discussed in chapter 3). Five seabed sediment stakes were embedded at selected points around the wreck (Cook and Kaye, 2000). These stakes monitor corrosion levels within buried sediments and also indicate sedimentation levels relative to the embedded rod. By repeating measurements of sediment levels at fixed intervals, an understanding of sedimentation processes can be gained (Plate 3.5).

Results

The vessel

The surviving timber structure covered an area 18.90 m long (E-W) and up to 5.30 m wide (N-S). The evidence for the orientation of the vessel is based on the position of several iron objects and of the hull remains at the east end of the site. At this point, cant-frames and outer planking at the run of the vessel lead to the base of two vertical timbers interpreted as remains of the sternpost structure (Fig. 5.3). A possible gudgeon or pintle strap and fittings from the stern of the ship, including a deck light and a small oven were also identified in this area, reinforcing this hypothesis. To the west there is no evidence of the stempost and the end piece of timber is heavily abraded. However, the existence of a folded stocked anchor which may have been a spare stowed in the bow locker and a bowsprit cap some distance off to the west of the main site points to this being the bow area. The presence of a large Armstrong-patent windlass down the slope at the western end of the site confirms this.

The length of the central structural timbers was 18.90 m, shorter than might have been expected from examination of the documentary records of the *John Preston* (*Lloyd's Register*, 1863). Any missing length, however, may be accounted for by the breaking off of the stempost, apron and deadwood and the subsequent erosion of the thinner forward end of the keel, which appears to have been exposed for some time. On the vessel's starboard side, the floor frames are fully exposed. The recorded length of the floors (2.30 or 2.10 m, see below) closely matches the documentary evidence for the *John Preston* (*Lloyd's Register*,

The *John Preston*

1863–4). On the port side, except in one or two places where the frame ends are visible, the frames remain buried (Fig. 5.4). Sections a and b (Fig. 5.3; Fig. 5.4) indicate that the vessel is listing at about 30° to port, with the result that the hull on the vessel's port side may be preserved up to the turn of the bilge under a layer of slate and seabed deposits. Excavation of trenches D and E to a depth of 60 cm revealed a sediment matrix consisting of a mid-grey clay (with a high organic content in the area around the timbers), capped by a 2–3-cm thick layer of loose sand and shell.

This excavation led to identification of the central structural timbers. The uppermost surviving timber was the rider keelson (Fig. 5.3; 5.4; Plate 5.2). This was 26 cm wide and 30 cm thick and survived for a length of 6.22 m. The presence of scarf joints at either end of the rider indicates that it was made up of three or four individual timbers. There was no evidence of any mast-step cut into the rider keelson. However, the presence of an area of heavy corrosion, measuring 1.12 m long by 0.26 m wide, located 5.60 m from the projected position of the stempost, indicates the presence of a substantial wooden mast-step or perhaps an iron plate bolted on to the rider. These features were used to spread the weight of a mast stepped in the vessel with an iron shoe.

The rider keelson rested directly on top of the keelson. This was a single timber 26 cm wide, 36 cm thick and surviving to a length of 10.96 m. Both ends terminated in heavily eroded breaks and the top surface of the timber was heavily abraded where the overlying rider was missing. In the area around the projected position of the mainmast, there were more bolt holes than was the case elsewhere, further evidence for the fastening of an iron plate to the overlying rider. Beneath the keelson, the surface of the keel was visible. It was 26 cm wide and survived to a length of 18.90 m, with a break approximately 6.50 m forward of the sternpost. This corresponds

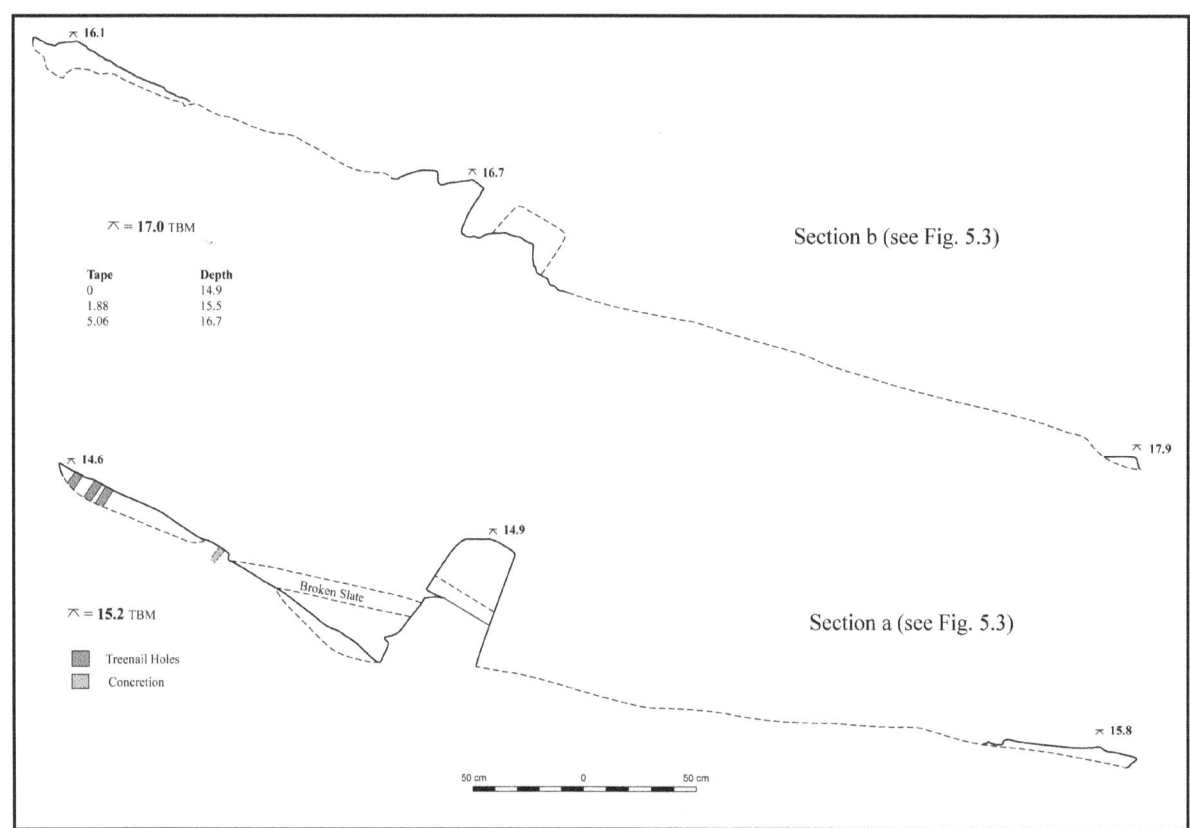

Fig. 5.4   Elevation sections through hull structure of the John Preston *(Antony Firth)*

with the broken end of the keelson, suggesting that the vessel may have broken her back at this point.

To the south of the keelson and in trench D, wooden beams were recorded running parallel to, and either side of, the keel line. They were 22 cm wide and 8–9 cm thick with a maximum visible length of 4.20 m (amidships on the port side) and probably represent the remains of narrow sister beams. The sisters abutted the keelson, but were only bolted on to the floor timbers.

The floors are exposed along the ship's starboard side, to varying degrees, along the full length of the vessel, but are buried on the port side. A few possible first futtocks were recorded on the starboard side but in all cases they had become detached from the floors. The floor timbers were all 16–20 cm wide by 23 cm thick and survived to a maximum of 2.10 m from the keel. The best preserved of these indicate that 20 cm (8 in) may have been the standard width. There was clear evidence for the pairing of floors. Evidence of fastenings was scarce. It appears that the paired floors may have been fastened together with treenails, rather than iron bolts, with only one of each pair bolted into the keel/keelson structure. A limber hole was identified by hand through the sediment, but not actually seen.

At the stern, the starboard cant frames were visible along the 4-m run of the vessel. These timbers, 20 cm wide and 5–24 cm thick, were fixed to the outer edge of the keel. They sloped out at an angle of 60–75° to the horizontal. These timbers were also paired and were fastened to the keel with treenails which also served to attach the outer planking. The cant frames gave way to horizontal floors at between 4 and 5.5 m from the aft edge of the heavily abraded sternpost.

The outer planking was visible only in one area between the starboard floors and along the run of the vessel. It was 6–7cm thick and was fastened to the frames with treenails in a diagonally paired pattern. Each strake was fixed to only one of the paired frames. The discovery of several pieces of copper sheet, each with nail-holes around the unbroken sides, has been taken to be evidence of the vessels sheathing. All recorded fragments were found to be broken along two sides. Probing in the stern area indicated that the underside of the vessel was still sheathed in at least that area. The ceiling planking survived in very poor condition in trenches D and E. It was 2–3cm thick with a maximum surviving width of 20 cm. The planks were fixed to the frames with occasional single treenails and iron nails.

The sternpost assembly survived as a confused mixture of ferrous concretion and fragments of timber. However two uprights, the outer and inner sternposts and what may be an impression of the aft end of the stern knee known as the sternson can be identified. The sternpost was 16 cm thick and the inner sternpost was 36 cm thick ('the moulded measurement'). Both were 28 cm wide ('the sided measurement') and were held together, just above the keel, by an iron strap. Immediately adjacent to this there was what may be another strap or the partial remains of a pintle or gudgeon. Forward of this the run of the vessel survived on the starboard side. In this area the keel was progressively recessed to accommodate the cant frames and outer planking. This allowed for a smooth run through to the sternpost.

Neither the stempost nor its associated timbers survived. An increase in the number of bolts was noted. These may have been fastenings for the stem knee. Probing by hand in this area confirmed that the bow timbers were missing rather than buried.

The keel assembly was fastened with iron clench (or through) bolts, secured on the upper surface of the rider keelson with square roves. The bolts were 3 cm in diameter and seemed to run right through from the bottom of the keel. Such a hypothesis is suggested by tracing the path of the bolts via gaps between the timbers though the base of the keel remained invisible. The roves were 6–7 cm square and 1 cm thick. Apart from the bolts, the main method of fastening the planking to the frames was with treenails. These were all 3 cm in diameter and in three well-preserved examples they were secured with a single central wedge.

A number of iron straps and knees were identified within the main body of the wreck and amongst the surrounding debris. Four or five straps were still attached to the floor timbers and these appeared to be long iron riders. In two cases, these were recorded to within 80 cm of the keelson/floor junction; thereafter they were covered. This suggests the straps were 10–12 cm wide and 2 cm thick. They were attached with round-headed iron bolts or spikes. The ends of each strap, where visible, were broken.

The iron hanging knees were all 10–12 cm wide and 2 cm thick and the length of the arms varied. The best preserved example had an intact upper (horizontal) arm measuring 86 cm. The other arm survived to a length of 80 cm and included a 6-cm outward kink 30 cm from the junction. It seems likely that the knees and the straps were both parts of long knee riders which ran from the deck down to the keelson. The strap distribution suggests that they were placed every 3–4 m along the length of the vessel. The kink in the upper end of the rider (see 'knee rider' in Fig. 5.3) would be required if the beam shelf projected out for the line of the ceiling planking (See Greenhill, 1988: 60, figs 11 and 12).

Fittings

Ship's fixtures and fittings have been found, scattered in an arc along the southern (down-slope) half of the site. Few fittings were found within the area of surviving timber. Towards the bow, a bowsprit cap lay on its own, 10 m to the west of the forward end of the keel. This was recorded in 1999. In 2000, monitoring visits identified the bowsprit cap, which had moved and broken in half. The cap consisted of an iron strap, 13cm wide by 3–4 cm thick, formed into a 'figure-of-eight'. On the lower end, two pierced lugs projected downwards forming an attachment for the martingale and bobstay. Of the two areas enclosed by the 'figure-of-eight', the upper one had a diameter of 25 cm and the lower one 23 cm. This seems to indicate that the jib-boom was thicker than the bowsprit at the point of the junction.

An Admiralty Pattern type of anchor lies folded on the starboard side of the forward end of the keel (Fig. 5.3). The shank is 14 cm in diameter and 130 cm long; at its upper end it terminated in a circular eye. The arms curved through a regular arc of 115 cm and the triangular flukes were fixed to the inner surface at each end. The stock was 5 cm in diameter and 140 cm long; a 124-cm long iron bar was concreted to one end. The anchor was hung by means of a circular iron

The *John Preston*

ring connected to the eye. There was no sign of any chain attached to the anchor.

In the area down-slope of the bow there was a large iron Armstrong-patent windlass (Guest and Guest, 2000). The central cogged wheel and pawl mechanism sat on four legs and the two barrels survived as a series of iron bars supported at their outer ends by further legs (Fig. 5.5). The wooden elements of the barrels had all decayed and in general little detail could be discerned amongst the corrosion during the 2000 survey. By 2001, it had collapsed into two sections, due in part to damage from being used to tie shot-lines to.

Amidships, four objects were found and recorded; they all appeared to be part of the same artefact. They consisted of two lengths of iron pipe, lying loose to the south of the keelson, an iron shoe fixed to the port side sister beam and the top of a possible additional shoe, just visible on the starboard side. The external diameter of the pipes matched the internal diameter of the shoe (12 cm). The port side shoe was bolted on to the sister beam at the centre point of the keel, its central hole continued through the sister and into the bilges. This was interpreted as the pipes and bottom flanges of the vessel's bilge-pump (Plate 5.3).

At the stern, several smaller fittings were recorded and four large iron objects. Of these, the most easily identifiable was the galley stove. This sat upright, 5.40 m to the east of the sternpost. It was the easternmost object on the site and anecdotal evidence suggests that sport divers may have moved it to its current position during the mid 1990s. It is a small solid-fuel-burning stove measuring 64 cm wide, 58 cm high and 56 cm deep. It is split into two halves with the left-hand side consisting of the firebox over which sits a narrow grill or plate warmer. The firebox is connected to a small flue which is positioned to the left of centre at the back of the stove. The right-hand side is taken up with the main oven, constructed of iron with ceramic tiles lining the internal surfaces. The stove sits on four short legs, giving it a 5 cm clearance off the cabin floor. The top surface, including the hot plates, does not survive.

Closer into the sternpost there are two complex corroded iron objects, not identical, but which both seem to fulfil the same function. Each consists of an iron pipe which runs at right-angles through the remains of two heavy timbers. The outer face is a teardrop-shaped iron plate, pierced in the centre by a triangular aperture (Fig. 5.6). Remains of lugs on the top edge suggest that the plate, or a missing cover, was hinged. The triangular aperture measures 17 cm along each side and is 8 cm deep and the pipes have a diameter of 8 cm. They appear to have provided a conduit through the side of the vessel via the beam shelf, possibly for the passage of chain or rope. The position at the stern and the fact that two very similar features were noted in the bow area suggest that that they may be hawse-holes or pipes for cable or mooring ropes.

Immediately adjacent to the sternpost lie the remains of a broken iron strap. Measuring 10 cm wide and 2 cm thick, it binds together the remains of four wooden beams. The beams, largely identified from timber impressions in the concretion and the build-up of concretion in the gaps between them, were 15 cm, 5 cm, 14 cm and over 8 cm wide and 15 cm thick. At the broken end of the strap a surviving piece of timber had a 2.5-cm diameter hole through it, suggesting that the beams were also bolted together. Firm identification of the function of this strap is not possible. However, it seems likely, given its form and

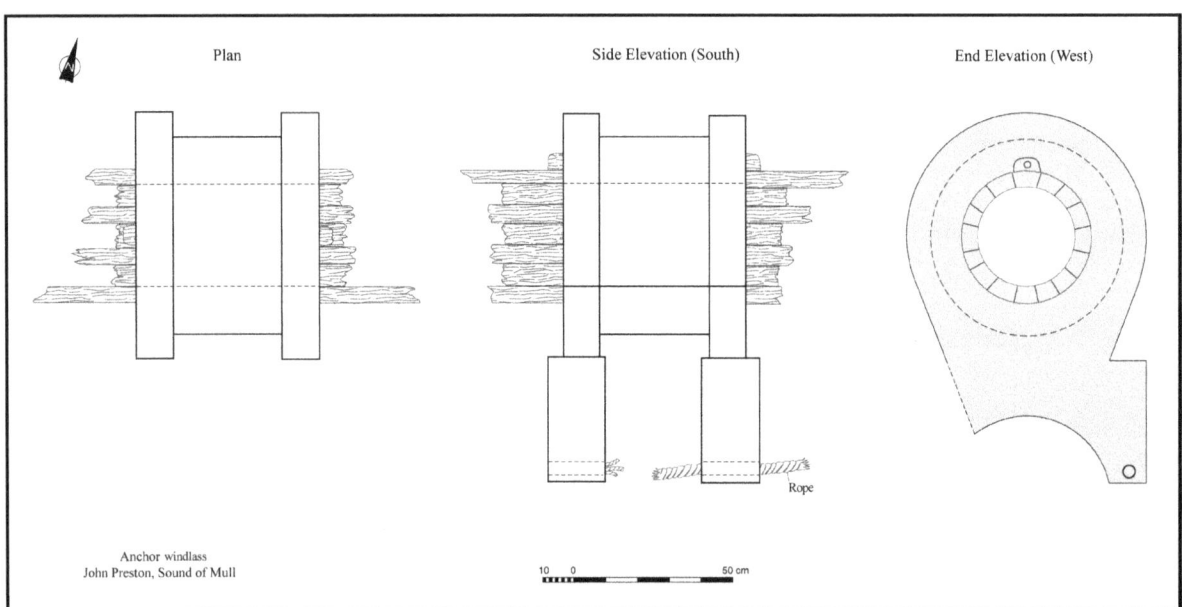

Fig. 5.5   The John Preston *anchor windlass (Jonie and Richard Guest; CFA Archaeology Ltd.)*

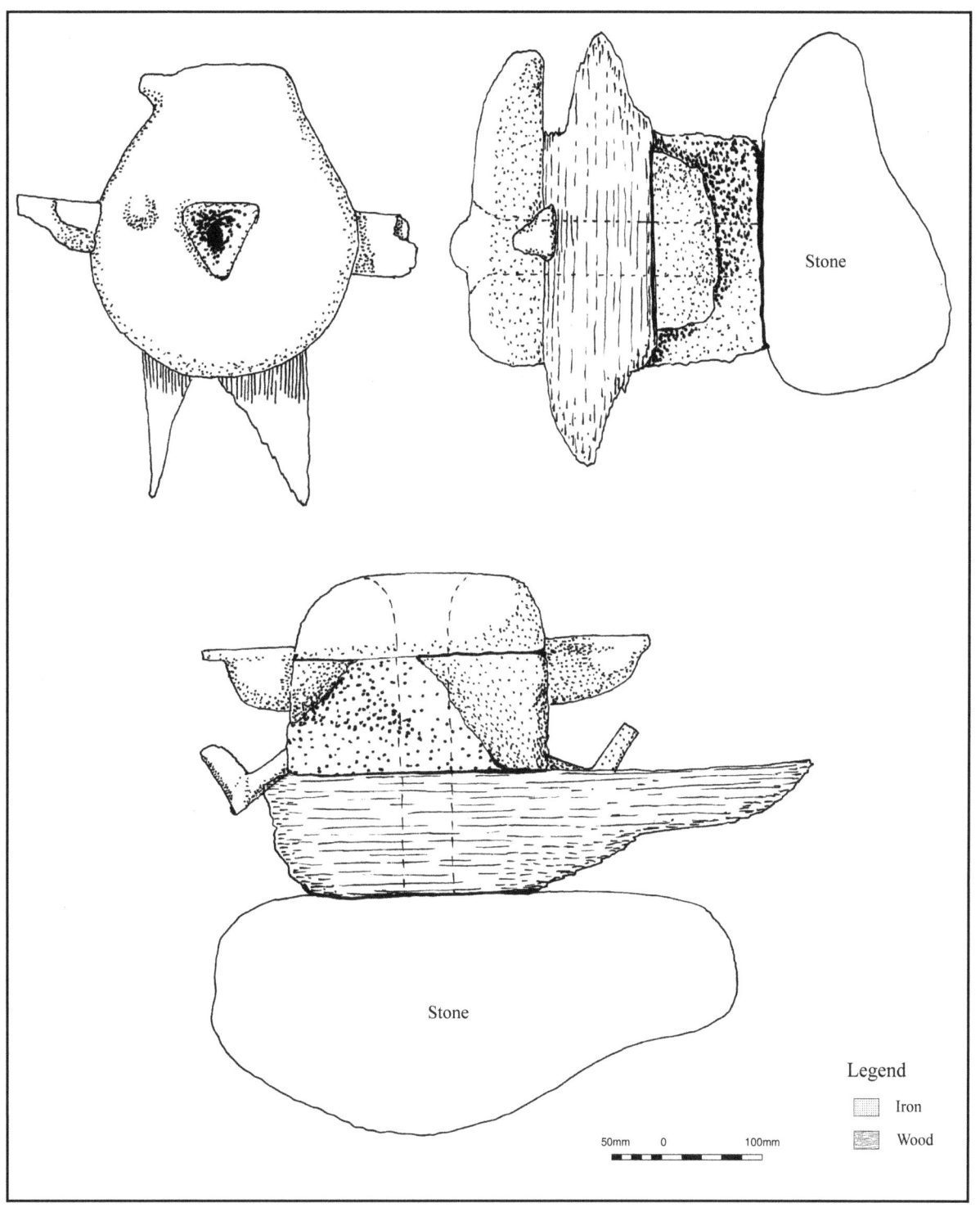

Fig. 5.6   Unidentified find from stern (Barry Kaye)

position, that it is either a broken pintle or gudgeon, or binding from around the top of the rudder (see reconstruction in Fig. 5.7). Probing around the object indicated the presence of further buried timbers in the area, suggesting that more of the structure may survive. Trench A also revealed a number of smaller objects, notably a glass deck light (inset in the deck to allow daylight through to the area below), wooden panelling and fragments of copper sheathing and angular lead channelling. The deck light was rectangular, measuring 20 by 7.5 cm, with a pyramidal prism on the underside (Fig. 5.8), identical in style to a prism recovered from the 1876 wreck of a fishing vessel in East Flevoland, Holland (Vlierman, 1994). There was a 1-cm wide lip around the prism, but no sign of any brass flange. The light lay beside two thin pine planks, with tongue-and-groove edges, which were interpreted as panelling from the stern

The *John Preston*

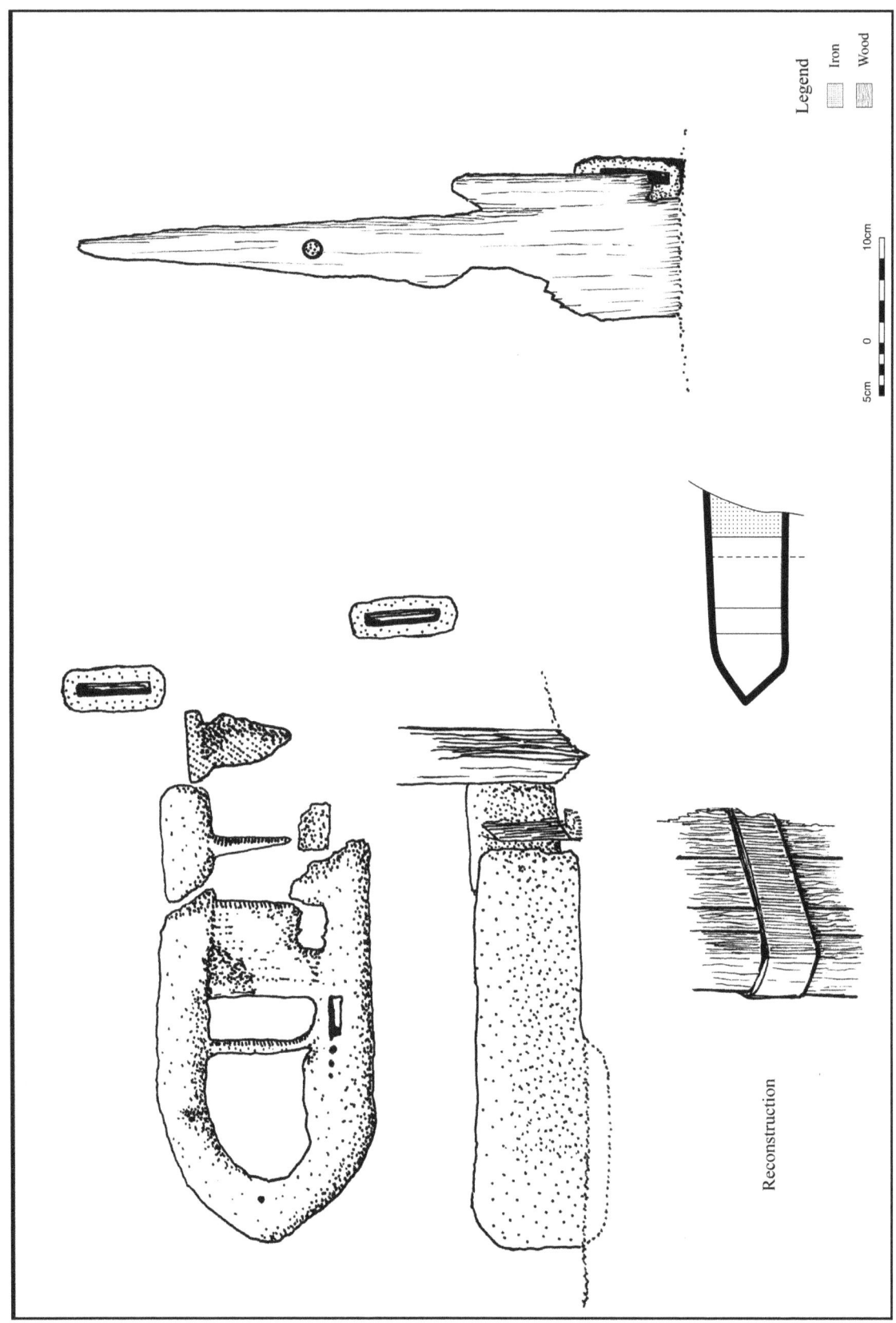

Fig. 5.7   Possible gudgeon at stern (Barry Kaye)

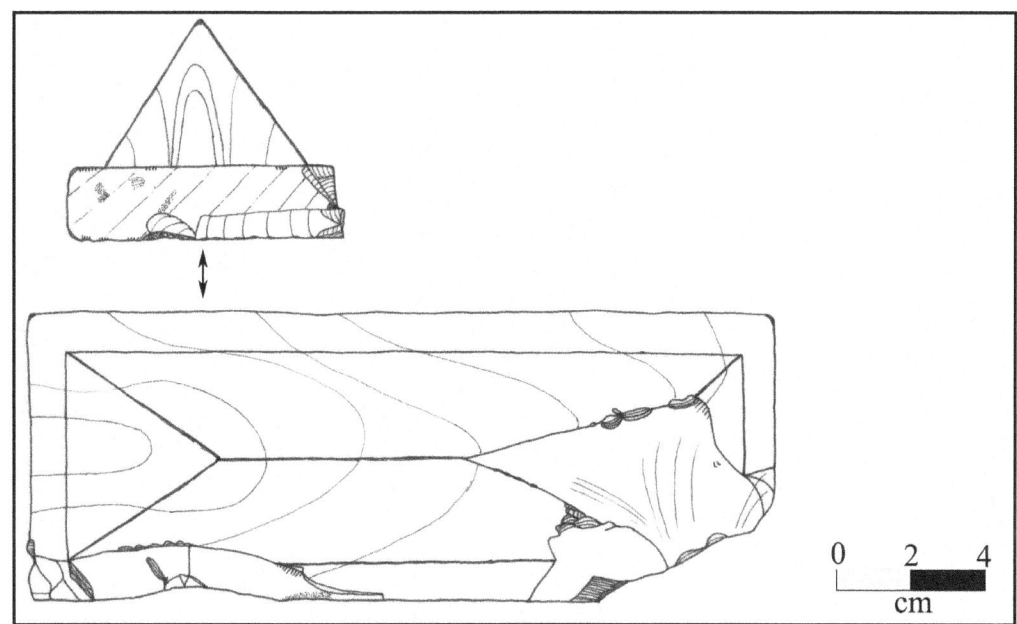

Fig. 5.8   Decklight from stern of the John Preston *drawn at 1:2 scale (Jo Cook)*

cabins. Three sections of rectangular lead sheet were recovered. They survived in variable condition, but all were folded into a right-angle and had their long edges perforated with nail holes. They may have been used to line the angle between the deck and the bulwarks and acted as gutters leading to the scuppers.

Several sheaves were found lying loose amidst the wreckage. They were for the most part mobile and only one was fully recorded. Six examples measured 2 cm thick with a diameter of 10 cm; one, located near the sternpost, was 3 cm thick with a diameter of 17 cm. All the sheaves had triangular recesses in one side to accommodate the bearing. One was attached to an iron concretion which may have been the remains of an iron cheek and head block.

Cargo

The vessel's cargo was the dominant feature of the site prior to its salvage. Grieve reported that when he first worked on the site the vessel itself was almost invisible. A thin layer of silt obscured a mound consisting of tightly-packed slate, layered in rows, and totally obscuring the vessel's hull. Today all that remains of the cargo is a scatter of slates covering the core of the site. The distribution is a product of several widely different factors: the wrecking and disintegration process, the salvage episodes and diver activity on the site.

The slates are not all of one size and were compared against the nomenclature suggested by Walsh (2000, table 2.4; p. 12). Richard Grieve reported 11 sizes of slate with the largest 457 x 305 mm (18 x 12 inches, 'countess small'). Of those remaining on the seabed, the majority have dimensions of 460–70 x 260–70 x 10 mm (18 x 10 inches, 'countess narrow'), with smaller sizes (360 by 210 by 10 mm, 14 x 8 inches, 'ladies small') present in smaller quantities. All have been dressed by chamfering the edge on one face. No nail holes were visible which is to be expected because a slater would pierce a nail hole as he progressed. Today, the largest concentration of slate lies on the up-slope side of the keelson, caught in an angle between the keelson and the floor timbers. Prior to this, the 1995 survey showed the area down-slope of the keelson to contain two to three times the number of slates. This dense concentration of slate occupied an area measuring 15 m E-W by 7 m N-S, restricted to the forward port side of the keelson.

Away from this area the slate density diminished considerably to the east, with little or no slate in the stern area. South and west of the main body of slate there was a thin spread, particularly in a rough line to the south-west. To the north the scatter petered out short of the cliff. Anecdotal evidence suggests that prior to the 1986 salvage the slates were still stacked as if in boxes, up to a height of 2 m in places. One example of this survives in the form of a box of slates. Preserved because of a covering of concreted iron chain, this shows that the slates were stacked vertically in rows back to back. Further evidence of vertical stacking exists in places on the starboard side where stacks of slate have fallen through rotten ceiling planking to become lodged between the floor timbers. By the 19th century at least, it was normal to stack slates on edge vertically with their faces parallel to the deck beams, to avoid a vertical wedging action which caused stress across the hull (pers. comm. Owain Roberts).

The *John Preston*

Discussion

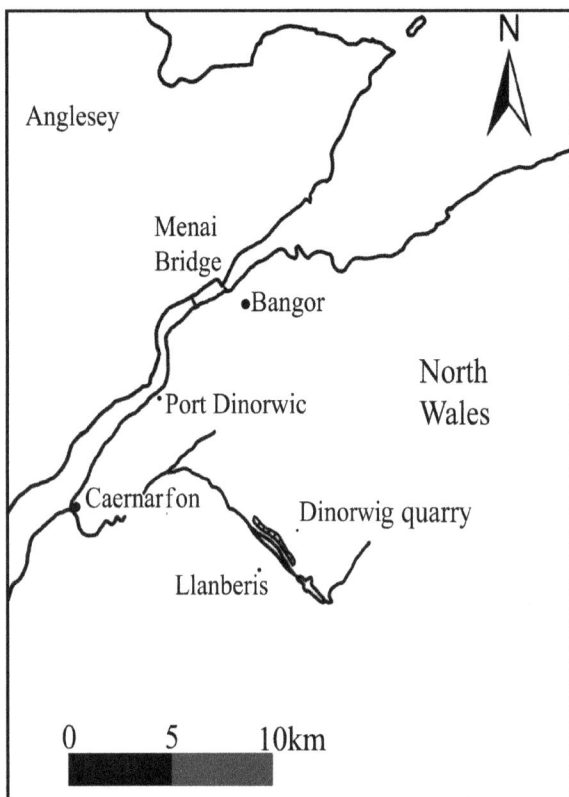

Fig. 5.9 (left) Location map, North Wales (Philip Robertson)

With a length-beam ratio of 4:1, in form and construction the *John Preston* appears typical of the smaller two-masted fore-and-aft schooner (as opposed to the larger three-masted schooner) and the coasting brigs and brigantines. Schooners were used in Britain as early as the end of the 18th century (Greenhill, 1988: 5). By virtue of combining a reasonable economic capacity with speed, by 1870, the schooner was well established in the mercantile navy list and it predominated in western ports of the British Isles (Greenhill, 1988: 21). Greenhill (1998: 180–2) confirms that Aberystwyth, Porthmadog, Nevin, Aberdovey, Port Dinorwic, Caernarfon and Bangor (among others) were all actively building schooners. Port Dinorwic (where the *John Preston* was built) launched at least 23 such vessels between 1759 and 1919 (Fig. 5.9).

Over the 27 years of her life, the *John Preston* had undergone three major refits, as was often the case, because the costs of substantial repair seldom exceeded the cost of a new build (Greenhill, 1988: 66). Evidence of iron strapping might suggest substantial repairs, illustrating the stresses and strains

Fig. 5.10   Port Dinorwic around 1880 'Llongau wrth cei llechi a'r bont haearn... Y Felinheli', by John Thomas (by permission of Llyfrgell Genedlaethol Cymru/National Library of Wales)

on the hull of this vessel during her many years of service. Although the documentary sources scarcely support this hypothesis, tentative evidence of copper sheathing might indicate that the *John Preston* was prepared for the deep-water trades (Greenhill, 1988: 63). However, between 1872 and 1875 downgrading by Lloyd's to AE1 limited her to carriage of dry or perishable goods on shorter voyages.

As was often the case during her service, the *John Preston*'s cargo on her final voyage was Welsh slate, on that occasion from Port Dinorwic to Fraserburgh. The vessel's Scottish connections are confirmed by her ownership position. By the 1870s slate-quarrying had become one of the most important of Welsh industries and Welsh slate had gained a reputation for its superior qualities of appearance and durability. It was smoother than Scottish slate, with fewer imperfections, and because it split into thinner pieces you got more for the weight. In 1882 the quarries of Caernarfon produced over 280,000 tons of finished roofing slates and Wales produced over four fifths of the total slate used in the UK. Its popularity clearly extended to Scotland despite the volume of slate being produced in Ballachulish and Easdale at the time.

Dinorwig was one of the largest and most important slate-quarries in North Wales, employing about 3000 men at its peak, and it was operational until 1969 (Jones, 2006). Much of this slate was transported by sea and the ports of the Menai Strait grew to service this trade, to the extent that over 3500 men were employed as seamen during the late 19th century. Slate was taken from the quarry on a 4-foot gauge railway to Port Dinorwic on the Menai Strait, 8 km west of Bangor (Fig. 5.9; 5.10). Along with the other smaller ports of the Menai Strait area, Port Dinorwic expanded in tandem with the slate industry. Greenhill (1988: 181) states that Port Dinorwic had its own fleet of schooners and larger craft in 1880. The *John Preston* was one of these vessels at the time of her loss.

Site formation

The evidence gathered on the timber, fittings and cargo distribution patterns allows some general observations to be made on the sequence of events involved in the formation of the site. These cover the wrecking, the disintegration of the wreck on the seabed, and diver-related disturbance.

Documentary details of the wrecking indicate that the *John Preston* was blown across the Sound of Mull onto Rubha Dearg. That she was upright when she struck and settled upright on the seabed, is suggested by the fact that her masts were just visible after her sinking. Although the heavy timbers at the bow of the vessel may have detached naturally during the disintegration of the hull, the fractured end of the structural timbers suggest that a traumatic impact may have occurred, possibly when the vessel hit the rocky shore head on. To this may be added the forward distribution of the cargo as suggested by concentrations of slate at the western end of the site. One possible interpretation may be that the vessel hit bow-end on and sank bow first, causing the cargo to shift forward during the sinking.

On the seabed, the *John Preston* settled into a natural hollow in the boulder slope, separating the shoreward cliff from a seaward drop-off. This, coupled with the weight of the cargo, was probably crucial in helping to preserve the site. A less secure location would surely have resulted in the vessel slipping down the slope and over the drop-off into deep water, where it would have been exposed to modern destructive impacts such as scallop dredging. The bottom of the hull survived because the hollow acted as a trap for sediment, settling in pockets over the hull. The irregular surface offered by the slate prevented blanket accumulation of sediment, preserving air pockets within the slate mounds. The effect of the slope has been to preserve the port side in greater detail than the starboard side, though this hypothesis has yet to be fully tested. In addition, some of the vessel's fixtures and fittings have tended to fall down-slope of the hull, probably shortly after the vessel was lost. Since the salvage of the slate, the exposure of timbers on the starboard side had hastened biological infestation to the extent that the frames are now extremely degraded. Their survival may be measured in years, but probably not in decades. The same may be true of even the largest iron artefacts such as the anchor windlass, the collapse of which was hastened by its use as a shot-line weight for divers.

Observations indicated that sedimentation and erosion rates over the site are not uniform. During the period of study, the eastern end of the site accumulated sediment while the western end was subject to erosion. Corrosion rates as viewed from the corrosion of the mild steel rods on the sediment stakes suggest that the sediment characteristics across the site appear to be fairly uniform. In fact, our observations suggest that the accumulation and erosion of sediment covering the site is a cyclical process, depending on storms, extreme tidal cycles and other environmental factors. In addition to dictating levels of sedimentation and erosion, currents across wreck sites can often cause movement of objects around the seabed. In the case of the *John Preston*, seabed currents may reach 1.5 knots at springs. This will not be sufficient to move larger objects, but more mobile artefacts and fragile organics will have been displaced.

Chapter 6 – Unknown: Scallastle Bay
(RCAHMS ref. NM63NE 8005)
Jane Maddocks

Background

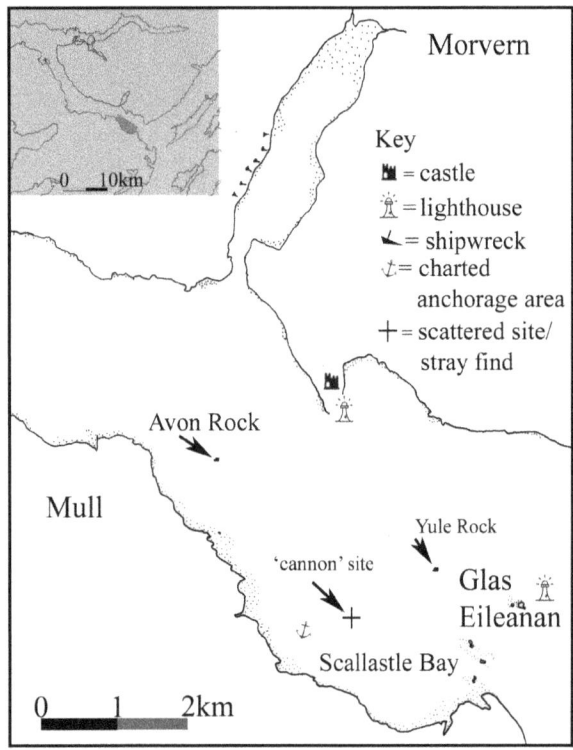

Fig. 6.1   Location map for Scallastle Bay (Philip Robertson)

Lochaline-based scallop diver George Forster discovered a collection of iron cannon in apparent isolation on the seabed at Scallastle Bay around 1991 (Fig. 6.1). The Archaeological Diving Unit (University of St Andrews) attempted to locate the site in 1994. Early in 1995, the area was searched by the Royal Navy minesweeper HMS *Berkeley*, under the command of Commander Bob Stewart. This search identified four strong targets with indications of 70% burial on impact (pers. comm. Bob Stewart). George Forster then took SOMAP divers out to the area and relocated the site in March 1995. An initial inspection in 1995 by the Archaeological Diving Unit prompted the suggestion that the assemblage might come from the wreck of HMS *Dartmouth* (lost 1690). She broke her anchor cable while sheltering in Scallastle Bay, before stranding on the island of Eilean Rubha an Ridire (Martin, 1998: 67 and chapter 4). This paper discusses SOMAP's survey of the site between 1995 and 1999 (Maddocks, 1996; Bailey *et al.*, 1998) and subsequent identification of the guns and associated finds. In addition the Scallastle Bay project has provided a practice ground for the development of methodologies for recording corroded cast-iron guns under water (Maddocks, 1998).

The site has been charted by remote sensing and DGPS at Lat/Long N56° 29.811', W5° 44.90', at a depth of 19–21 m on a gradual gravel/mud slope in the middle of Scallastle Bay (Fig. 6.1). Scalistal (Scallastle Bay) was marked as an anchorage by McKenzie Senior (1788). By virtue of the shelter afforded it by the hills of Mull from prevailing south-westerly winds, this open bay is still used by ships for shelter during bad weather. Scallastle Bay is also a popular scallop dredging area and the side-scan data from 2003 has identified the seabed scouring caused by dredging activity, close to this site (Plate 6.1)

Survey work

In 1995 and 1996, SOMAP divers carried out a tape-measure survey of the three guns originally identified. The results were plotted by hand and the measurements checked using Web for Windows (Rule, 1989). In 1996 circular searches of the surrounding seabed delineated the visible extent of the site, identifying two more guns. A hand-held metal detector grid-survey conducted in 1997 over an area of 108 m^2 identified several buried anomalies, including the sixth gun. Hand fanning was used to expose for recording the partially buried guns which were plotted in to the site-plan (Fig. 6.2). This limited excavation identified two lead apron covers and one clay-pipe bowl. One of the apron covers was re-buried. The second was recovered along with the pipe bowl because of the risk of the items being lifted by sport divers. They were photographed, drawn, and then conserved by SOMAP participant Dr Barry Kaye.

Detailed gun recording

Recovery of the guns was not an option and the emphasis was on recording them *in situ*. This was initially done by taking rudimentary measurements. However, the thick corrosion products evident on the guns obscured important diagnostic features and staff at the Royal Armouries (Fort Nelson, Portsmouth) and Priddy's Hard Museum of Naval Ordnance (Portsmouth) could not identify them from the information we provided. In 1998, the author developed an easy-to-use pro forma suitable for use by volunteers in British waters (Maddocks, 1998).

Sound of Mull Archaeological Project

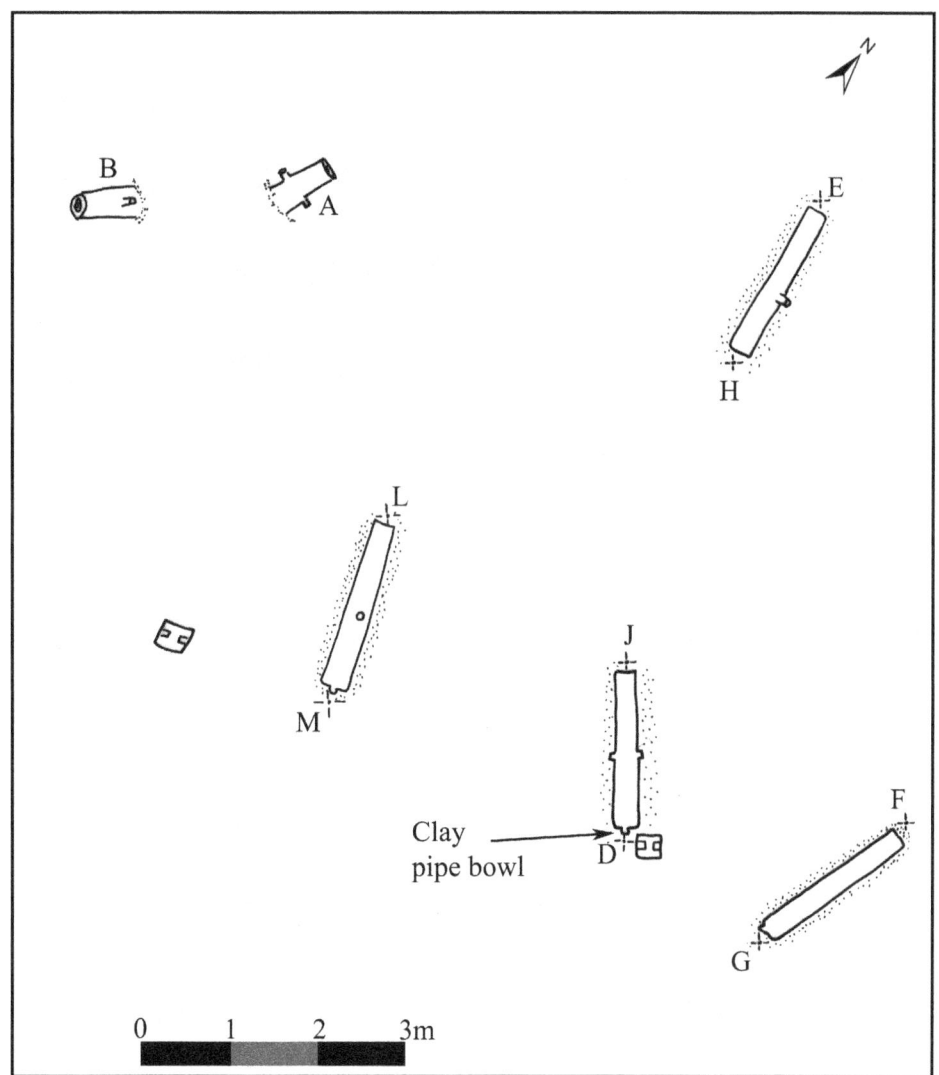

Fig. 6.2   Cannons site plan (Philip Robertson)

Designing the pro forma, however, proved more difficult than had been envisaged. The reporting and recording of naval ordnance or historic artillery has never been straightforward and available recording sheets for naval ordnance are highly detailed. Smith (1988) and Roth (1989) have discussed appropriate terminologies and recording methods in an attempt to standardise methodology, but that suggested by Roth itemises over 90 measurements for a cast-iron gun. While fillets and astragals (small parts of a reinforcing ring) are visible and measurable when the gun is on land and has been conserved, they are invisible under water on heavily-concreted guns. Dean *et al* (1992: 317) provides an alternative which is again more suited for recording guns already raised, requiring 58 measurements following reduction of ferrous oxide.

The conventions and terminology used by SOMAP are those used by the Royal Armouries, the National Maritime Museum (Greenwich), Caruana (1997) and Munday (1987: 6). Munday suggests that the essential features for identifying date and size of gun are the cascabel end, the number of reinforcing rings and the shape of the muzzle. The poundage of the gun can be estimated by measuring the length from base ring to the front of the face, length from base ring to first reinforce, base ring to centre of trunnions and the length from centre of each trunnion to front of face. It was also thought important to record whether the trunnions were high or low in relation to the centre-line and the widths of face and mouth. The finalised recording-form incorporates these considerations, with the required measurements listed for ease of progression underwater. A diagram is provided on the form to explain the measurements that are required (Fig. 6.3).

Where possible, each gun was partially exposed by hand fanning and use of a trowel. Once exposed each horizontal gun was measured according to the gun-recording-sheet data. In addition, each gun was drawn at 1:20 using a 0.5 m planning-frame and photographed by stills photography and video.

Unknown: Scallastle Bay

```
SOMAP 1998 gun recording form
Gun name


Cascabel end type: button/ring/combination of both
Cascabel to base ring:_____


Base ring to 1st reinforce:_____
Base ring to centre of trunnion:_____


1st reinforce to 2nd reinforce:_____


Length of chase:_____


Muzzle neck:_____
Width of face_____ width of mouth_____
Muzzle face to centre of trunnion:_____



Muzzle shape in profile (sketch).                Tulip / flat


Overall length of base ring to face:_____


Other comments
```

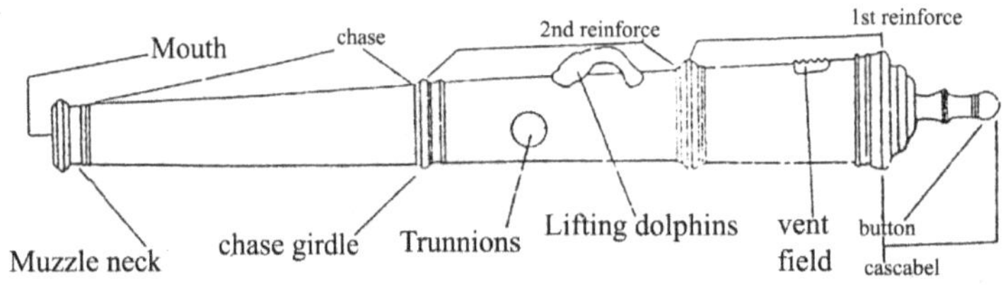

Fig. 6.3   Gun recording form (Jane Maddocks)

Results

The six guns are closely grouped in an area 9 by 12 m. Two lie vertical or nearly so and partially buried, muzzle end up with their trunnions at seabed level (Plate 6.2); the other four lie horizontally. Due to burial, only three could be measured overall and a further two were only partially recordable. Gun L-M was buried in 1998 and the record completed in 1997 when it was exposed was not sufficiently informative to allow full analysis.

The results of the gun recording measurements from the 1998 survey are provided in Table 6.1.

Discussions with staff from the Royal Armouries have helped to pinpoint the most notable features on the recorded guns, as follows. Gun D-J had a button with the rounded shaping characteristic of the Armstrong design. Previous button ends had been elongated, a particular feature of many guns cast prior to the reign of George II (1727-60). Gun G-F (Fig. 6.2) has the appearance of a Blomefield pattern gun, with an offset ring (Plate 6.3), but no evidence of the button that should be with it (this may have been struck off at some time). The ring is typologically incorrect for the later hinged-ring gun, but it was almost certainly cast after 1788, the earliest known use of the breeching ring (pers. comm. R. Roth). Gun H-E has no visible cascabel. Guns A and B are lying vertical with the cascabel end buried, but, like the other recordable guns, the presence of a classic 'tulip' mouth suggests – and the appearance of the ring on the 'second reinforce' further indicates – a manufacture date prior to 1840. After that date, guns changed shape and the mouth became flat, without any characteristic flare.

Lead apron 1 (Plate 6.4) was recovered from a partially buried context, close to Gun D-J, the Armstrong pattern gun. The apron is square and measures 26 by 26 cm (approximate thickness is 2 cm), with moulded features relating to its associated iron gun and a possible Roman numeral inscription (Plate 6.5). Lead apron 2 was found 2m from gun L-M, but it may have been semi-mobile. It appeared to be identical to lead apron 1 and it was reburied without detailed recording. Excavation of the cascabel of Gun D-J to facilitate recording resulted in location of a clay-pipe bowl (Fig. 6.4), moulded with a raised Red Hand of Ulster and an oval bearing the indented initials R M.

Detail	Gun				
	A	B	D-J	H-E	G-F
Cascabel end type	N/A	N/A	button	Lost	Ring ? button
Cascabel to base ring	N/A	N/A	25 cm	Lost	18 cm
Base ring to 1st reinforce	N/A	N/A	50 cm	50 cm	53 cm
Base ring to centre of trunnion	N/A	N/A	79 cm	79 cm	80 cm
1st reinforce to 2nd reinforce	52 cm	52 cm	?40 cm	51 cm	51 cm
Length of chase	?68/60 cm	60 cm	65 cm	53 cm	52 cm
Muzzle neck	25 cm	25 cm	30 cm	25 cm	?29/25 cm
Width of face	24 cm	25 cm	24 cm	32 cm	30 cm
Width of mouth	10 cm	10 cm	10 cm	N/A	?19 cm
Muzzle face to centre of trunnion	106 cm	110 cm	105 cm	110 cm	108 cm
Muzzle shape tulip (T) or flat (F)	T	T	T	T	T
Length face to base ring	N/A	N/A	185 cm	184 cm	185 cm

Table 6.1

Discussion

The use of a specially designed form enabled divers with no previous experience of gun recording to record relevant information in an effective manner. However, despite common terminology and pre-dive briefings some misunderstandings did arise. Two divers misinterpreted the width of the face as being the muzzle flare. In the future, this could be solved by adding a muzzle front view to the form. Variations within the measurements of the guns are fairly small and can be explained by differences in the extent of corrosion and debris covering each gun, differences in casting, as well as by differences in survey practice.

The presence of 'tulip' mouths on five of the guns and a breech ring on one gun leads us to conclude that the guns were variously manufactured sometime between 1788 and 1840. A deposition date in the first half of the 19th century is suggested by the presence of the clay-pipe bowl (manufactured between 1800 and 1830). These dates rule out any association with HMS *Dartmouth*. The lengths of the fully-visible guns tentatively indicate that these all fired six or nine pound shot. This size of gun was commonplace in the Royal Navy and the British merchant fleet in the latter

Unknown: Scallastle Bay

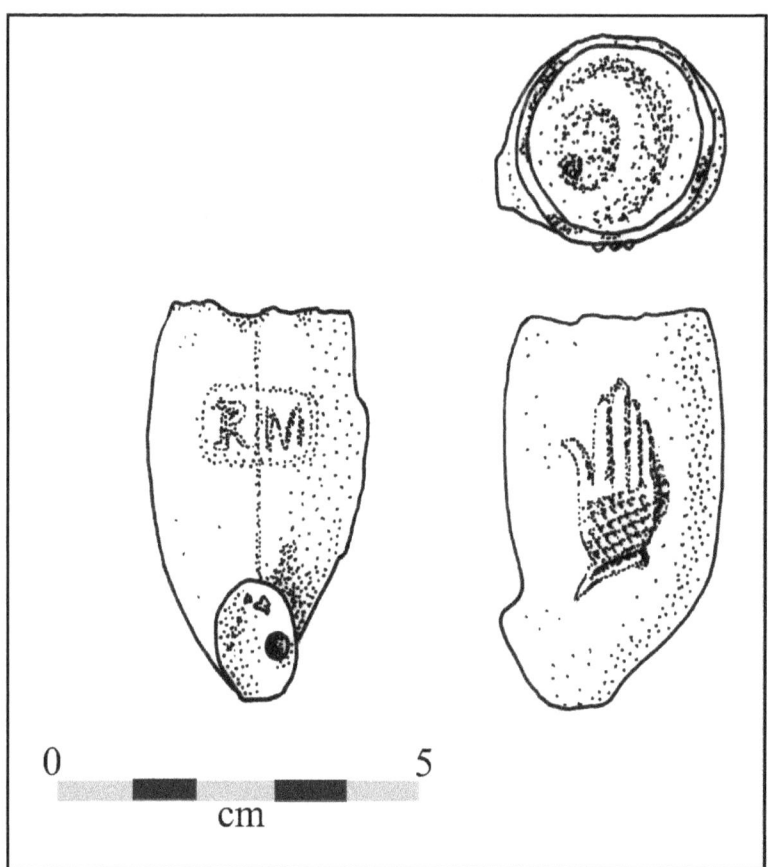

Fig. 6.4   Clay pipe drawn at 1:1 scale (Alo Parfitt)

half of the 18th century. In ordnance terms, these guns were relatively small and were often placed on an upper deck.

The enigmatic vertical presentation of two guns is interpreted as a result of the immediate wrecking process. It seems likely that these two guns hit the seabed with considerable impact, probably because they were jettisoned without gun carriages. It is just possible that the missing cascabel buttons on guns H-E and G-F also resulted from the wrecking process. However, in our view it is more likely that these two guns were not serviceable at the time of loss: a missing cascabel would have meant that these guns could not be restrained during firing and this would have been a hazard on board ship. By contrast, the discovery of two vent aprons suggests two other guns were serviceable, if not actually in operational readiness. On the basis of the finds discovered so far and the absence of any obvious candidate from documentary sources, this site is not interpreted as a shipwreck, but as a jettisoned scatter of guns and associated finds within a busy anchorage area. Certainly, jettisoning heavy material from a ship if it was in danger of foundering is a known practice.

It is just possible that some of the guns were due to be re-cast. It is understood that Blomefield pattern guns in the early years of their development tended to fail after firing several rounds. The Armstrong pattern guns failed at proof when they were fired from cold. Armstrong guns were made from Wealden iron; the Blomefield gun from ironstone found in the Midlands. This source of iron was rich in sulphides, which made the gun porous and frail when fired hot. Gun founders re-cast the guns using metal from the older Armstrong-pattern guns, which reduced the sulphides, made the casting more fluid and allowed the ring to be cast before the rest of the gun had cooled. This ensured the integrity of the gun and reduced the rate of failures at proof.

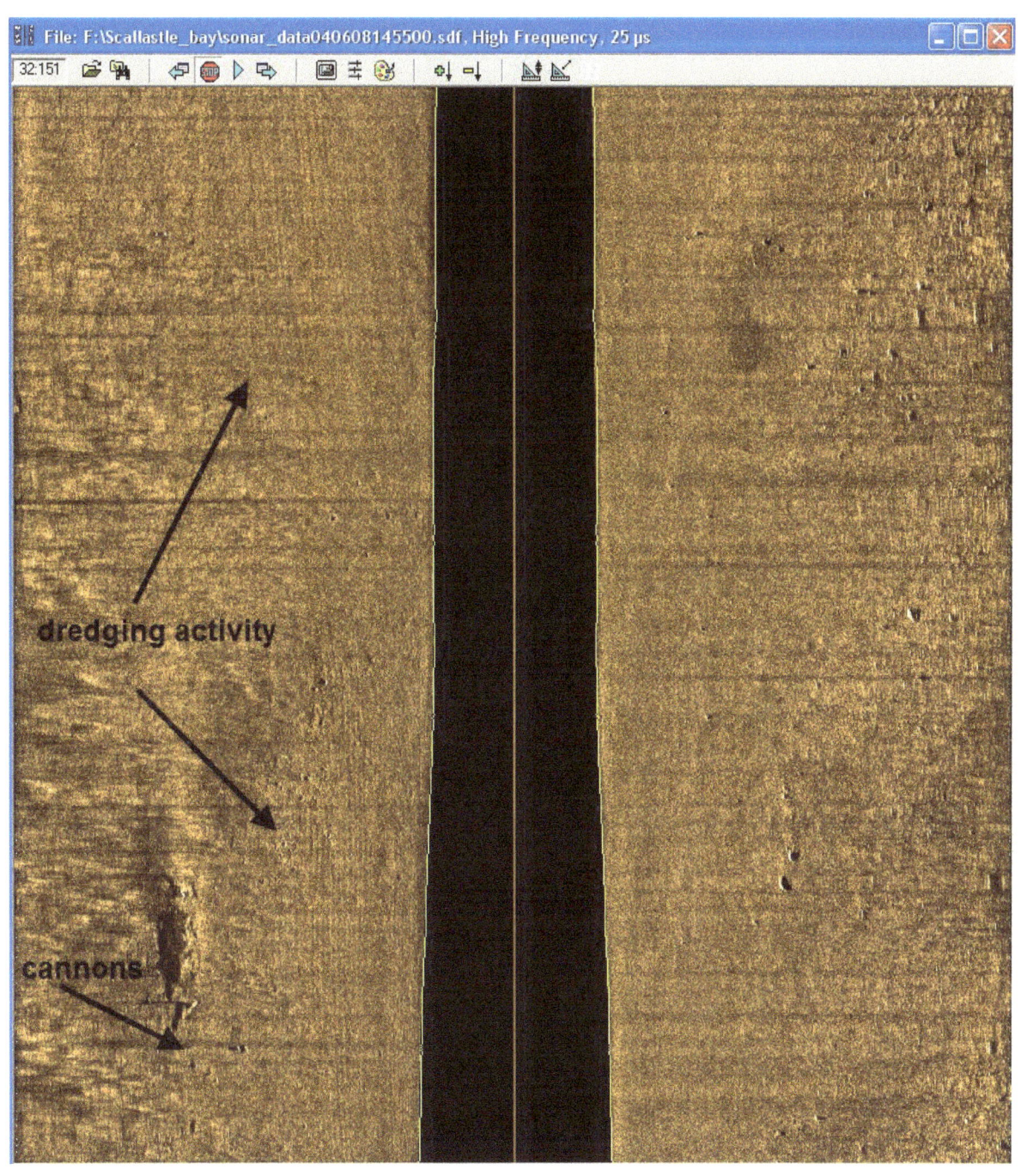

Plate 6.1   Dredging activity in Scallastle Bay, close to cannon site (© Sound of Mull Mapping Consortium)

Plate 6.2 Cannon under water (Philip Robertson)

Plate 6.4 Lead apron; this object measures 26 cm by 26 cm (Edward Martin)

Plate 6.3 Breeching loop close-up, the scale divisions are 5cm (Philip Robertson)

Plate 6.5 Lead apron close-up of possible inscription (Edward Martin)

Plate. 7.1 Foredeck hold frames and missing plating on the starboard side of the Thesis *(© Simon Volpe)*

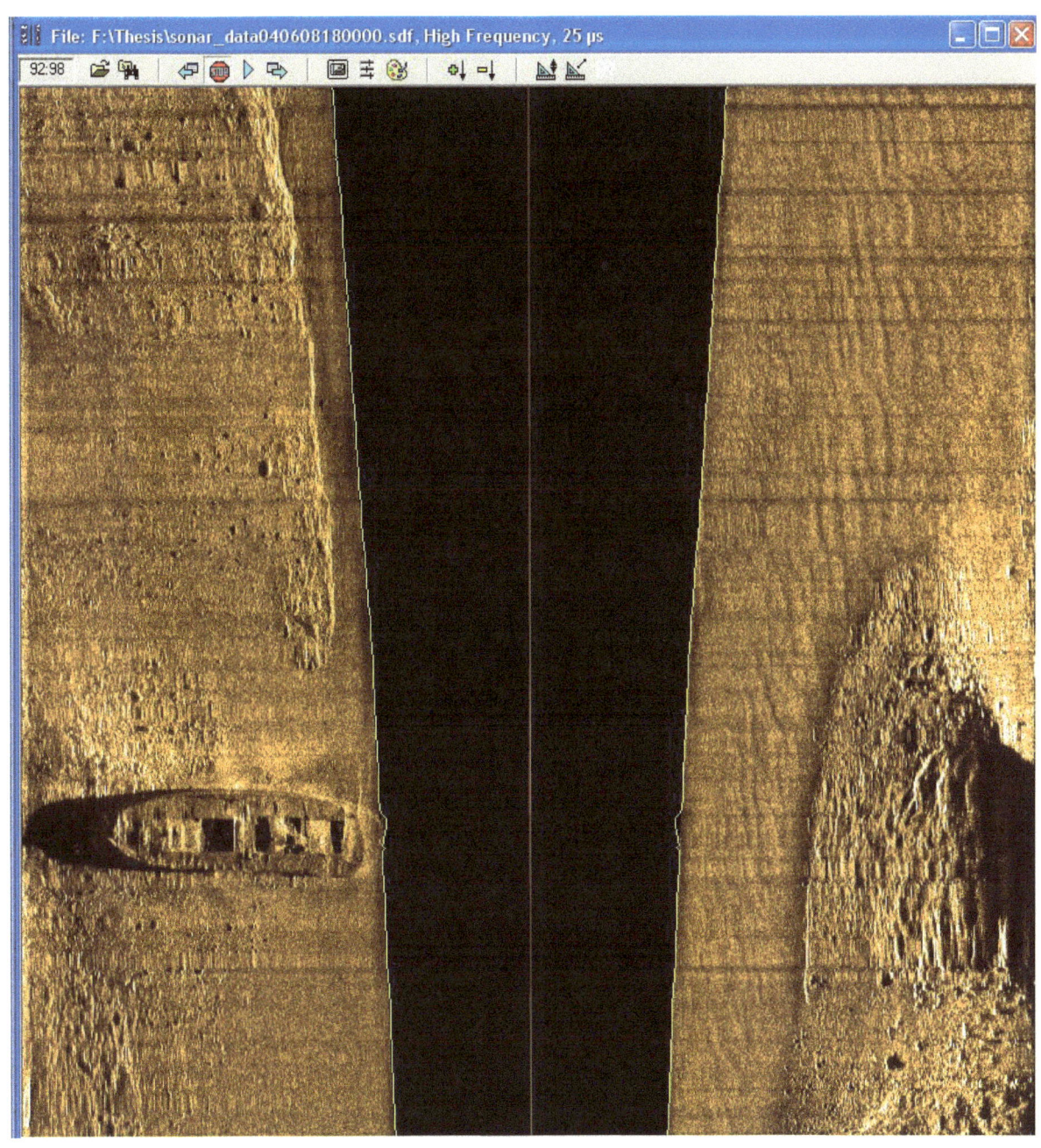

Plate 7.2   Side-scan sonargraph showing the Thesis *and surrounding seabed (© Sound of Mull Mapping Consortium)*

Plate. 7.3 Remains of stern frame, lying on seabed close to vessel's starboard bow (Clive Field)

Plate 7.4 Reversing wheel in engine compartment (Philip Robertson)

*Plate 7.5 Deadman's fingers (*Alcyonium digitatum*) on an exposed frame on the vessel's starboard bow (Philip Robertson)*

Chapter 7 – An integrated study of the *Thesis*: Rubha an Ridire
(RCAHMS ref. NM74SW 8001)

> Dirty British Coaster with a salt caked smoke stack,
> Butting through the Channel in the mad March days,
> With a cargo of Tyne coal, road-rail, pig-lead,
> Firewood, iron-ware and cheap tin trays.
>
> (*Cargoes*, John Masefield)

Introduction, significance and aims

The loss of the SS *Thesis* around midnight on 16 October 1889 has bequeathed to Scottish archaeology the substantially intact remains of an example of the typical, unsophisticated steamship which formed the basis of the British merchant fleet at the height of its worldwide presence and during a period of heavy and expanding coastal trade around the UK.

The *Thesis* was built by MacIlwaine, Lewis and Co. at Belfast and launched on 25 June 1887. Less than two years after entry into service and apparently still in unmodified condition, while on passage from Belfast to Middlesbrough, she stranded on Inninmore Point (Morvern) at the south eastern entrance to the Sound of Mull (Fig. 7.1). All 11 crewmen rowed to safety. The wreck lies at N56° 30.0333′, W5° 41.4333′ and is not indicated on the current edition of the Hydrographic Office chart (no. 2390, surveyed 1976, amended 1991). Selection of this popular tourist wreck for detailed study was prompted by an initial inspection in June 2000 which revealed apparent deck collapse towards the bow.

Background research has demonstrated the quality, quantity and limitations of documentary evidence that may be available for a wreck of this period lost in British waters. Although Lyon (1974) and Muckelroy (1980: 10) questioned the value of archaeological investigations for the study of documentarily attested iron and steel wrecks of this period, the significance of illustrative examples should not be underestimated. There is a worldwide dearth of preserved examples of vessels such as this. The *Robin* (built 1890 and preserved at India Dock, Port of London) is comparable in size, but is a long raised-quarter deck steamship with an engine at the rear (http://www.nhsc.org.uk). Only two more closely comparable vessels survive anywhere. The *Amadeo* (built 1884 by Liverpool Forge Company), held by the Chilean Navy at Punta Arenas, is closely comparable, though smaller and without her original compound steam engine (Brouwer, 1999: 54). The *Calderon* (built in Glasgow in 1884), grounded at Guayaquil in Equador, is smaller, but comparable in construction and possibly appearance (Brouwer, 1999: 67). The majority of surviving examples lie at the bottom of the sea. However, iron, steel and steamship wrecks on the seabed are rapidly deteriorating (McCarthy, 2000: 187) and Flemming (1988: 198–200) has called for prioritising of the study of iron wrecks because 'iron will not last for ever'. Investigations by McCarthy (2000) of the *Xantho* (lost in 1872 off Port Gregory, Western Australia) provided SOMAP with a significant and instructive methodological parallel for steamship archaeology.

Against this background, the project's objectives were as follows:

1. to develop an appropriate methodology for the three-dimensional recording of a substantial wreck by recreational divers using basic archaeological techniques available at limited cost;

2. to develop basic techniques of scientific and environmental recording to elucidate the condition of the remains and the processes affecting it and to produce plans of sufficient quality to facilitate the monitoring of significant changes to the wreck in the future;

3. to investigate available documentary and oral sources and to produce plans, drawings, photographs, video and written accounts of the vessel, its function, history and loss.

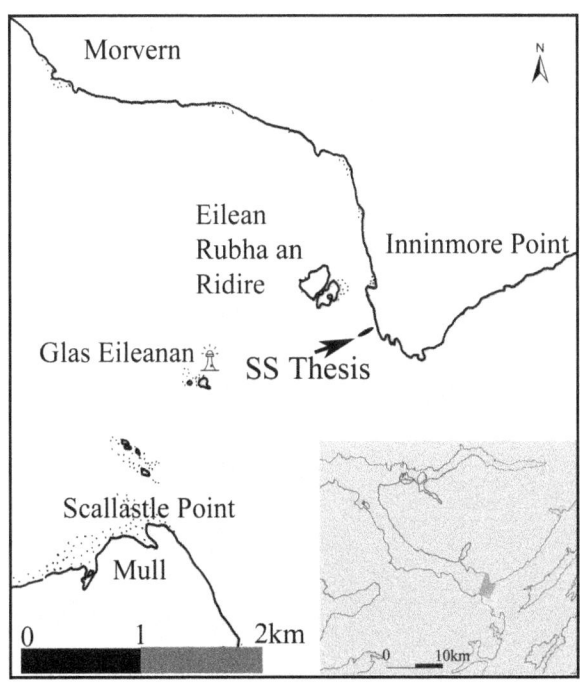

Fig. 7.1   Location of the Thesis *(Philip Robertson)*

An integrated study of the *Thesis*

Documentary research

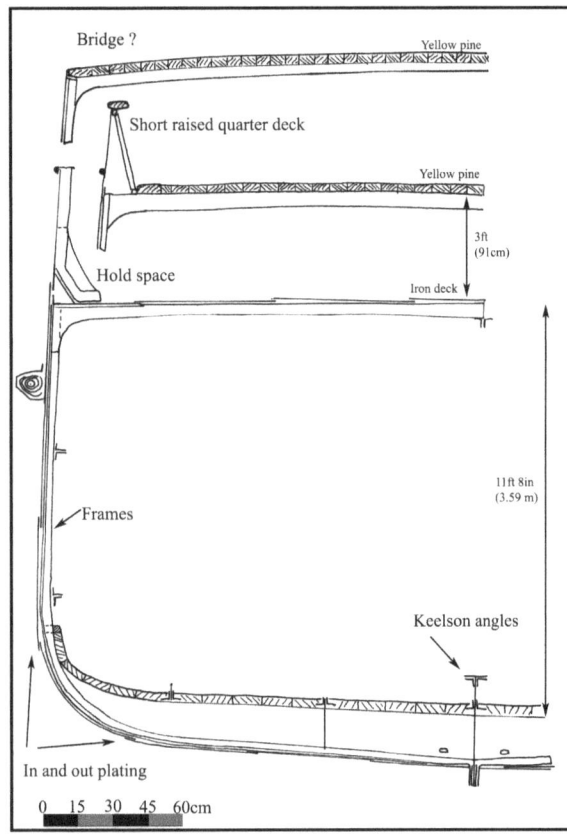

Fig. 7.2   Midship section of the Thesis *(adapted from Lloyd's Survey 3303, with permission from National Maritime Museum)*

The specifications and building history of the *Thesis* are furnished in some detail in a series of Lloyd's Survey reports which involved at least 32 surveyor's visits between 18 August 1885 and 24 March 1887 during her construction (*Lloyd's Register*, 1887). These reports are hereafter referred to as the *Construction Survey*. Transcriptions are included in Appendix 1. Searches for the ship's plan have located only a half-body plan (Fig. 7.2). No photographs of the ship have been found, but Fig. 7.3 shows the SS *Theme*, another MacIlwaine and Lewis steam ship of similar size and date, built for William Grainger (pers. comm. Roy Fenton,).

The loss of the *Thesis* is described by two contemporary sources, *The Oban Times* (October 1889) and *Lloyd's List*. The site is also listed in the summary of wreck losses in Scotland by Larn and Larn (1995: DF 16/10/1889) and in dive guides by Butland and Siedlecki (1989, 39, no. 119), Ridley (1990, 32, no. 618;), Baird (1995, 151-2), Macdonald (2000, 56–60), Liddiard (2001) and Moir and Crawford (2003, 198). Dive guides have provided an entrée for investigating the complex history of the vessel since its discovery. Where possible, these accounts have been checked by personal contact with salvage divers and others who claim discovery of the wreck.

Fig. 7.3   Photograph of the Theme, *renamed the* Glenarn *(© J and M Clarkson)*

Remote sensing

The *Thesis* was surveyed by multibeam and side-scan sonar in 2004 (see Chapter 3) with the aim of recording the site and its immediate environmental context and thereby providing geophysical data to compare with the diver survey. Unfortunately, for various reasons, due to problems in post processing, the *Thesis* multibeam survey did not yield the point-resolution that might have been expected.

Tape measure survey and detailed recording underwater

Between 2000 and 2004, some 160 survey dives by 38 divers (amounting to about 80 hours under water) generated records and led to the award of at least four NAS part II training certificates on the basis of practical project work (Young, 2000; Cleasby, 2001; Fish, 2003; Restell and Restell, 2004). The underwater survey initially aimed to enhance and test available historical evidence. Following a thorough reconnaissance of the wreck and its surrounding debris field, work began in 2000 on compilation of a deck plan. This was undertaken using tape-measure survey and work began at the bow. A baseline was laid and offset measurements were used to plot deck features and the deck edge (Young, 2000).

Because the *Thesis* is a popular dive site, the team removed baselines at the end of each dive, re-locating them at the start of the next. Apart from the inevitable loss of time, large inaccuracies resulted, prompting a change of approach in 2002. A control network was established on the holds, assuming that they were of a regular size and shape (incorrectly as it turned out) and in a central location and that their four corners were plotted by trilateration. Once fixed, smaller features and the principal areas of cracking and deck collapse were measured in around them. Results were drawn up manually at 1:50 and checked using Web for Windows (Rule, 1989). The survey of the bow section was completed by summer 2002. That of the stern, though deeper, was completed in one week the same year. Scuba equipment was used throughout and the majority of work was undertaken by divers breathing oxygen enriched air (nitrox) as a means of maximising bottom-time and quality of work, particularly at 20–30 m depth.

Detailed recording was required of features such as the steering-gear, engine and boiler compartments, to aid understanding of the complex arrangements of twisted and corroded metal. Safety considerations precluded penetration into some parts of the structure such as under the deck on the port side of the boiler. Recording involved compilation of measured drawings, supported by extensive use of video and still (latterly digital) photography. Videography proved invaluable as a recording medium when used in conjunction with a tape-measure baseline for monitoring areas of continuing deterioration and as a de-briefing tool. All images and video have been retained as part of the site archive.

In 2002, recording of the profile began with the deployment of plumb bobs to drop verticals to the seabed on the port side (where the angle of heel allowed for this). Relative depth measurements along the deck edge and at surveyed points over the entire deck completed the process. The bow was recorded by photo-mosaic and measured drawing; the impressive counter-stern was recorded by measured sketch and mathematics, because of its depth, angle of heel and a lack of available light. Measured drawings of the internal compartments of the ship enabled comparison with the *Construction Survey*. Detailed measurements of identifiable features enabled comparisons to be made between the *Survey* and the wreck on the seabed to assess the validity of the recording exercise and to identify any divergence from the surveyors' record (Restell and Restell, 2004).

Qualitative recording of biological remains

Notwithstanding the damaging presence of engine oil and other pollutants, metal hulls can enhance the natural environment by providing an artificial reef for biological colonisation. In turn, the presence of sessile species of marine organisms can have considerable effects on the corrosion of metal-hulled wrecks (Lenihan *et al.*, 1989: 117–56). Within the limitations of time and resources, qualitative recording of resident marine biological species was conducted to aid understanding of the interaction of the *Thesis* with its surrounding environment. This recording work was undertaken by SOMAP members in association with the Marine Conservation Society's Seasearch programme (pers. comm. Calum Duncan). In the interests of species identification, some biological samples were raised for microscopic examination ashore.

Material and environmental sampling

Two samples of already-broken iron fragments were recovered and de-concreted to reveal the remaining iron. Both samples were then measured and drawn and the remaining metal was weighed. Following recording, the samples were re-buried as test stakes to enable periodic inspection of corrosion rates. In 2004, a sample of ferrous sediment was recovered from 30 cm beneath the surface layer of sediment in the

An integrated study of the *Thesis*

forward hold and a large lump of coal was recovered from the coal bunker. Both samples were analysed by British Geological Survey, Keyworth, Nottingham (Fortey *et al*, 2005).

Results of background research

Accounts by James Turpin, Surveyor to *Lloyd's Register* (signed and dated Tuesday 12 April 1887) describe an iron-hulled, single deck vessel of very good workmanship. The *Thesis* had an L.O.A. of 165.8 ft (50.54 m), a gross displacement of 377.76 tons (383.80 tonnes) and 'a raised quarter deck 21.9 ft (6.68 m) long, an unenclosed forecastle 30.6 ft (9.33 m) and a bridge (unenclosed, open at both ends) 45.6 ft (13.9 m) long'. She was propelled by one double cylinder compound engine developing 60 hp. The vessel was built MacIlwaine, Lewis and Co. in accordance with *Lloyd's Rules for the Construction of Iron Vessels* formulated in 1855 (*Lloyd's Register*, 1934: 80) and revised in 1863 (*Lloyd's Register* 1934: 90). She was classified Lloyd's 100A1 with a +LMC classification for her machinery, until her loss in 1889.

The yard of MacIlwaine, Lewis and Co. was established in premises known as the Ulster Iron Works on the newly opened Abercorn Basin, Belfast, in 1867 (Lynch, 2001: 19). Initially established as a partnership, they provided engineering and ship repairing services, not launching their first vessel until 1876. Around 1885, at the time when construction of the *Thesis* started, the firm was undergoing considerable change and the partnership was dissolved. John MacIlwaine was joined in business by Hector Macoll and the new firm was established as a limited company before acquiring a new yard next to Harland and Wolff (Lynch, 2001: 20). Messrs MacIlwaine and Macoll Ltd went into liquidation in 1893 as a result of the cyclical nature of shipbuilding demand and a failure to attract major clients (Lynch, 2001: 21). However, in the intervening years, Belfast's third shipping firm (after Workman and Clark, and Harland and Wolfe) completed 58 vessels, mostly small coasters and tugs for small ship-owning companies involved in coastal and cross-channel trade.

Purpose and trade of William Grainger's vessels

William Grainger acquired his first ship in 1876 and his first steamship the *Tolka*, in 1878. His small fleet of 11 steamships comprised mostly newly built vessels, of which four were ordered from MacIlwaine and Lewis (Lynch, 2001: 21). The similar *Theme* (later renamed *Glenarn*), was built by MacIlwaine, Lewis and Co. for William Grainger in 1884. She had much the same specifications (315 gross tons, 159.2 ft L.O.A., with a short raised quarter deck, but a raised forecastle) and propulsion system, a two cylinder 60 hp compound engine (Fig. 7.3). Until Grainger's death in 1915, casualty details suggest that his fleet operated in the usual west coast trades, with coal from Lancashire or South Wales for Irish ports and occasionally further afield and ore from Antrim for north-east England. The Spanish voyage of the large *Galvanic* seems to have been exceptional. Five of Grainger's 11 steamships were lost at sea (pers. comm. Roy Fenton).

Circumstances of loss

Larn and Larn (1995: DF 16/10/1889) and the *Oban Times* (October 1889) detail the loss of the *Thesis*, but with substantial discrepancies. Larn and Larn (1995: DF 16/10/1889), quoting the *Board of Trade Wreck Returns* (1889, Appx C Table 1 p. 120 (652)), postulate a journey from Belfast to Middlesbrough under the command of G. Wallace. The same route is given by *Diver* magazine (1982). By contrast, a Middlesbrough to Belfast voyage appears in the *Oban Times* (October 1889) and Moir and Crawford (2003: 201). The vessel's cargo is variously described as pig-iron (*Oban Times*, October 1889; Moir and Crawford, 2003: 201) or iron ore and unspecified pottery (Larn and Larn, 1995: DF 16/10/1889).

Ridley (1990) relates how the iron plates around the vessel's bows were removed by salvage teams trying to recover her, but there is little evidence for this. Local scallop divers Mike Campbell and Richard Grieve (Salen, Mull) claim to have discovered the *Thesis* some time during the late 1970s while working close to Eilean Rubha an Ridire (pers. comm.). Grieve remembers that, at the time, much of the plating around the bows had already fallen away and this persuaded him to nickname her 'the skeleton wreck' (Plate 7.1). The pair undertook some rudimentary salvage work; Campbell recovered the vessel's bell and a Walker log that he sold via Sotheby's (pers. comm.) and Grieve recovered a steam whistle (pers. comm.). Campbell presented the builders' name-plate to Dave Tye at Oban Divers. This, the bell and the brass letters '*Thesis*' recovered from the seabed in 1988 (RCAHMS, MS/829/35) confirm the identity of the ship.

A subsequent, and possibly more intense, salvage operation was carried out by Neil Brown, a scallop-diver operating out of Oban, who worked the site intermittently for two years in 1979 or thereabouts, when scallops were thin on the ground (pers. comm. Mike Campbell). Brown died while scallop diving in 1981, but his boatman at the time, Andy Sproat, confirmed that no explosives were used (pers. comm. Andy Sproat). Third-party reports, denied by Sproat, suggested that Brown used to tie his fishing-boat into the wreck at low water, using the flood tide to lift bits off the ship. By the early 1980s, the wreck was already popular with the growing number of sport divers visiting the area, as is still the case today. Neither Grieve nor Campbell remembers seeing any pottery on the vessel, though diver guides mention its presence 'in two holds' (Butland and Siediecki, 1989: 39, no. 119). As was common in British waters, many souvenirs were recovered. A few finds have been declared to the Receiver of Wreck (see www.rcahms.gov.uk). However, pottery recoveries have not been reported and extensive efforts by SOMAP to trace pottery items ashore have been unsuccessful.

The gradual deterioration of the wreck structure evident from these accounts is corroborated by extracts from Roger Mathieson's logbook: 'Thursday 16/5/96 10:30 am – dived *Thesis*, shot was attached to winch on foredeck & as was usual at the time you went down shot then across foredeck and inside via a hole in hull plating on the stbd bow. We were the only divers on site at the time and perhaps naively tied-up our two RIBs to the shot, just before leaving site our boats were suddenly pulled forward about 10ft by the shot-rope - didn't think much of it at the time'. 'Saturday 18/5/96 16:08 pm – dived *Thesis,* tied-up to shot again. Went down shot and found that it now disappeared thro' a hole in the foredeck – the hole was obviously new, bright red with iron rust and had distinct holes around it where rivets had popped out. Went thro' hole and found that winch plus a section of deck plating was now precariously balanced on the edge of what must have been a 'tween-deck (or intermediate) area. I cut shot line from winch and re-attached it back up on the foredeck then went back down thro' hole and after checking area below buddy & I pushed the winch over the edge & it fell to base of wreck'.

Results of fieldwork

The wreck of the *Thesis* is located on a shelving slope close to the Morvern shore, west of Inninmore Point and in the lee of Eilean Rubha an Ridire. This is a moderate- to high-energy environment: although Inninmore Point shelters the wreck from the flood (NW-flowing) tide, the ebb current can exceed 2 knots (*c*.1 m per second) at full flow. The site is seldom inaccessible due to adverse weather, but winds from the south can create a short, sharp sea for a limited duration.

The remains comprise the semi-intact hull of a steamship within a narrow debris field (Fig. 7.4; Plate 7.2). The collapse of the non-ferrous deck superstructure, masts, rigging and hull plating, together with the removal of almost all non-ferrous artefacts, leave the wreck with an anomalous flush-decked appearance. As is to be expected of a vessel of her date and type, the *Thesis* displays a parallel middle-body form and a flat bottom. The dimensions of the wreck accord closely with the *Construction Survey*. Investigations have confirmed the extent of structural distortion of the hull. There is a twist towards the bow of approximately 0.5 m to port which is evident from the angle of heel at deck level. From the stern, moving forwards as far as the front of the boiler compartment, the deck is at 6° off the horizontal. Within a short distance, forward of hold 1, the angle of heel increases to 8° degrees and at the rear end of main hatch, the angle of heel is 10° (Fig. 7.5). Investigations around hold 1 on the starboard side have revealed two missing ribs, bowing of bulkhead plating and buckling of deck plates. On the port side, 10 m forward from the stokehole and 1m above seabed level, some of the plates appear to have been compressed and are lifting away from their rivets. A longitudinal crack running along the starboard deck from aft of the engine compartment to forward of hold 1 may also indicate that the hull has been under stress. The edges of this crack are very heavily concreted, suggesting that the crack may have occurred some time ago.

The seabed depth at the impressive counter-stern is 31 m below chart datum (Fig. 7.6; 7.7). Although a bedrock reef is exposed close to the starboard quarter there has been a substantial accumulation of sediment around the stern and the keel appears to be buried to a depth of 2 m or more in coarse sandy gravel and small pebbles. The rudder and sternpost have become detached from the ship. A large cast-iron feature was identified close to the vessel's starboard side in the debris field approximately 50 m from the stern. This feature was 3.8 m long (Plate 7.3). In form and dimensions it mirrors a diagram of the sternpost recorded by Lloyd's surveyors in the *Construction Survey*. The most likely explanation for this is that it was ripped out of the bottom of the ship when she first impacted with the seabed on sinking and before slipping back into deeper water. The bow overlies a bedrock reef at 14 m below chart datum. The stempost has become detached from the bow frames and lies on the seabed, pointing to starboard with one end underpinning the vessel's bow (Fish, 2003).

An integrated study of the *Thesis*

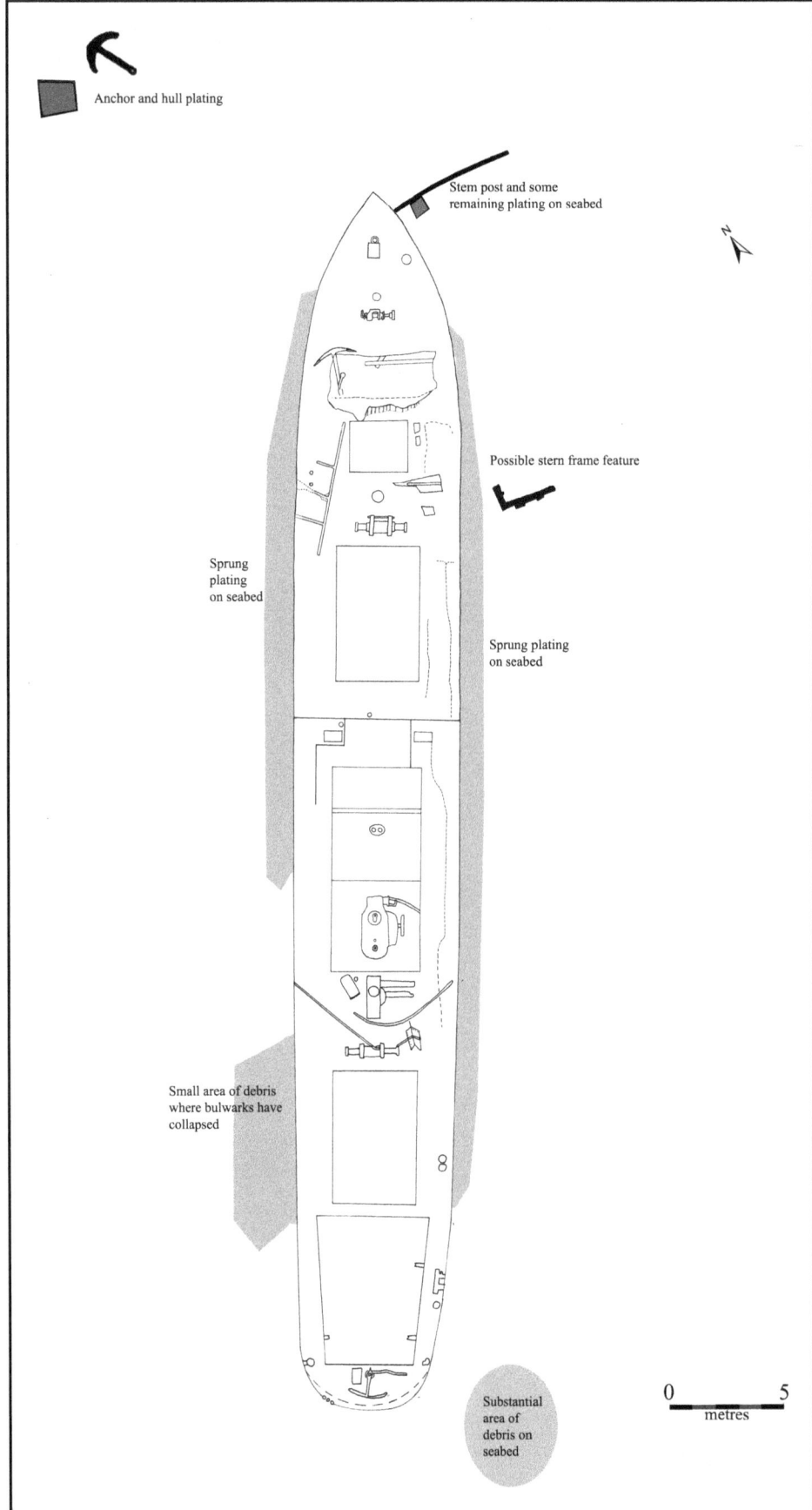

Fig. 7.4 Spread of debris on the seabed surrounding the Thesis, shown in relation to the deck plan. Only the key features and the approximate coverage are delineated (Barry Kaye, Philip Robertson)

Sound of Mull Archaeological Project

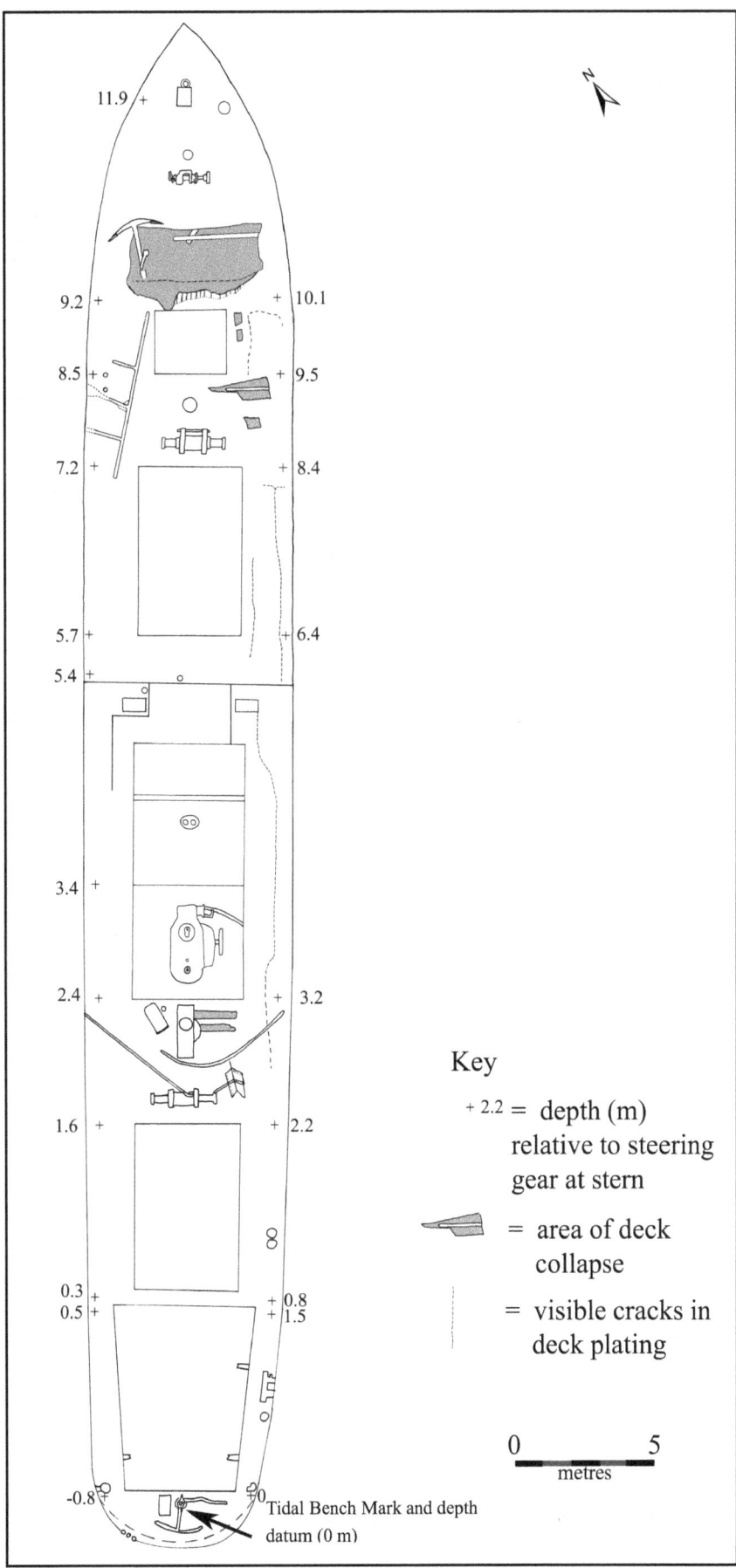

Fig. 7.5   Angle of heel at deck level and evidence of other deterioration (Barry Kaye, Philip Roberston)

An integrated study of the *Thesis*

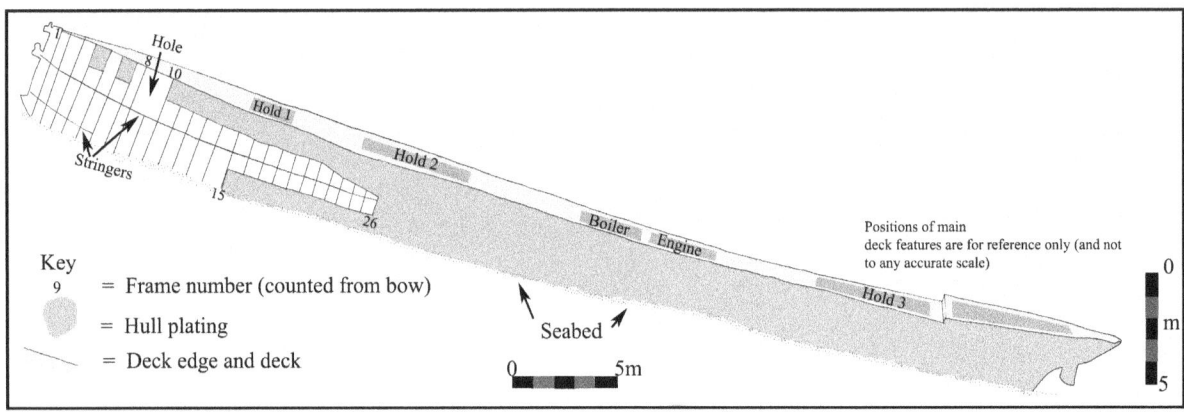

Fig. 7.6   Plating survey and profile of port side (Barry Kaye, Gwynn Hodges, Philip Robertson)

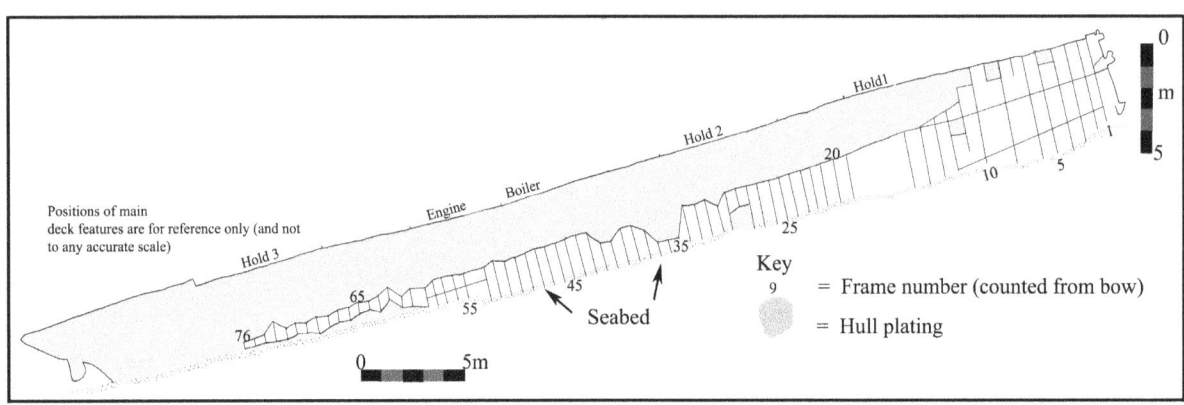

Fig. 7.7   Plating survey and profile of starboard side (Barry Kaye, Vic Tomalin, Philip Robertson)

Construction details

The stempost is made of cast iron, rectangular in section. Including its curvature, the post is almost 8 m long and its uppermost surface is 0.2 m wide along the majority of its length. Two small sections of iron plate remain attached to it (Fish, 2003: 8). Reconstructions based on recording of the stempost confirm a 'straight' bow (Fig. 7.8) characteristic of this period (Admiralty Manual of Seamanship, 1952: 16).

The stempost is made of cast iron, rectangular in Including its curvature, the post is almost 8 mlong and its uppermost surface is 0.2 m wide along the majority of its length. Two small sections of iron plate remain attached to it (Fish, 2003: 8). Reconstructions based on recording of the stempost confirm a 'straight' bow (Fig. 7.8) characteristic of this period (Admiralty Manual of Seamanship, 1952: 16).

The iron plates are attached to the frames by rivets according to the 'raised and sunken' or 'in and out' method of plating (Fig. 7.2). The plating thickness varies at different points on the hull (see the *Construction Survey*). It was not possible accurately to record thickness of hull-plating due to heavy corrosion, but in places around the bridge deck it was possible to put a hand through some of the plating. The degraded condition of these plates and rivets may explain why, forward of the boiler compartment, many of the hull-plates are no longer attached to the frames. On the starboard side (Fig. 7.7), frames are exposed as far back as the rear end of the quarter hatch (frame 76 counted from the bow). On the port side (Fig. 7.6), the plating is complete aft of frame 26 (counted from the bow).

Frames were investigated at the bow, in the main hold and inside the raised quarter deck void. Measurements of frame dimensions (width and thickness) on the seabed regularly give figures 2.54 cm smaller than the *Construction Survey*. In the vicinity of the main hold and raised quarter deck void, frame spacing (centre to centre) appeared fairly consistent with the 21 inches (53.34 cm) specified. However, unexpected extra small knees were found fitted to frames either side of small 2.54cm wide frames in the main hold area. In the raised quarter deck void, the frame widths seemed at complete variance with the *Construction Survey*, with no sign of the supporting knees detailed there.

At the bow, the frames appear heavily corroded; a missing frame was noted on the starboard side aft of the forward bulkhead and one partially-broken frame was recovered for observation ashore. To investigate structural condition in more detail, starboard frame 12 (counted from the bow) was partly broken at the

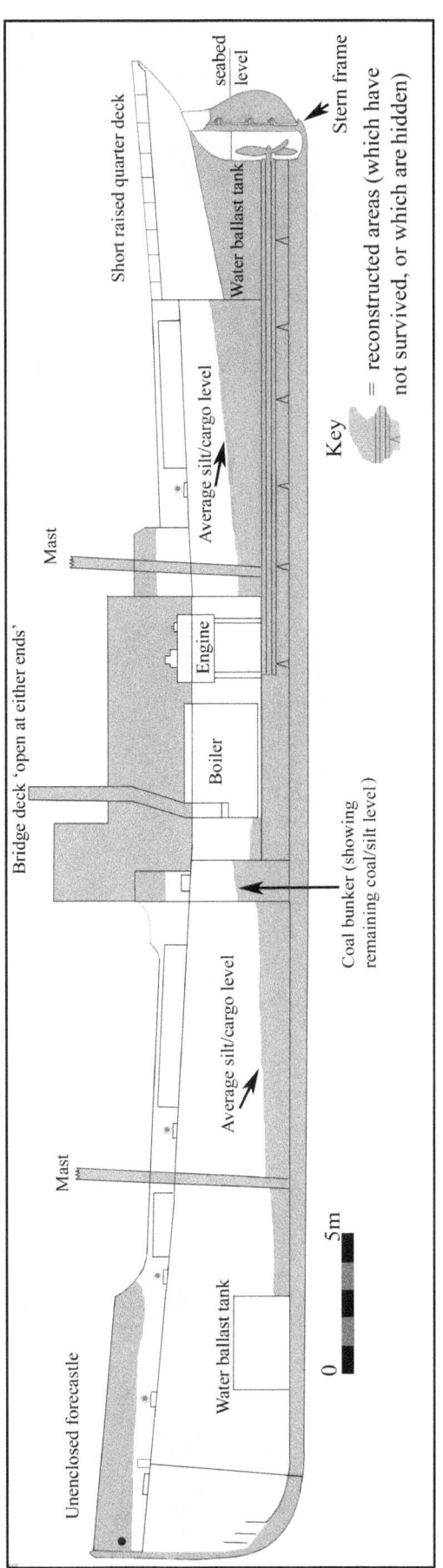

Fig. 7.8   *General arrangement and tentative reconstruction (Philip Robertson)*

An integrated study of the *Thesis*

upper joint with the upper stringer and was still partly attached to the lower stringer. A loose section 70 cm long was recovered to the surface and measured sketches and digital photographs were taken. The concretion layer varied in thickness between 5 and 10 mm thick throughout and comprised a black brittle substance with a covering of deadman's fingers (*Alcyonium digitatum*). The concretion was then broken off and the metal cleaned using soap, to reveal signs of preferential corrosion around the rivets. Thickness of 'sound' metal varies from a sharp edge to approximately 5 mm at the centre of the angle. Comparisons with figures from the *Construction Survey* suggest that as much as 50% of the frame recovered has formed a concretion layer. The resulting loss of strength cannot be accurately estimated, but may be considerable.

The *Construction Survey* indicates five watertight bulkheads within the hull structure, one more than was required by Lloyd's Rules. The foremost of these is a collision bulkhead dividing the cargo hold from a chain-locker accessed by a small hatch in the deck. The plate on this bulkhead measured about 5 cm thick in a heavily corroded state, although the bulkhead plating thickness was originally ¼ in (6.35 mm). A second forward bulkhead is situated between hold 1 and the coal stoker's hold, but it has a large hole in it.

Further bulkheads were found at the aft end of the engine compartment, at the forward end of the raised quarter deck and at its aft end next to the aft trimming tank. The midship section in the *Construction Survey* shows the keelson (Fig. 7.2) and this is visible forward of the intermediate deck where no cover plate was fitted. The top plate is 0.39 in (10 mm) thick compared to the Lloyd's figure of 0.56 in (14 mm), consistent with the effects of corrosion and biological colonisation (Restell and Restell, 2004).

Above deck configuration

Amidships, the *Thesis* had a bridge deck 'open at either end'. This structure no longer exists, but steel stanchions and plating, intact in places to a height of 2.2 m on both edges of the vessel around the engine area, presumably supported it. A large davit overlies the boilers and this may have been used for the long boat and the smaller dinghy mentioned in the *Construction Survey*, which were stowed on top of the bridge-deck. It is likely that there was accommodation on the bridge-deck, at least for the engineer, captain and bo'sun, but this is not mentioned in the *Construction Survey* and no evidence remains. However, Mike Campbell recovered several gimballed paraffin lamps from this area, further strengthening this argument (pers. comm.).

At the stern, *Thesis* has a short raised quarter deck 6.7 m long with a vertical step up to the raised quarter deck, 0.6 m high. This poop-like area has a large trapezoidal hole in the deck, close to the deck edge. The edges of this void are diagonal and there is no hatch coaming. The slope of the counter-stern beneath means that the void is not deep, nor is there cargo-handling equipment to suggest that this was an additional hold. Underneath the deck at the rear of the void, an after-peak tank with a capacity of 36 tons can be seen. At deck level, wooden beams 20 cm wide on either side of the void suggest that there was a wooden deck covering. Initially it was thought that a lightly-constructed wooden shelter might have existed too, but no evidence remains. Photographs of the contemporary and similar *Theme* show a similar short raised quarter deck, a stern steering position and a hatch and deck light, possibly providing stairway access to poop-storage below, but no shelter (Fig. 7.3). It is tempting to think that the configuration of the *Thesis* was similar to this contemporary vessel.

At the bow, the vessel had an 'unenclosed forecastle 30 ft (9.14 m) in length' (*Construction Survey*). The presence of a large capstan, a fore-peak hatch and the patent deck windlass at deck level suggest that this forecastle amounted to nothing more than an area with high stanchions and bulwarks, of which no direct evidence remains. However, the dimensions of the stempost identified on the seabed suggest that these probably extended us much as 2 m above the deck.

Propulsion and machinery

One cylindrical Scotch boiler is positioned forward of the engine. According to the *Construction Survey* the boiler has a diameter of 12ft. 9in (3.93 m) and developed 90 psi (6.21 bar). There is a visible outline of the uptake and smoke box on the boiler's front face, though the box itself is missing and this has exposed the smoke-tubes to view. The dome on top of the boiler is missing too. Calculations based on an established rule of thumb suggest that this boiler would have required approximately 120 lb (54 kg) of coal per hour at cruising speed (Jarvis, 1993, 168–70). The *Thesis* also had a donkey boiler developing 50 psi (3.45 bar) and this may still be found on the starboard side of the main boiler close to the stoke hole.

The bunker and ash-pit at the boiler's forward end are buried in silt and debris and some scattered remains of bunker coal, with an estimated depth of 1.5 m. The coal was loaded aboard ship via two stoking-hatches on either side of the deck. Judging from the size of the bunker, the *Thesis* could have carried a maximum of

13 m³ of coal. Some coal has also spilled onto the seabed close to the ship's starboard coal bunker. The bunker coal sample that was analysed has the characteristics of a medium-volatile coking coal (Fortey *et al.*, 2005). Coal of this sort was used mainly for coke manufacture in the steel industry, as distinct from low-volatile coals which were the preferred fuel for powering naval ships. Merchant shipping tended to use less expensive high-volatile coals. This coal may be a rogue sample (perhaps from contaminated loading) and further sampling would be required to ascertain for certain whether her crew were making use of coking coal in her boilers, contrary to standard practice.

Manufactured by MacIlwaine, Lewis and Co., the engine may be recognised on the seabed by its twin high- and low-pressure cylinders of 20 and 38 inch (50.8 and 96.5 cm) diameters respectively. The engine is housed vertically in a trough, protruding above deck level. A large reversing-wheel with a diameter of 90 cm may be seen on the starboard side (Plate 7.4). The engine appears to be complete with the exception of the brass pipe-fittings removed by salvage divers. The condenser remains visible, built into the engine-bed arrangement. Brown considered removing it and the boiler, but decided against it because it was not readily accessible and explosives would have been required (pers. comm. Andy Sproat).

The drive-shaft and dog-clutch are obscured under deck level, preventing examination of these features, but the *Construction Survey* provides extensive dimensional details. Steerage was by means of chain connections to a steering cam pulley and attached through the counter-stern to the rudder assembly. There is no evidence remaining for steam hydraulic steerage, although this may have been present. Four steering pulley fittings have been identified at the stern, two on either side of the vessel and appear consistent with chain steerage of some sort (Restell and Restell, 2004: 21–4). The steering quadrant is visible at the stern and is inclined to port. Photographs of the similar *Theme* display a stern steering position and it is possible that one existed on the *Thesis* too.

The *Thesis* also had one donkey engine but the location could not be confirmed by diver survey. It may be inaccessible under a section of deck plating. Neither the rudder nor the propeller (which would have been made of iron) has been identified. Given that the sternpost (which has been located) was ripped from the stern of the ship on impact with the seabed, the same is almost certainly true of the rudder and propeller.

Holds and cargo

The *Thesis* has two cargo holds, one forward, the other aft of the bridge deck (Fig. 7.9).

In both holds, iron pillars with a measured circumference of 34 cm are located along the ship's centre-line supporting the deck structure above. The stern hold is located between the raised quarter deck and the engine compartment and is accessed from above by the quarter hatch. A build-up of debris on the hold floor prevented examination of the base of the ship. On the port side at the aft end of the hold, this depth of sediment is estimated to exceed 2 m in places.

Between the forecastle and well deck hold, a gaping hole in the deck plating may be seen directly above a 'tween deck (intermediate deck). This is clad with wooden decking and it overlies a forward water ballast trimming tank 10 ft 3 in long (3.1 m) with a water capacity of 28 tons (Fig. 7.8). This tank remains apparently intact. It is likely that this 'tween deck and the void forward of this provided extra storage and possibly extra accommodation for the crew, perhaps accessed via steps and a hatch onto deck level, evidence of which has been removed by deck and internal collapse.

The well deck hold forward of the engine and boiler compartments is accessed by two hatches. The fore hatch was presumably used for loading and offloading general cargo. On the ship's last voyage, it may have contained the vessel's aforementioned pottery consignment, none of which has been identified on the seabed. The main hatch was used to access the main hold area. There is a considerable build-up of sediment which obscures the base of the holds. Reconstructions suggest that the sediment on the port side and at the aft end of the hold probably exceeds 1 m depth in places. The sediment appears to consist of a thin layer of organic material mixed in with granular ferrous material, almost certainly originating from the ship's cargo and possibly interspersed with corrosion residues from the superstructure. The iron ore sample recovered from 30 cm beneath the surface layer appeared to consist of fragments of earthy iron oxide. The analysis carried out by British Geological Survey (Fortey *et al.*, 2005) indicates that the sample is an iron ore rather than material that had already been smelted (such as pig-iron). However, the presence of magnetite in the sample is confusing since the Rosedale mines near Middlesbrough provide the only possible British source for such an ore. Given that the most trustworthy documentary source indicates a

Belfast to Middlesbrough routing, it is tempting to look for another explanation for the presence of magnetite. It may be that the results have been rendered unreliable by an ongoing reaction of ferrous material with seawater, creating what is an ore in the making.

An integrated study of the *Thesis*

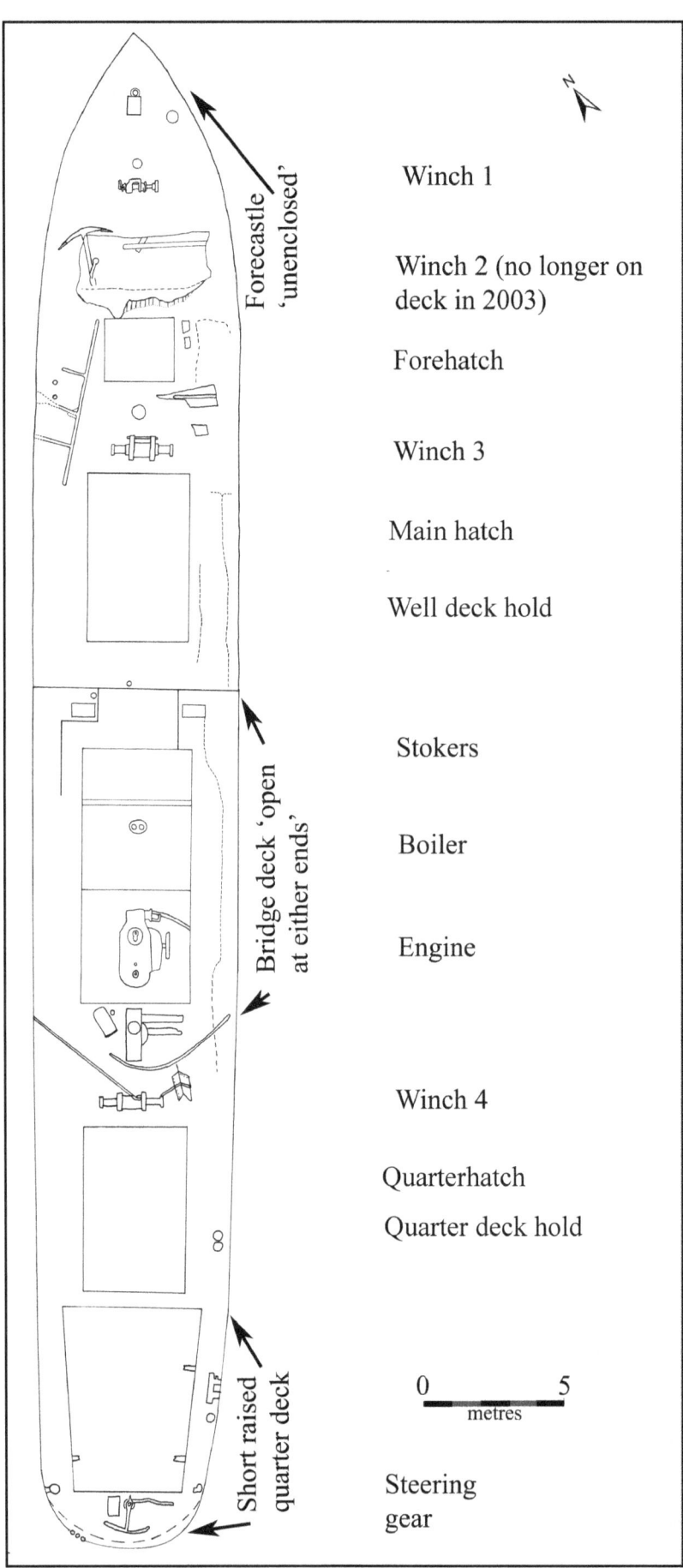

Fig. 7.9 *Deck plan, showing general arrangement (Barry Kaye, Philip Robertson)*

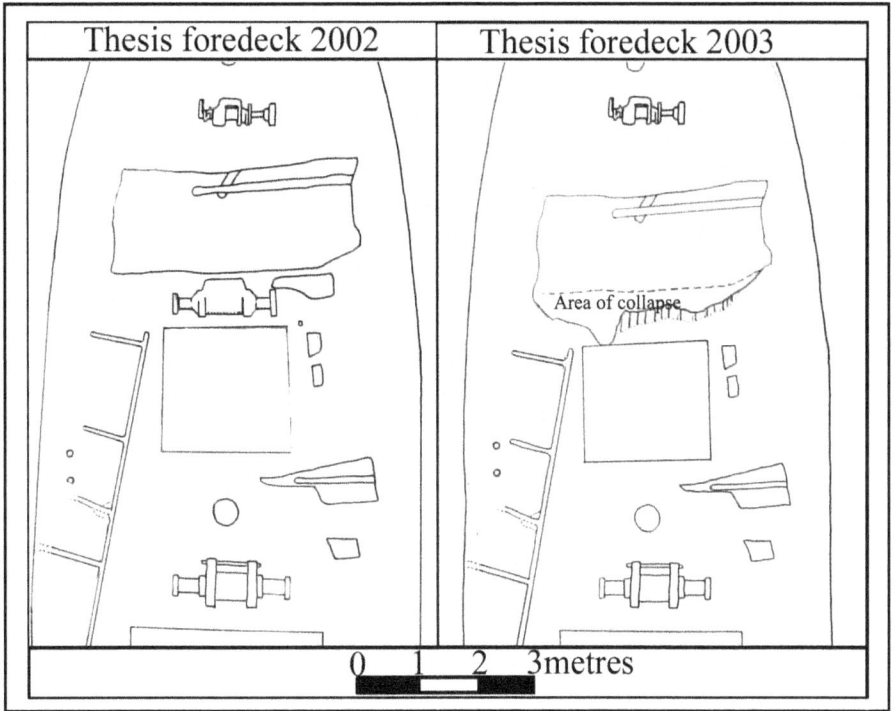

Fig. 7.10   Foredeck collapse 2002–3 (Barry Kaye, Philip Robertson)

Ancillary fittings

The *Thesis* was rigged as a schooner with two 'pitch pine pole masts'. A barely recognisable hole situated between the two well deck hatches probably held the foremast. This was 77.4 ft (23.6 m) long and 17 inches (43.2 cm) in diameter. The aft mast, 74.4 ft long (22.7 m) and 17 inches (43.2 cm) in diameter was probably located directly aft of the engine room where a circular hole in the deck was located with an average diameter measured at 16.65 inches (42.3 cm) (Restell and Restell, 2004: 26). The shorter length of the aft mast presumably took into account the higher stepping position in the aft hold (where the propeller shaft tunnel reduced cargo hold space).

The two masts also served as cargo-handling derricks for the two cargo holds, in conjunction with two sets of steam deck winches. Two circular holes in the deck provide evidence for two derricks forward of the quarter hatch and between the two well deck hatches and there may have been a third derrick forward of the fore hatch, but the deck has collapsed at this point removing any evidence. Alternatively, the off-centre positioning of the associated winches either side of the single mast derrick may suggest that this derrick was used for unloading both hatches. Further evidence for the fragility of the vessel's forward end comes from the collapse during the autumn and winter of 2002–2003 of the winch forward of the fore hatch into the hold, removing approximately 1.5 m of iron deck at the same time (Fig. 7.10). Observations of the thin layer of remaining metal on the deck that was visible shortly after the collapse confirm that the loss of strength due to corrosion at this point has caused the collapse.

Detailed measurements of all hatches were undertaken to enable comparisons with the *Construction Survey* and as indicators for twisting of the hull (Restell and Restell, 2004). Measurements of the fore hatch accord closely with the documentary evidence. On the main hatch lateral measurements were found to be up to 4 inches (10 cm) below the expected results. The diagonal measurements differed by –3 inches and –4 inches (–7.6 and –10 cm), although these were taken over a distance of 22 ft (6.7 m). Similar discrepancies were found in the quarter hatch: three of the lateral measurements are 1½ to 3¾ in (3.8 to 9.5 cm) smaller (over 12 and 19 ft – 3.7 and 5.8 m) whilst the port edge is +2½ inches (+6.35 cm) longer. The diagonal measurements differed by 4 in over 22 ft (10 cm over 6.7 m). While some of the errors in these figures may be explained by surveying difficulties, it is likely that the discrepancies do corroborate a degree of damage and twisting to the hull of the *Thesis* forward of the boiler and engine area, as suggested by the site plan and reconstructions (Fig. 7.4).

The cargoes were covered during voyage by hatch covers attached over the hatch coaming which Lloyd's recorded as being 30 inches (76.2 cm) above the deck level around all hatches (*Lloyd's Register*, 1887). On the fore hatch the coaming remains intact

An integrated study of the *Thesis*

to its full height. On the main hatch the coaming is also intact on the starboard side to its full height, but fragmented on the other three. On the quarter hatch the coaming only remains along the aft and port sides of the hold and its height was measured at three places. At the aft starboard corner it was 2 ft 9½ inches (85 cm), at the aft port corner as 2 ft 1½ inches (63.5 cm) and halfway along the port side as 3 ft (91.4 cm), some 6 inches (15 cm) in excess of the Lloyd's figure.

The presence of large cargo hatches on an open-decked ship required scuppers in the bulwarks to ensure that any water shipped would clear off the decks. On the *Thesis*, there were two scuppers and two freeing ports before the bridge bulkhead and three scuppers and two freeing ports abaft this point on either side, but it is now impossible to identify these due to corrosion and heavy colonisation of deadman's fingers (*Alcyonium digitatum*). The bulwarks on either side of the ship have been constructed of angle-iron and solid iron plating throughout. In a few places, the bulwarks remain intact to their full height, but the plating between the uprights has disintegrated throughout.

The forward most deck winch is a patent windlass for anchor-handling. The *Thesis* carried five anchors consisting of three bowers, one stream and one kedge and 90 fathoms (165 m) of $1^1/_{16}$ inch (2.7 cm) anchor chain. There is tentative evidence of some concreted anchor chain lying on the foredeck close to the gear hatch, but only one of her anchors remains on the hull. It has a stock 2 m long and is of swivelling arm design of Admiralty Pattern. It now lies crown end up in the holds but was originally tied to the bulwarks on the port side. A second anchor also of the swivelling arm Admiralty Pattern design lies off the port bow. There is no chain between the wreck and this anchor. A third anchor was recovered (pers. comm. Paul Gallacher) and it now lies in Tobermory High Street. Unfortunately it did not prove possible to identify this anchor among the three or four which decorate the same location. Only the first can be conclusively linked with the *Thesis* and it probably represents one of the vessel's bower anchors. The outstanding anchors cannot be accounted for, but the remains of a capstan at the bow can still be seen on the deck.

Environmental parameters

The full range of species identified on the hull and surrounding seabed is covered in Appendix 2. In summary, the flat surfaces of the deck are covered in faunal growth, mostly hydroids and sea firs (*Delesseria sanguinea* or *Phycodrys rubens*). A sea fir from the starboard deck edge was examined under microscope and small pink anemone polyps (species unidentified), a praying shrimp (species unidentified) and microscopic fragments of grit were observed. Sea firs were also identified alongside colonies of tubeworms (*Pomatoceros triqueter*) and peacock worms (*Tubularia larynx*) under the counter-stern and towards the stern on the starboard side. The tubeworms are 20–40 cm long with *c*.30 cm separation. Deadman's fingers (*Alcyonium digitatum*) have colonised upstanding deck features, such as deck winches, as well as the sides of the ship (Fig. 7.15). On the port side above the rubbing strake, where exposed frames have provided an excellent surface for colonisation, there is almost 100% coverage with individual specimens up to 35 cm long. The same coverage may be found amidships where the plating remains, though the density of specimens is far less beneath the rubbing strake. The density reduces towards the stern with specimens 1–15 cm long and there is less coverage on the starboard side, which is more sheltered from the current.

The seabed surrounding the wreck consists of gravel, mixed cobbles and pebbles, with exposed bedrock at the bow. At the stern the sea anemone (*Epizoanthus couchii*) was found on the seabed, as well as some examples of the rare featherstar (*Leptometra celtica*). Close to the wreck, plating on the sea floor has some coverage of deadman's fingers (*Alcyonium digitatum*), though individuals are smaller in size and less concentrated than on the wreck. This is generally the case with the exception of sea urchins (*Echinus esculentus*), which were more abundant on the seabed, but sparse on the wreck.

Discussion

Trilateration proved to be the best method for compiling a basic record of the deck plan and Web for Windows (Rule, 1989) was useful in checking survey accuracy. Still and video photography proved invaluable for detailed recording. Measuring and drawing artefacts under water provided a far greater understanding of complex features. However, the task of recording a large 3D structure such as the counter-stern (at a depth of at least 30 m) proved challenging from the point of view of both survey methodology and safety. Plumb bobs and dive-computers were effective tools in recording the angle of heel of the vessel and compiling a side-on view. The multibeam survey achieved the complicated task of recording the wreck within its wider context with speed and efficiency, a task that would have been beyond the SOMAP dive team, even given available time and safety backup.

Minor discrepancies (of 1 inch – 2.54 cm – in measuring detail and 3–4 inches – 7.6–10 cm – in measuring distances of 22 ft – 6.7 m) between actual and expected measurements were noted and might be expected on any survey of a steamship wreck. Errors can be assigned to a variety of causes. Corrosion reduced the original metal dimensions, yet added oxidised deposits. Marine growth was extensive in some areas, at once increasing the visible size and subsequently producing layer upon layer of concretion. Measurement methods contributed to inaccuracy; flexible tapes stretch with use giving inaccurate readings and also bow in strong current producing increased dimensions.

Larger differences are less easily explained and are worthy of further investigation. The variation in the coaming height of the quarter hatch, rising to a full 6 inches (15 cm) above the expected height, is puzzling. It is possible that this was an alteration made to the ship after the survey or, alternatively, the hatch may have been wrenched out above the deck during the sinking. Equally puzzling are other areas where small additional frames or larger sections or extra knees were found. Presumably the shipbuilder felt these were necessary. After all, the rules were designed to benefit the insurance company by specifying minimum manufacturing standards in order to reduce their risk.

Despite the abundance of documentary information for wrecks of this period, some of the historical reports relating to the route, the cargo and the loss of the ship proved to be contradictory. Archaeological evidence for the twisting of the bow to port suggests that the *Thesis* hit the rocks of Inninmore Point at speed with a glancing blow while entering the Sound of Mull from the south-west. She was clearly afloat long enough for her crew to abandon ship, but, once she sank, the impact of the stern on the seabed caused the sternpost and rudder to be ripped from the hull before the wreck slid further back into deeper water. The position and orientation of the wreck all point strongly to her being on passage between Belfast and Middlesbrough, as was indicated originally by *Lloyd's List*. It is likely that *Oban Times* account was inaccurate at the time and has been recycled in later accounts. According to scientific testing there is a possibility that the iron ore was a Rosedale ore from magnetite-rich mines close to Middlesbrough. While scientific analysis does corroborate seabed observations that the cargo was iron ore as opposed to pig-iron, Kaye (pers. comm.) has argued that the samples may represent an ore in the making due to chemical changes of the sample in reaction with sea water and the Rosedale provenance is therefore not definite. This counter hypothesis has not been denied by Fortey as a possibility (pers. comm.). In summary therefore, it is likely that the cargo was an ore from the iron-ore mines in County Antrim, Province of Ulster. These were in operation from 1867 until 1933, with much of the iron ore exported to England from Red Bay pier. After 1876 export from Red Bay declined when a railway linked the mines to Ballymena and hence to the larger ports of Larne and Belfast. With the opening of the railway, ore production rose steadily each year to peak at 230,000 tons in 1880.[1]

By the 1870s and 1880s, screw steamships like the *Thesis*, with engines amidships, were becoming common, particularly large merchant vessels over 225 ft. – 69 m (Waine, 1980: 99). This design reduced weight in the stern and avoided a change in trim in the vessel as the bunker coal was consumed. However, a long shaft-tunnel reduced cargo capacity in the after holds and there was a risk that a vessel would trim by the head (Robertson and Hagan, 1953: 28). To regain the lost space and to correct the trim, a raised quarter deck evolved. By the 1890s, the long raised quarter deck, extending extra space to the bridge, had become popular (Waine, 1980: 10).

Using standard nomenclature (Admiralty Manual of Seamanship, 1952: 16) the hull shape of the *Thesis* might best be described as a '2–3 hull'. There is no extended raised quarter deck to provide extra space in the after hold, but short raised quarter deck possibly to allow some storage space above the tunnel shaft and water tanks. Her well deck and forecastle are flush in the manner of the first steamships and this is perhaps strange, given that many screw steamships with engine amidships at this period, including other vessels built by MacIlwaine and Lewis for Grainger (such as the *Theme* and the *Lough Fisher*) had a raised forecastle (including winches etc.) and a cargo hatch at lower level. The forecastle mentioned in the *Construction Survey* exists entirely beneath deck level, probably providing rudimentary accommodation space for sailors, as was common at the time (Robertson and Hagan, 1953: 20). The presence of a 'tween deck in the forward hold accessed by a small hatch is of interest too, since 'tween deck levels were not common on coasting tramps designed for carrying bulk cargoes like coal (Robertson and Hagan, 1953: 10). The pillars that support the deck on the *Thesis* were not desirable in bulk cargo carriers. By 1900, pillars were replaced by cantilever brackets (Robertson and Hagan, 1953: 10).

Given the sum of available evidence, it seems likely that the *Thesis* was designed for carrying mixed cargoes, probably reflecting the type of coastal trade Grainger's vessels worked. This trade may be illustrated by the cargo carried on her final voyage, a combination of iron-ore and pottery, of which the pottery, if indeed it did exist, may have been no more than a few crates (pers. comm. Roy Fenton). It may be that the *Thesis* represents a stage in the evolution of the coastal tramp steamer, incorporating elements of

---

1 See www.antrim.net

An integrated study of the *Thesis*

sailing design as well as the raised quarter deck. Though the basic design illustrated by the *Thesis* was to continue well into the 20th century, she was the last of her breed in a number of ways. By 1888, iron hull construction was on its way out and 90% of ships were built with steel hulls (*Lloyd's Register*, 1934: 139). By 1890 triple-expansion engines (patented in 1871), with their extra power and efficiency, were used to propel large coasters, though smaller coasters (under 140 feet – 43m L.O.A.) continued to use twin-cylinder compound engines for some time because of the space saving (Waine, 1980: 37).

The analysis of the bunker coal sample may suggest that in addition to higher grade fuels, coking coals were sometimes used on the earlier Belfast merchant steamers. Given the nature of coastal trade in low-value bulk goods, it is tempting to suppose that ship-owners accepted cheap fuel wherever they could get it – even if it was not of the highest quality. Bearing in mind the low efficiencies of marine boilers and engines at the time, cheap fuel of this sort might not have made a huge difference anyway.

It is possible that the *Thesis* and the *Theme* reflect a Belfast coaster design tradition that may have been distinct from other acknowledged coastal tramp types such the Glasgow steamships (mostly raised quarter deck steamships with engine and machinery aft). This is most probably a reflection of the particular needs of the Northern Irish coastal trade, as well as of the infrastructure for loading and unloading cargoes at Belfast and the various ports of destination.

The biodiversity of the *Thesis* suggests a moderate- to high-energy environment with a strong unidirectional current. The most obvious illustration of this is that species (e.g., deadman's fingers – *Alcyonium digitatum*) favouring a high-current habitat appear to have colonised the vessel's exposed port side more thickly than the sheltered starboard side.

It is likely that the twisting in the hull and other signs of buckling were caused during the wrecking process when the ship went down by 'the bows'. The preferential corrosion evident around the rivets suggests strongly that the loss of plating at the bow has occurred due to corrosion of the rivets and not due to salvage. Collapse of plating will have further weakened the hull-structure and exacerbated any twisting of the forward end. The absence of plating towards the bow will have increased the flow of oxygenated water through the hull and so has probably increased the rate of corrosion of metal deck plating. In places, the surviving deck plating is so corroded that it has collapsed under the weight of large fittings such as winches. The durability of the deck has not been helped by the use of deck beams and deck fittings as shot-line anchor points for diver tourism purposes. The frames also appear to be in very poor condition with very little intact metal remaining on the one sample examined. Moreover, the collapse of deck fittings through the deck suggests that, for safety reasons, divers should beware of entering the bow area.

Salvage and souvenir hunting have accounted for removal of the brassware and non-ferrous fittings, leaving only the shell of a ship on the seabed. As alluded to in dive guides, it may be presumed that divers have removed the pottery; the salvors do not recollect seeing any of it. Throughout the project it has proved difficult to reconcile evidence of the remains of the vessel with the sometimes conflicting oral testimonies of divers and salvors. For reasons of commercial confidentiality, personal grievances and worries over legal reprimand, perhaps these accounts should all be taken with a pinch of salt. Accounts in diving guides are very useful as introductions, but they often rely heavily on recycled, sometimes inaccurate, versions of history and little seabed research. It is possible that the accumulation of sediments at the stern may contain material from the ship's raised quarter deck of which little material evidence has been found.

Conclusions

Despite the inherent inaccuracies in recording corroding iron underwater and the abundant availability of documentary information for any wreck of 19th-century date, archaeological work on the *Thesis* has added knowledge. Recording of the wreck has illustrated some peculiarities of construction not observed by Lloyd's surveyors, who were content perhaps simply to check compliance with Lloyd's Rules and to minimise risk for the insurance company. SOMAP surveys have succeeded in reconciling conflicts in historical accounts, thereby arriving at a more complete history of the route, cargo and loss of the ship. Before this project, the post-wrecking history of the ship was inadequately recorded: salvage events left no documentary record and the seabed evidence made little sense. Hopefully now the picture is clearer. Yet, in every respect, work on this fairly recent, well-documented wreck has highlighted the major challenges archaeologists face in eliciting the truth about a wreck site from the material evidence on the seabed.

With the exception of shipping company records (e.g. Cuthbert, 1956) and a few analytical accounts (Waine, 1980; Robertson and Hagan, 1953), steam coasters and short sea traders have not received much attention by historians. Commentators (e.g. Gardiner and Greenhill, 1993) have tended to record technological advances and innovations, preferring the passenger liners and trans-oceanic traders to the coastal tramp. Yet archaeology is often at its most relevant when recording the commonplace and the *Thesis* was certainly commonplace in her time. Built by the thousand, such steam coasters contributed considerably to the rise of Britain as an industrial power. Although recorded in old photographs, oral testimonies and ships' plans, the vessels that survived to the ends of their days were mostly broken up for scrap. The best, unaltered, examples may lie at the bottom of the sea where they are important as full-scale illustrations of the innovation, engineering and design of the maritime industrial age. This resource is potentially huge; entries so far to the RCAHMS database suggest that approximately 4000 steamships (including liners, lighters and trawlers) may have been lost around the coast of Scotland since 1900 (pers. comm. Bob Mowat)

In this case, salvage work and the side effects of dive tourism have unfortunately diminished her archaeological value. Environmental factors too have taken their toll in common with most metal wrecks. It is very difficult to put an accurate timescale on her collapse, but within 100 years, she will probably exist only as a pile of scrap metal, with some centrally visible features such as the engine and boiler exposed amidships. The *Thesis* was wrecked in a fairly sheltered coastal environment. The numerous 19th-century metal hulled wrecks located in less favourable burial conditions around Scottish coasts may not last as long.

Chapter 8 – Summary and conclusions

Despite widespread use of the Sound of Mull since prehistory, the earliest underwater site so far discovered dates from the 16th century. However, given the preservation conditions evident from the Duart Point wreck (1653), it is reasonable to suppose that earlier material will be preserved, albeit partially or wholly buried and therefore difficult to locate. Wreck sites of 18th to 20th century date are often upstanding and easier to locate by divers using standard echo sounders. As a result, most of the known sites date to this period.

It is perhaps also no coincidence that the abundance of post-medieval maritime archaeology in the Sound of Mull relates to a period of expansion in shipping activity. Blessed with deep navigation channels and open, but sheltered anchorage areas, a route through the Sound of Mull provided ships with a coastal route away from exposed Atlantic shores. These factors were favoured particularly during bad weather. Despite advances in cartography, navigation and lighthouses, many vessels met their end in the Sound of Mull during this period.

For the 18th – 20th centuries, there are extensive documentary accounts of shipping and aircraft losses off Scottish coasts. There have been two aircraft losses in the Sound. Anchor dragging incidents and strandings appear to have been a common cause of loss for sailing vessels, equipment failure and navigational error for steamships and other powered vessels. In summary, written sources suggest that 68 incidents in the Sound resulted in a total loss (see Appendix 3). We are aware of current or recent existence of archaeological remains from 21 of these. The other 71 incidents relate to strandings and such events, which have probably not yielded a significant archaeological record, if any at all (see Appendix 3). The discrepancy between identified sites and total losses suggests that more sites remain to be discovered. The sites recorded by SOMAP can be broadly categorised as follows.

Harbours and shipping infrastructure

The collapsed quay at Ardtornish Bay is just one example recorded by SOMAP of the numerous small harbours and cleared landing places that scatter the coast edge, linking land with sea.

Debris sites

In popular anchorage areas, harbours and landing places, ships have left behind seabed debris associated with their activities. For instance, the holed stones discovered on the seabed near Eilean Rubha an Ridire are probably connected with nearby quarrying. Isolated anchors and the collection of cannon and associated finds in Scallastle Bay all recall the use of this bay as an anchorage area.

Wreck sites

In the Sound of Mull, there are wrecks of steam drifters, puffers, sailing schooners, steam coasters (small and large) and small sailing warships, some of the major vessel types that evolved in Britain during the post-medieval period. But what was their purpose in the Sound of Mull?

Vessels such as the *Buitenzorg*, the *Shuna*, the *Hispania* and the *Rondo* were using this channel on passages between ports far afield. Until the moment of wrecking, they played only a transitory role in the fabric of local life. But, with cargoes originating from or destined for countries such as India and Scandinavia, we are reminded that wreck sites in isolated locations around the Scottish coasts can provide information linking communities across oceans and continents. Other vessels were in transit too, but between British ports. For instance, the *John Preston* was carrying Welsh slate to Fraserburgh on the north-east coast of Scotland. Trade from Wales to Orkney and the ports of the east coast of Scotland accounted for five other incidents between 1869 and 1896 (the *Menai*; the *Margaret*; the *New Blessing*; the *Louisa*; the *Elizabeth*).

Some had a clear purpose on Mull, Morvern or other communities on the west coast of Scotland. The HMS *Dartmouth* and the small warship wrecked off Duart Point in 1653 (along with the five other vessels in the same squadron) were engaged in naval sorties against clan strongholds during the political uncertainties of the 17th century. Vessels such as the *Pelican* (local coal storage hulk), the *Anna Bhan* (a smack used for transporting livestock and coal between Mull and the mainland) and the *Logan* (supply of coal to Skye) were tools of trade in a rural highland economy which depended on the sea for prosperity and survival. When a wreck occurred on shore a busy recovery operation sprang into life and stranded vessels were soon patched up and pressed back into service. Early salvage work on the sunken Tobermory galleon around 1677 provides ample illustration of the scale of human invention where a profit was to be made. In more recent times, salvors have worked on the *John Preston*, the *Hispania*, the *Rondo*, the *Thesis* and the *Buitenzorg*. The salvage tradition continues to this day.

Level of preservation

Muckelroy (1978: 164) classifies wreck sites in British waters into three groups: coherent; scattered and ordered; and scattered and disordered. On balance, the SOMAP surveys confirm that the wreck sites in the Sound of Mull fall within the two better preserved categories. Muckelroy (1978: 160–75) also illustrates how the formation of an archaeological site on the seabed is a result of a complex interplay of environmental and man-made 'drivers' of change.

The environment has a major part to play and this is a complex area of science. However, SOMAP's remote sensing has hinted at the role of currents and sediment regimes in this process: noticeable scouring and sediment accretion patterns have been seen on the *Thesis*, the *Hispania*, the *Buitenzorg* and the Duart Point wreck. The effects of souvenir hunting and salvage have been widely discussed, but the effects of commercial fishing techniques on submerged archaeological sites are poorly understood. SOMAP has documented evidence of scallop or nephrops trawl activity close to the wrecks of the *Buitenzorg*, the *Shuna*, the *Hispania* and the *Rondo*. Impacts by scallop-dredging equipment to the *Hispania* have also been observed, while evidence for heavy dredging activity in Scallastle Bay may help to explain the scattered characterisation of its seabed archaeology.

At first glance, the wooden vessels appear to have been preserved where soft sediments have partially buried their hull structures (e.g. Duart Point wreck; the HMS *Dartmouth*; the *John Preston*); the more recent metal wrecks are structurally intact. The *Shuna* appears to be the best preserved of these, perhaps because she is located within a tidally benign environment. She was the last of the metal wrecks to be discovered and has not been targeted by salvage interests. However, on closer inspection, structural deterioration evident on the *Thesis* and changes to the *Hispania* might suggest that the metal wrecks are in a phase of rapid evolution, by interaction with a chemically and mechanically challenging environment. Similar findings have arisen from repeat surveys of the remaining seven wrecks from the German High Seas fleet scuttled in Scapa Flow in 1919 (pers. comm. Bobby Forbes).

Significance

Except for the Duart Point wreck and the *Dartmouth*, none of the sites in the Sound of Mull has any statutory designation signifying national importance. Certainly vessels like the *Shuna*, the *John Preston*, the *Rondo*, the *Hispania* and the *Thesis* are well documented in written sources. Nevertheless, the wrecks of these ships may be of some illustrative importance as examples of once common cargo-vessel types of which few unaltered examples exist within maritime museums (Brouwer, 1999). These vessels played an important part in a period of burgeoning maritime trade around the British Isles and across the British Empire during the 19th and 20th centuries.

Approaches to survey and recording

Sites like the *John Preston* and the *Thesis* provide valuable opportunities for budding archaeologists to learn and improve their skills while contributing knowledge. These are relatively durable sites which are of some importance, but they are not the nation's most prized historic assets: better a misplaced fin kick on the *John Preston* than on a more fragile and unique historic wreck. It is certainly true that mistakes have been made and lessons learned. Planning frame survey worked better on the *John Preston* than endless tape measurements; initial attempts to use baseline and offset survey on the *Thesis* proved impossible given tidal constraints. However, when issues of methodology have been resolved, diver surveys have resulted in very detailed recording of three sites. This in turn has allowed detailed archaeological analysis and interpretation to take place.

Diver based survey was inevitably time-consuming and was limited in its coverage to wreck sites and defined areas of seabed. Remote sensing provided a means of rapidly surveying large areas of seabed. Of the systems used, high-resolution multibeam bathymetry proved useful for rapid recording of complex three-dimensional wrecks and the surrounding seabed. High resolution side-scan worked best as a tool to locate sites, to provide a detailed overview of large intact wrecks and their debris fields and to enable differentiation between geological features and archaeology. However, despite the obvious benefits of these systems, archaeological interpretation of specific features within a site was most effective when the remote-sensing data was used in conjunction with diver survey and not in isolation; although all the sites identified relate to a period that is well documented, SOMAP's research has added value. As far as we are aware, the Scallastle Bay cannon site does not appear in documentary sources. The location of the *Evelyn Rose* has succeeded in matching a documented loss to seabed remains. Surveys on the *Thesis* have helped to resolve inconsistencies in oral tradition and historical accounts. On the *John Preston*, work has illustrated a perhaps mundane, but nevertheless important aspect of coastal trade.

Summary and conclusions

Implications for resource management

The sites described in this monograph are under pressure from man-made and environmental factors. In this respect, more integrated management may help to ensure that the interests of the historic environment are safeguarded from inadvertent damage. Fortunately, this monograph has come to fruition at a time when management of the marine environment according to the principles of Integrated Coastal Zone Management (ICZM) is high on the policy agenda.

In December 2006, the Scottish Executive announced that the Sound of Mull is to be the fourth in a network of pilot projects under the Scottish Sustainable Marine Environment Initiative (SSMEI) banner. The three-year Sound of Mull pilot will develop and implement a marine spatial plan through partnership between stakeholders and regulators.[1] In March 2007, DEFRA issued a Marine Bill White Paper proposing, amongst other things, a system of marine spatial planning for the UK.

Within this policy context, sound decisions can only be made with sound data. For the historic environment, the lack of quality data is an issue: so far we have located on the seabed only 15% of the 15,000 or so maritime records in the RCAHMS database. As we seek to identify what actually lies on the seabed, there must surely be a role for the 'enthusiast'. Over a decade and more, given appropriate guidance and support from external organisations, 200 or more enthusiasts have contributed to a major recording exercise, overcoming considerable logistical challenges, to document and monitor a resource that is out of sight for most Scots, but need not be out of mind.

As SOMAP continues into the future, what will be the key challenges? More sites remain to be found and more need to be recorded in detail. As efforts continue better to understand the timescales and processes of deterioration, continued remote-sensing and diver based surveys will provide an effective baseline for monitoring change. At this stage, it seems unlikely that the pace of deterioration can easily be delayed. If this is the case, then SOMAP has at least started a programme of preservation by record which will ensure that future generations can benefit from a legacy of sorts. In this regard, the collection of iron and steel wrecks in the Sound of Mull provide an important research opportunity. Work on the *Thesis* has helped to demonstrate that archaeological surveys can contribute knowledge to sites which are well documented. A research project led by academia might help to investigate further where archaeological fieldwork on a wider range of iron and steel wrecks can add knowledge. This would help curators to prioritise funding to those sites where most can be learned and before they become nothing more than a pile of iron ore on the seabed.

Although SOMAP has cost the taxpayer relatively little, its 200 or more participants have contributed their own time and money, for nothing in return but hard graft on holiday in the Sound of Mull. Not everyone has the same time, energy or inclination to participate in this way. Therefore, it is important that future initiatives offer encouragement to those divers or non-divers who merely want to look and learn about what lies beneath the waves. For the diving tourists, there is a clear case for continuing the visitor schemes to ensure that as many visitors as possible can enjoy Scotland's most significant historic wrecks, without long-term detriment to the sites themselves. Museums and exhibitions, boat and submarine tours and virtual dives by computer visualisation all provide means whereby non-divers can penetrate the depths of the Sound of Mull.

Closing comments

For those communities who have inhabited the shores of the Sound of Mull since prehistory, its sheltered waters have provided an important seaway for transport and communication, trade and prosperity. The Sound of Mull has also been a thoroughfare for shipping from far afield. From the 17th century at least, much of the coastal shipping traffic on passage between the North of Scotland and the Irish Sea passed through it. Many incidents occurred. However, these sheltered, sediment rich waters have bequeathed to Scottish archaeology some well preserved examples of significant vessel types from the post-medieval period of British shipping. The archaeological potential of a sheltered seaway such as the Sound of Mull may also be reflected in other coastal locations within Scotland, such as the Clyde and Forth estuaries, where even greater concentrations of diverse archaeology may be found underwater in environments also conducive to the long term survival of archaeological remains.

---

1   http://www.thecrownestate.co.uk/print/newscontent/92_marine_spatial_planning_sound_of_mull.htm

Appendix 1 – Abridged transcriptions of Lloyd's survey report 3303 on the SS *Thesis* (metric conversions added where appropriate)

General Remarks (State quality of workmanship, opinions as to class etc.)

Iron Ship		
Survey held at	Belfast	
Date, First Survey	August 13 1885	
Date, Last Survey	March 23 1887	
On the	Iron Screw steamship *Thesis*	
Master	J Ferguson 1877–1887	
Built at	Belfast	
When built	1886-7	
Launched	January 25 1887	
Owners	W.A. Grainger	
Port Belonging to	Belfast	
Destined voyage	Coasting	
If Surveyed while Building, afloat, or in Dry Dock	Specially Surveyed while Building	
Detail	**Detail or Imperial measurement**	**Metric**
Gross tonnage	377.76 tons	383.80 tonnes
Net tonnage	151.05 tons	153.46 tonnes
Tonnage under Tonnage Deck	346.45 tons	351.99 toones
Ditto of Third, Spar or Awning deck	-	
Ditto of Raised Qr.Dk.	13.21 tons	13.42 tonnes
Ditto of Houses on Deck	6.21 tons	6.31 tonnes
Ditto of Hatch ways	11.89 tons	12.08 tonnes
Length	165.8 ft	50.54 m
Breadth	25 ft	7.62 m
Depth (upper part of keel to upper deck beams)	13.16 ft	4.01 m
Depth (top of floors to upper deck level)	11.8 ft	3.6 m
Proportions - Breadth to length	1:6.63	
Depths to Length – Upper deck to Keel	1:12.6	
Construction specifications		
Keel (depth by thickness)	7¼ by 1⅞ in	18.4 by 4.8 cm
Stem (moulding by thickness)	7¼ by 1⅞ in	18.4 by 4.8 cm
Sternpost for rudder (moulding by thickness)	7 by 3½ in	17,8 by 8.9 cm
Do. for propeller (moulding by thickness)	7 by 3½ in	17,8 by 8.9 cm
Distance of Frames from moulding edge to moulding edge, all fore and aft	21 in	53.3 cm
Frames, Angle iron, for 3/5 length amidships	3 by 3 by 7 in	7.6 by 7.6 by 17.8 cm
Do. For 1/5 at each end	3 by 3 by 6 in	7.6 by 7.6 by 17.8 cm
Reversed frames, Angle iron	2½ by 2½ in	6.35 by 6.35 cm
Floors depth and thickness of floor plate at mid line for half length amidships	18 by 6 in	45.7 by 15.2 cm
Depth at ¾ the half-breadth	13 in	33 cm
Height extended at the bilges	29 in	73,7 cm
Beams, Upper Single angle iron bulb iron	5 by 3 by 6 in	12.7 by 7.6 by 15.2 cm
Do. hatch beam	6 by 3 by 6 in	15.2 by 7.6 by 15.2 cm
Single angle iron on upper edge	4 by 3 by 7 in	10.2 by 7.6 by 17.8 cm
Average spacing	21 in	53.3 cm
Beams, Rear Quarter Deck		
Single angle iron bulb iron	5½ by 3 by 7 in	14 by 7.6 by 17.8 cm
Average spacing	42 in	106.7 cm
Beams, Forecastle	5 by 2½ by 6 in	12.7 by 6.35 by 15.2 cm
Average spacing	42 in	106.7 cm
Keelson Centre line single plate	11 by 9 in	27.9 by 22.9 cm

Thesis – Construction Survey

Rider plate	7½ by 9 in	19.05 by 22.9 cm
Bulb plate	3½ by 3 by 6 in	8.9 by 7.6 by 15.2 cm
Angle irons	3½ by 3 by 6 in	8.9 by 7.6 by 15.2 cm
Double Angle Iron Side Keelson	3½ by 3 by 6 in	8.9 by 7.6 by 15.2 cm
Side intercostals plate	6 in thick	15.2 cm
Attached to outside plating with angle iron	3 by 3 by 6 in	7.6 by 7.6 by 15.2 cm
Bilge Angle Irons	3½ by 3 by 6 in	8.9 by 7.6 by 15.2 cm
Do. Bulb iron	6 in for $^3/_5$ by 6 in	15.2 cm for $^3/_5$ by 15.2 cm
Bilge Stringer Angle irons	3½ by 3 by 6 in	8.9 by 7.6 by 15.2 cm
Plates in garboard strakes, breadth and thickness	43 by 9 in	109.2 by 22.9 cm

General Remarks (State quality of workmanship, opinions as to class etc.,
Bed-plate machined and brasses fitted and crank shaft bedded in place all shafts turned low pressure cylinder bored and high pressure cylinder cast, condenser in shop, piston and connecting rods turned, details of valve gear and pumps in hand. Shell plates of boilers bent and furnaces and combustion chambers partially built. The material and workmanship of the machinery of this vessel, so far as same has been examined by me, was found to be good and satisfactory
    Signed Duncan Ritchie

The machinery of the above vessel has been completed satisfactorily in accordance with the approved place of main boiler, the Secretary's letter to the Barrow Surveyors, dated 3rd Sept. 1885, the Rules of the Society for machinery built under Special Survey and to the Satisfaction of the undersigned. The boilers when finished were tested under hydraulic pressure the main to 180lbs and the donkey to 100lbs per sq, inch, and under steam pressure when the Safety valves were adjusted to 90lbs, + 50 lbs per sq. inch respectively.

The machinery was tried under steam, the engines working smoothly and efficiently. Both main and donkey pumps were tested and move satisfactorily. I am therefore of opinion that the machinery is eligible for the notification +LMC with a date attached and would respectively recommend that the same receive the favourable consideration and approval of the Committee.
    Signed James Maxton
Engineer Surveyor to Lloyd's Register of British and Foreign Shipping
Dated 24th March 1887
Minuted by the Committee with a note approving certification at + LMC on 31st March 1887

Boiler

Detail	Detail or Imperial measurement	Metric
Description	Single Multi tubular steel boiler	
Working Pressure	90 psi	6.206 bar
Tested by hydraulic pressure to	180 psi	12.42 bar
Date of test	5 January 1887	
Description of superheating apparatus or steam chest	None fitted	
Description of safety valves	Cockburns	
Number to each boiler	Two	
…… of each valve	9.6 (no units given)	
Are they fitted with easing gear	Yes	
Smallest distance between boilers and bunkers or woodwork	6 ft Main, 12½ in to Donkey	18.3 m 31.75 cm
Diameter of boilers	12 ft 9 in	3.93 m
…. Of boilers	19ft 3 in	5.88 m
Description of riveting of shell long, seams	DB Straps, D Rivd	
Circum. Seams	lap, D Rived	
Thickness of shell plates	$^{13}/_{16}$ in	2.1 cm
Diameter of rivet holes	$1^1/_{16}$ in	2.7 cm
Whether punched or drilled	Drilled	
Pitch of rivets	3½	
Lap of plating	Butt straps 13 in wide	33 cm
….age of strength of longitudinal joining	69.6 (no units given)	

Working pressure of shell by rules	96.1 psi	6.627 bar
Size of manholes in shell	15 by 12 in	38.1 by 30.5 cm
……compensating rings	w.iron 5½ by 1 in	14 by 2.5 cm
No. of furnaces in boiler	Three	
….diameter	2 ft 9 in	88.4 cm
Length, top	6 ft	1.83 m
Bottom	8 ft 6 in	2.62 m
Thickness of plates	½ in	1.3 cm
Description of joint	DB Straps, D Rivd	
If rings are fitted	Bottom plate stiffened by T irons	
Working pressure of furnace by the rules	113 psi	7.792 bar
Combustion chamber plating, thickness, sides	½	1.3 cm
Back	½	1.3 cm
Top	½	1.3 cm
….stays to ditto, sides	9¼ by 9	23.5 by 22.9 cm
Back	9¼ by 9	23.5 by 22.9 cm
Top	9¼ by 9	23.5 by 22.9 cm
If stays are fitted with nuts or riveted heads	Nuts	
Working pressure of plating by the rules	90 psi	6.206 bar
Diameter of stays at smallest part	1¼ in	3.2 cm
Working pressure of ditto by rules	88.6 psi	6.109 bar
End plates in steam space thickness	¾ in	1.9 cm
….stays to ditto	16 in by 16 in	40.6 by 40.6 cm
How stays are secured	Double nuts and washers	
Working pressure by rules	90 psi	6.206 bar
Diameter of stays at smallest part	2¼ in	5.7 cm
Working pressure by rules	93.2 psi	6.427 bar
Front plates at bottom, thickness	$^{9}/_{16}$ in	1.4 cm
Back plates, thickness	$^{9}/_{16}$ in	1.4 cm
How stays are secured	10¼ in	26 cm
Greatest pitch of stays		
Working pressure by rules	100 bar	6.90 bar
Diameter of tubes	3 in	7.6 cm
Pitch of tubes	4⅜ in by 4⅜ in	11.1 by 11.1 cm
Thickness of tube plates, front	No dimension given	
…plates, front	⅝ in	1.6 cm
Back	⅝ in	1.6 cm
How stayed	Stay tubes	
Pitch of stays	13⅛ in by 13⅛ in	33.3 by 33.3 cm
Width of water spaces	Between boxes 3½ in Sides of do. 5 in Wide space between tubes 9 in Narrow….do 1⅞ in	8.9 cm 12.7 cm 22.9 cm 4.8 cm
Material of shell plates	Siemens Steel	
Do. Stays (longitudinal and screw)	Iron	
Ditto End Plates	Steel	
Ditto Furnaces	Steel	
Ditto Combustion Chamber Plating	Steel	
Ditto Other Parts	All steel except comb. Box, girders and tubes which are iron	

Thesis – Construction Survey

Donkey boiler

Detail	Detail or Imperial measurement	Metric
Description	Cylindrical Vertical with Firebox, all plates of steel	
Made at	Belfast	
By whom made	McIlwaine, Lewis, and Co Ltd.,	
When made	1886 + 7	
Where fixed	Starboard of stokehold	
Working Pressure	50 psi	3.448 bar
Tested by hydraulic pressure to	100 psi	6.895 bar
No. of certificate	13	
Fire grate area	13 sq ft	1.2 sq.m
Description of safety valves	Cockburns patent	
Number of safety valves	One	
Area of each	7.07 sq ft	0.66 sq.m
Fitted with easing gear	Yes	
If steam from main boilers can enter the donkey boiler	No	
Diameter of donkey boiler	4 ft 9 in	1.49 m
Length	9 ft	2.74 m
Description of riveting	Longitudinal lap, double riveted	
Thickness of shell plates	⅜ steel	9.5 mm
Diameter of rivet holes	$^{13}/_{16}$ in.	2.1 cm
Whether punched or drilled	Drilled	
Pitch of rivets	2½ in	6.35 cm
Lap of plating	4⅛ in	10.5 cm
Percentage of strength of joint	67.5	
Thickness off crown plates	$^{7}/_{16}$ in	11 mm
Stayed by	Three 1½in iron stays and disked top	38 mm
Diameter of furnace, top	45 in	114.3 cm
Bottom	49 in	124.5 cm
Length of furnace	5 ft	1.52 m
Thickness of plates	⅜ in	4 mm
Description of joint	…….(illegible)	
Thickness of furnace crown plates	$^{7}/_{16}$ in	11 mm
Stayed by	Uptake only 3 stays 1½ diameter of convex crown	38 mm
Working pressure of shell by rules	88.7 psi	6.116 bar
Working pressure of furnace by rules	53.6 psi	3.696 bar
Diameter of uptake	14½ in	36.8 cm
Thickness of plates	$^{7}/_{16}$ in	11mm
Thickness of water tubes	⅜ in 10 in diameter	4 mm/25.4cm
Spare gear – State the articles supplied: 2 connecting rod top end bolts and nuts; 2 connecting rod bottom end bolts and nuts; 2 main bearing bolts; 1 set of coupling bolts; 1 set of feed and bilge pump valves; 1 set of piston springs and a quantity of assorted bolts and nuts and iron of various sizes. The foregoing is a correct description Signed Manufacturer, John H MacIlwaine on behalf of MacIlwaine, Lewis and Co., Ltd.		

Engine

Detail	Detail or Imperial measurement	Metric
Description	Single compound inverted surface condensing	
Diameter of cylinders	20 by 38 in	50.8 by 96.5 cm
Length of stroke	33 in	83.8 cm
Number of revs per minute	75	

Point of cut off, high pressure	17⅜ in	44.15 cm
Low pressure	⅝ (no units given)	
Diameter of Screw shaft	7½ in	19.05 cm
Diameter of Tunnel shaft	7⅛ in	18.1 cm
Diameter of Crank shaft journals	7½ in	19.05 cm
Diameter of Crank pin	7½ in	19.05 cm
Size of Crank webs	8½ by 5¼ in	21.6 by 13.3 cm
Diameter of screw	10 ft 6 in	3.2 m
Pitch of screw	11ft 2 in to 16ft 2 in	3.4 m to 4.9 m
Number of blades	Four	
Total surface	34 square feet	3.16 sq.m
Number of feed pumps	One	
Diameter ditto	3 ¼ in	8.3 cm
Stroke	14 ¾ in	37.5 cm
Can one by overhauled while the other is at work	Yes	
Number of bilge pumps	One	
Diameter of ditto	3 ¼ in	8.3 cm
Stroke	14 ¾ in	37.5 cm
Can one be overhauled while the other is at work	Yes	
Where do they pump from	Feed pump pumps from hot well and bilge pump pumps from all bilges and from fore peak	
Number of donkey engines	Two	
Size of pumps	Illegible entry	
Where do they pump from		
Are all the bilge suctions pipes fitted with roses	Yes	
Are the roses always accessible	Yes	
Are the sluices on engine room bulkheads always accessible	Yes	
Number of bilge injections	One	
And sizes	3 ½ in	8.9 cm
Are they connected to condenser or to circulating pump	Circulating pump	
How are the pumps worked	By link and levers from cross head of after engine	
Are all connections with the sea direct on the skin of the ship	Yes	
Are they valves or cocks	Yes	
Are they fixed sufficiently high on the ship's side to be seen without lifting the stokehold plates	Yes	
Are the discharge pipes above or below the deep water line	Above	
Are they each fitted with a discharge valve always accessible on the plating of the vessel	Yes	
Are the blow off cocks fitted with a spigot and brass covering plate	Yes	
What pipes, cocks, valves, and pumps in connections with the machinery accessible at all times	Yes	
How are they protected	Boxed in with wood alongside centre keelson	
Are all pipes cocks valves and pumps in connection with the machinery accessible at all times	Yes	

Thesis – Construction Survey

Are the pipes, cocks and valves arranged so as to prevent an unintentional connection between the sea and the bilges	Yes
When were stern tube, propeller, screw shaft, and all connections examined in dry dock	Before launching 22nd Jan 1887
Is the screw shaft tunnel watertight	Yes
And fitted with a sluice door	Yes
Worked from	Main deck

Cargo handling gear and other fittings

Detail	Detail or Imperial measurement	Metric
Masts, Bowsprit, Yards etc	All in good condition and sufficient in size and length	
Length and diameter of lower masts ~~and bowsprit~~	Schooner rigged as auxiliary to steam power with two pitch pine pole masts. Fore mast extreme 77 ft 4 in by 17 in diam. Main mast 74 ft 4 in by 17 in diam.	Fore mast extreme 23.59 m by 43.18 cm diam. Main mast 227 by 43.18 cm diam.
Sails		
One complete suit	Fore sails, fore top sails, fore topmast stay sails, main sails, main top sails	
Cables		
Chain	90 fathoms of $1\,^{1}/_{16}$ in chain 75 fathoms, 2½ ft of $1\,^{1}/_{16}$ in chain	164.6 m of 2.7 cm chain 137.9 m of 2.7 cm chain
Iron steam chain or steel wire	60.1 fathoms length of $1^{1}/_{16}$ in thickness	109.9 m of 2.7 cm
Towline, Hemp or Steel wire	75 fathoms of 7½ in 90 fathoms of 5½ in	137.92 m of 19.05 cm 164.6 m of 13.4 cm
Hawser	150 fathoms of 4½ in	274.3 m of 11.4 cm
Warp	120 fathoms of 3½ in	219.5 m of 8.9 cm
Anchors		
Bower (weight ex. Stock)	8.1.21 [cwt.quarters.pounds]	429 kg
	8.0.0	406 kg
	7.2.0	381 kg
Stream	2.2.20	136 kg
Kedge	1.2.2	77 kg
Standing and Running Rigging	Wire and hemp sufficient in size and good in quality	
She has	One long boat	
And	A dingy	
The windlass is	Patent and good	
Capstan	Good	
And Rudder	Good	
Pumps	Good	
Engine Room Skylights – How constructed?	Of teak on iron comings 24 in above the Bridge Deck	61 cm above the bridge deck
How secured in ordinary weather?	Screw bolts and nuts	
What arrangements for deadlights in bad weather?	Solid top with bull's eyes	
Coal bunker openings – How constructed?	Plates & angles	
How are lids secured?	With hatch bars	
Height above deck?	12 in	30.5 cm
Scuppers etc., What arrangements for clearing upper deck of water, in case of shipping a sea?	2 scuppers & 2 freeing ports before the bridge bulkhead, and 3 scuppers and 2 freeing ports abaft each side	

Cargo hatchways – how formed	Of plates and angles, comings 30 in above the deck	
State size – Main hatch	19 feet 3 in by 12 feet	5.88 m by 3.66 m
Fore hatch	7 feet by 8 feet	2.13 m by 2.44 m
Quarter hatch	19 feet 3 in by 12 feet	5.88 m by 3.66 m
If of extraordinary size, state how framed and secured	A deep web plate and 3 fore and afters in each of the main and after hatchways, and 1 fore and after in the fore hatch	
Hatches, if strong and efficient?	Yes, 3 in. solid	7. 6 cm

General remarks (state quality of workmanship etc,)

This vessel has been built in accordance with the accompanying approved sketch of midship section, in compliance with the Secretary's letter dated as above, and in general conformity with the rules. The pumping arrangement has been carried out as approved for similar vessels built by this firm. She is a one deck vessel, having a raised quarter deck 21 ft 9 in (6.68m) long, a forecastle (unenclosed) 30 ft 6in (9.33m), and a bridge (unenclosed, open at both ends) 45 ft 6 in long (13.9m). A trimming tank at the fore end of the fore hold 10ft 3 in (3.14m) long with water capacity for 28 tons and an after peak tank with a water capacity for 36 tons, both tested as required by the Rules.

The materials and workmanship are very good.

How are the surfaces preserved from oxidation?	Inside – cement and paint. Outside - paint	
I am of the opinion this Vessel should be classed	100 A1	
Surveyor to Lloyd's Register of British and Foreign Shipping	James Turpin (signed)	
Committee's Minute	Tuesday 12 April 1887	

Appendix 2 – Table of marine species identified on the wreck of the SS *Thesis* (pers. comm. Calum Duncan, Marine Conservation Society)

Species	*	Typical habitat
Sea weeds		
Delesseria sanguinea	C	On rocks, deep shady lower inter-tidal pools and sub-tidal, generally distributed, commonest in spring.
Phycodrys rubens		On rock or epiphytic, especially on *Laminaria hyperborea* stipes, lower inter-tidal pools and sub-tidal, generally distributed, common.
Flustra foliacea 'hornwrack'		Found on coarse sediment and rocky substrate in the shallow sub-littoral, where it favours current-swept rocky grounds.
Porifera		
Halichondria panicea	O	An opportunistic species found in a wide range of habitats from the mid-shore to the lower circa-littoral and under a wide variety of physical conditions.
Hymedesmia 'Blue sponge'	R	Hard rocky bottom and current exposed locations
Hydroids Indet.,	C	
Abietinaria abietina	O	Hydroid usually found attached to bedrock and boulders in strong tidal streams, but can also grow on shells and cobbles.
Tubularia larynx	O	This hydroid is usually found on rocks and attached to algae in moderate to strong tidal streams. It is commonest in shallow water, fouling piers and the undersides of boats, down to 25 m or more in strong tidal streams
Aglaephenia pluma	O	
Cnidaria		
Epizoanthus couchii	O	Encrusting on rocks and shells from low water of spring tide level to 100 m depth often overgrown by other species and easily overlooked when its polyps are retracted. Common in habitats subject to moderate tidal streams and some sediment scour.
Alcyonium digitatum 'deadmans' fingers'	C	Attached to rocks, shells and stones where the otherwise dominant algae are inhibited by a lack of light and occasionally on living crabs and gastropods. Generally found in situations where strong water movement prevails. Occasionally on the lower shore, but more common sub-littorally, down to about 50 m.
Caryophyllia smithii 'Devonshire cup coral'	F	Lives on rocks, stones, shells, etc., from the lower shore to 100 m or more.
Annelida		
Sabella pavonina 'peacock worm'	C	Found on stones in sand and mud, at and below low water.
Pomatoceros triqueter 'tubeworm'	F	Encrusts stones, rocks and shells, and the carapace of some species of decapods. They are predominantly sub-littoral to depths of 70 m.
Crustacea		
Pagarus bernhardus 'hermit crab'	O	Ubiquitous
Munida rugosa 'squat lobster'	O	Normally found in deep water (50–150 m) on sandy or soft substrata.
Bryozoans		
Umbonula littoralis	O	A characteristic species of the sub-littoral fringe and under-boulder habitats. Occurs on rock and on *Laminaria spp.* holdfasts and *Himanthalia elongata* buttons.
Echinoderms		
Asterias rubens	O	The commonest British starfish inter-tidally and in the sub-littoral. Particularly common on mussels in the shallow sub-littoral and on soft sediments. One of the few echinoderms which can tolerate brackish conditions.
Antedon bifida	O	Found in a variety of habitats both sheltered and moderately exposed, attached to rocks, algae and sedentary animals. *Antedon bifida* often occurs in large numbers and may dominate areas of rock in suitable habitats.

Leptometra celtica	R	Deep water featherstar which has only recently been discovered in water as shallow as 20 m in sheltered localities and sea lochs in western Scotland.
Crossaster papposus 'sunstar'	R	Found in sheltered sites with moderate tidal streams and semi-exposed rocky or bouldery sites. Frequent in brittle-star beds.
Henricia oculata 'bloody henry starfish'	O	Found on a variety of substrata on open coasts
Echinus esculentus 'edible sea urchin'	C	Common on most coasts of the British Isles, but absent from most of east coast of England, the eastern English Channel and some parts of north Wales.
Fish		
Pollock		
Saithe		
Labrus bergylta 'Ballan wrasse'	O	*Labrus bergylta* is found in inshore waters amongst weed covered rocks or in lower shore pools. It is also found in the algal zone on rocky coasts from 5–30 m
Ctenolabrus rupestris 'goldsinny wrasse'		Inhabits rocks or algae (particularly eelgrass) at depths between 1–50 m. Adults inhabit deeper waters, while young can be found further inshore and even inhabiting rock pools.

* A = abundant, C = common, F = frequent, O = occasional, R = rare.

Appendix 3
Gazetteer of incidents, sites and scattered finds

Name	RCAHMS Ref. or other source	Type of vessel/ find	Port of registry	Date of incident	Cargo	Purpose in the Sound of Mull	Approximate location of incident	Total loss?
Speedwell: Duart Point	NM73NW 8009	Sailing vessel Scotland				local/west of	Duart Point	☑
Scattered find: Scallastle Bay	SOMAP	Anchor				isolated find	Scallastle Bay	☐
Scattered find: Eilean Rubha an Ridire	SOMAP	Bellarmine pot				isolated find	Inninmore	☐
Scattered find: Eilean Rubha an Ridire	SOMAP	Scupper liner				isolated find	Inninmore	☐
Scattered find: Eilean Rubha an Ridire	SOMAP	Quern stone				isolated find	Inninmore	☐
Unknown: Lochaline	SOMAP	Small fishing boat				local/west of Scotland	Lochaline	☑
Scattered find: Lochaline narrows marmalade jar	SOMAP	Scattered find				isolated find	Lochaline	☐
Ardfern [Possibly]: Eilean Rubha An Ridire	NM74SW 8006	Motor fishing vessel				local/west of Scotland	Eilean Rubha an Ridire	☑
Unknown: Fishnish Bay	SOMAP	Small fishing boat			Creels	local/west of Scotland	Fishnish	☐
Unknown: Tobermory Pier, Tobermory Bay,	NM55NW 8010					uncertain	Tobermory Pier	☑
Swan: Duart Point,	NM73NW 8005	Sailing vessel				local/west of Scotland	Duart Point	☑
Thomas: Sound of Mull	Whittaker, 1998: 296	Sloop	Inverness			uncertain	Duart Bay	☐

Sound of Mull Archaeological Project

Name RCAHMS Ref. or other source		Type of vessel/ find	Port of registry	Date of incident	Cargo	Purpose in the Sound of Mull	Approximate location of incident	Total loss?
Martha & Margaret: Duart Point	NM73NW 8008	Sailing vessel				local/west of Scotland	Duart Point	☑
Maid: Sound of Mull	Whittaker, 1998: 296	Sloop	Tobermory				Sound of Mull	☐
Unknown: Calve Island, Doirlinn A' Chailbhe,	NM55SW 8012	Transport Craft; Cargo				uncertain	Calve Island, Doirlinn A' Chailbhe,	☑
Unknown: Calve Island, Tobermory Bay,	NM55SW 8017	Transport Craft; Cargo				local/west of Scotland	Calve Island	☑
Glen Carradale: Loch Aline Jetty,	NM64NE 8003	Ring-net motor fishing			None	local/west of Scotland	head of Loch Aline	☐
Emerald: Sound of Mull	NM64NW 8015	Brigantine	Montrose		Slates	local/west of Scotland	Sound of Mull (south side)	☐
Lohada: Doirlinn A' Chailbhe	NM55SW 8005					uncertain	Doirlinn A' Chailbhe	☐
Morning Star [Possibly]: An Corr Eilean	NM55SE 8002	Fishing Vessel				uncertain	Dun Ban	☑
Scattered find: Rubha Dear	SOMAP	Quern stone				isolated find	Lochaline	☐
Unknown: Scallastle Bay	NM63NE 8005					uncertain	Scallastle Bay	☐
Unknown: Tobermory Pier, Tobermory Bay,	M55NW 8009	Barge?				uncertain	Tobermory Bay	☑
Unknown: Eilean Glasa	NM54NE 8003					uncertain	Eilean Glasa, or Salen Pier	☐
San Juan de Sicilia	NM55NW 8013	Sailing vessel	Ragusa?			in transit	Tobermory Bay	☑

Gazetteer of incidents and finds

Name RCAHMS Ref. or other source		Type of vessel/ find	Port of registry	Date of incident	Cargo	Purpose in the Sound of Mull	Approximate location of incident	Total loss?
Unknown: Calve Island, Doirlinn A' Chailbhe,	NM55SW 8011					uncertain	Calve Island, Tobermory	☑
Cull Castle: Tobermory Bay, Mull, Sound of	NM55NW 8023	Smack				uncertain	Tobermory Bay	☐
Anna Bhan: Tobermory Bay	NM55SW 8008	Smack?				local/west of Scotland	Calve Island, Tobermory	☑
Unknown: Tobermory Pier, Tobermory Bay,	NM55NW 8008					uncertain	Tobermory Pier, Tobermory Bay	☐
Unknown: Dun Ban	NM55SE 8001	Fishing vessel				uncertain	Dun Ban	☑
Unknown: Bogha Eilean Nan Geodh, Calve Island	NM55SW 8007	Unknown				uncertain	Calve Island, Tobermory	☑
Dartmouth: Eilean Rubha An Ridire	NM74SW 8002	5th-Rate frigate	London	9/10/1690		local/west of Scotland	Inninmore	☑
Hawke: Sound of Mull	NM64NW 8003			17/11/1772		uncertain	Sound of Mull	☐
Union: Sound of Mull	NM64NW 8004			9/2/1787		in transit	Sound of Mull	☐
Fame: Sound of Mull	NM64NW 8005			1/12/1795		in transit	Sound of Mull	☑
Alert: Tobermory Bay, Sound of Mull	NM55NW 8017			29/1/1796	Unspecified	in transit	Tobermory Harbour	☐
Three Brothers: Sound of Mull	NM64NW 8006			4/10/1796		uncertain	Sound of Mull	☐
Wildam: Sound of Mull	NM55NW 8030			3/8/1813	Unspecified	in transit	Near Tobermory	☐

Sound of Mull Archaeological Project

Name RCAHMS Ref. or other source	Type of vessel/ find	Port of registry	Date of incident	Cargo	Purpose in the Sound of Mull	Approximate location of incident	Total loss?
Industry: Sound of Mull	NM64NW 8007			26/11/1813		uncertain	Sound of Mull	☐
Enigton: Sound of Mull	NM64NW 8008			26/1/1815		in transit	Sound of Mull	☑
Anniehetta: Ardtornish,	NM64SE 8010	Sailing vessel		28/2/1815		local/west of Scotland	Near Ardtornish	☐
Neptune: Tobermory, Sound of Mull	NM55NW 8018			1/4/1819	Unspecified (assumed slate)	local/west of Scotland	'near Tobermory'	☑
Rambler: Eilean Rubha An Ridire	NM74SW 8013		Peterhead	23/9/1824		local/west of Scotland	Eilean Rubha an Ridire	☐
Fortuna: Morvern,	NM55SW 8014			22/9/1830		in transit	Morvern	☐
Betsey and Janet: Duart Point,	NM73NW 8012			18/10/1830		uncertain	Duart Point	☐
Eclair: Tobermory, Sound of Mull	NM55NW 8026			1/12/1830		in transit	Tobermory Harbour	☐
Unknown: Sound of Mull	NM64NW 8020			24/10/1833		uncertain	Sound of Mull	☑
Two Sisters: Tobermory, Sound of Mull	NM55NW 8036			14/5/1835		uncertain	Tobermory	☑
Victory: Sound of Mull	NM55NW 8034	Smack	Stranraer	1/7/1836	Unspecified	uncertain	Near Tobermory	☑
Mary: Sound of Mull	NM64NW 8016	Sloop	Glasgow	31/10/1837	Herring, salt and casks	local/west of Scotland	Sound of Mull or (Loch Broom)	☐
Crispin: Sound of Mull	NM64NW 8017			18/12/1843		in transit	Sound of Mull	☐

Gazetteer of incidents and finds

Name RCAHMS Ref. or other source		Type of vessel/ find	Port of registry	Date of incident	Cargo	Purpose in the Sound of Mull	Approximate location of incident	Total loss?
Eliza: Scallastle Bay,	NM63NE 8007	Schooner	Kirkwall	25/1/1845	Salt	in transit	Scallastle Bay	☐
Vibilia: Duart Bay	NM73NW 8017			26/1/1845		in transit	Duart Bay	☐
Providence: Sound of Mull	NM64NW 8018			30/1/1845		uncertain	Sound of Mull	☐
Astoria: Sound of Mull	NM64NW 8019		Kinloch	26/7/1845		local/west of Scotland	Sound of Mull	☐
Adventure: Sound of Mull	NM74SW 8010	Brig	Holyhead	15/2/1847	Unspecified	uncertain	South entrance to Sound of Mull	☐
Hetty: Tobermory, Sound of Mull	NM55NW 8021			16/4/1847		uncertain	Near Tobermory	☐
Thebes: Tobermory, Sound of Mull	NM55NW 8022			4/5/1847		uncertain	Tobermory Harbour	☐
Mary Clark: Tobermory Bay	NM55NW 8004	Sloop	Greenock	21/8/1847	Unspecified	local/west of Scotland	Off Tobermory	☑
Aid: Tobermory Bay, Sound of Mull	NM55NW 8012	Schooner		22/8/1847	Unspecified	in transit	Tobermory, Mull	☐
Joseph Howe: Tobermory, Sound of Mull	NM55NW 8041		Liverpool	16/12/1848		in transit	Tobermory	☐
Fox: Tobermory, Sound of Mull	NM55NW 8040			17/12/1848		uncertain	Tobermory	☐
Isabella: Morvern, Sound of Mull	NM55NW 8033	Smack	Belfast	3/10/1851	Unspecified	in transit	Opposite Tobermory	☐
Marquess of Stafford: Salachan Point	NM64NW 8012	Sloop		19/1/1852		in transit	Salachan Point	☑

Sound of Mull Archaeological Project

Name RCAHMS Ref. or other source		Type of vessel/ find	Port of registry	Date of incident	Cargo	Purpose in the Sound of Mull	Approximate location of incident	Total loss?
Dean Swift: Tobermory Bay	NM55NW 8003	Smack	Irvine	17/3/1854	Unspecified	local/west of Scotland	off Tobermory or Blackmill Bay - uncertain	☑
Duke of Argyll: Sound of Mull	Whittaker 1998: 294	Paddle steamship	Glasgow	12/1/1858		uncertain	Sound of Mull	☐
Duart Castle: Morvern, Sound of Mull	NM55NW 8032	Smack	Campbeltown	17/1/1858	Unspecified	local/west of Scotland	On Morvern Shore	☑
Mary Mackenzie: Sound of Mull	NM74SW 8011	Schooner/brigantine	Stornoway	31/3/1858	Shell lime	local/west of Scotland	entrance to the Sound of Mull	☐
John: Tobermory	NM555NW 8043			23/12/1858		local/west of Scotland	Drimnin	☐
Thomas Graham: Duart Bay	NM73NW 8013	Schooner		27/2/1860	Salt	in transit	Duart Bay	☐
Liberty: Duart Bay	NM73NW8014	Smack		27/2/1860	Unspecified	uncertain	Duart Bay	☑
Kitty: Drimnin	NM55SW 8001	Smack		3/10/1860	Coal and one passenger	local/west of Scotland	Drimnin	☐
Mary Dawson: Scallastle Bay,	NM63NE 8009	Smack	Campbeltown Scotland	3/10/1860	Herring, salt	local/west of Scotland	Scallastle Bay	☑
Elizabeth: Drimnin, Morvern	NM55SW 8010	Smack		5/10/1860	Sheep and one passenger	local/west of Scotland	Drimnin	☑
Ardnamurchan Packet: Sound of Mull	NM55NW 8028	Smack		5/10/1860	Coals	local/west of Scotland	Near Tobermory	☐
Unknown: Scallastle Point	NM73NW 8015			2/2/1861		uncertain	Scallastle Point	☑
Onyx: Ardinrider Point	NM45NE 8006	Schooner	Porthmadog	20/2/1861	Potatoes	in transit	Rubha an Ridire (Ardinrider Point)	☑

Gazetteer of incidents and finds

Name RCAHMS Ref. or other source		Type of vessel/find	Port of registry	Date of incident	Cargo	Purpose in the Sound of Mull	Approximate location of incident	Total loss?
Friends: Scallastle Bay,	NM63NE 8010		Arendal	8/10/1863	In ballast	in transit	Scallastle Bay	☑
Petrel: Duart Bay	NM73NW 8016		Wexford	8/10/1869	Unspecified	in transit	Duart Bay	☐
Elizabeth: Sound of Mull	NM74SW 8012	Smack	Kirkwall	18/11/1869	Slates	in transit	Sound of Mull	☐
Telegram: Calve Island,	NM55SW 8015	Sloop	Stornoway	17/11/1870	Coal and general cargo	local/west of Scotland	Calve Island, Tobermory	☐
Louisa: Sound of Mull	NM64NW 8014	Schooner		29/10/1872	Slates	in transit	Sound of Mull	☑
Unknown: Tobermory, Sound of Mull	NM55NW 8025			17/2/1873		uncertain	Tobermory Bay	☑
Hero: Glas Eileanan	NM54NE 8002	Brigantine	Belfast	15/9/1878	Pig iron	in transit	'Grey' or 'Scaladale' Island	☑
Margaret: Tobermory Bay, Sound of Mull	NM55NW 8024	Schooner	Caernarvon	16/9/1878	Slates	in transit	Tobermorys Bay	☐
Roseneath: Craignure Bay	NM73NW 8010	Schooner	Greenock	30/10/1878	Hemp	in transit	Craignure Bay	☐
Robert Norras: Craignure	NM73NW 8002	Schooner (wood)		23/9/1879		uncertain	Craignure Bay	☐
Katherine Ellen: Craignure	NM73NW 8001	Schooner (wood)		23/9/1879		uncertain	Craignure	☐
Unknown: Scallastle Bay	NM63NE 8006	Schooner		27/12/1879		uncertain	Scallastle Bay	☑
Jane Shearer: Scallastle Bay	NM63NE 8004	Brigantine		28/12/1879	Coal	in transit	Scallastle Bay	☑

Sound of Mull Archaeological Project

Name RCAHMS Ref. or other source		Type of vessel/ find	Port of registry	Date of incident	Cargo	Purpose in the Sound of Mull	Approximate location of incident	Total loss?
Slater: Tobermory, Sound of Mull	NM55NW 8038	Schooner		13/2/1880	Slates	uncertain	Grey Rock	☐
Elizabeth: Tobermory Bay,	NM55SW 8013	Smack	Glasgow	6/1/1882	In ballast	local/west of Scotland	Calve Island	☑
Ranger: Glenmorven,	NM55SE 8006	Yacht (wood)		1/10/1882	In ballast	local/west of Scotland	Glenmorvern	☑
John Preston: Rubha Dearg,	NM64SE 8005	Schooner (wood)	Caernarvon	2/12/1882	Slates	in transit	Rubha Dearg Lochaline	☑
New Blessing: Duart Point	NM73NW 8006	Brigantine (wood)	Caernarvon	12/12/1883	Slates	in transit	Duart Point	☑
Kalafish: Lochaline,	NM64SE 8009	Schooner (wood)	London	22/8/1885	Ballast	local/west of Scotland	off Lochaline	☐
Cartsdyke: Craignure	NM73NW 8007	Schooner	Greenock	1/12/1886	In ballast	local/west of Scotland	Craignure	☐
Clara R: Scallastle Bay,	NM63NE 8003	Brig (wood)	Dublin	15/1/1887	Rock salt	in transit	Scallastle Bay	☐
Industry: Craignure	NM73NW 8004	Schooner (wood)	Inverness	8/2/1889	Coal	in transit	Craignure	☐
Thesis: Rubha An Ridire	NM74SW 8001	Steamship (iron)	Belfast	16/10/1889	iron ore	in transit	Innimore	☑
Jubilee: Loch Eishort Skye	NG61NW 8003	Smack (wood)	Stornoway	17/11/1893	Herring	uncertain	Duart Bay	☐
Malachite: Tobermory, Sound of Mull	NM55NW 8037	Steamship		20/11/1894	Unspecified	uncertain	Tobermory	☐
Fiery Cross: Sound of Mull	NM64NW 8010	Lugger (wood)		13/3/1895	Slates, cement and nails	local/west of Scotland	Morvern	☐

Gazetteer of incidents and finds

Name RCAHMS Ref. or other source	Type of vessel/ find	Port of registry	Date of incident	Cargo	Purpose in the Sound of Mull	Approximate location of incident	Total loss?
Seal: Poll Arinnis, NM64NW 8001	Steamship (steel)	Glasgow	28/8/1895	Pit-wood	in transit	Lochaline	☑
Pelican: Calve Island, Doirlinn A' Chailbhe, NM55SW 8009	Paddle steamship	Glasgow	6/12/1895	Bunker coal	local/west of Scotland	Calve Island	☑
Glenarm: Scallastle Bay NM63NE 8001	steamship (iron)	Belfast	24/12/1895	Unspecified	uncertain	Scallastle Bay	☐
Maid of Lorne: The Stirks, Sound of Mull NM55NW 8014			1/4/1896		uncertain	The Stirks, Auliston	☐
Menai: Scallastle Bay NM63NE 8002	Schooner (wood)	Caernarvon	8/4/1896	Slates	in transit	Scallastle Bay	☑
Lady O' The Lake: Calve Island, Sound of Mull NM55NNW 8015	Steamship (steel)		16/3/1900	Unspecified	uncertain	Calve Island, Tobermory	☐
Unknown: Duart Point Admiralty Chart 2390			11/2/1905		uncertain	Duart	☑
Aleksander: Eilean Rubha An Ridire, NM74SW 8007			23/5/1905		local/west of Scotland	Eilean Rubha An Ridire,	☑
Urania: Lochaline SOMAP	Motor vessel (steel)	Hamburg?	22/6/1905	silica sand	local/west of Scotland	Lochaline	☐
Crane: the Stirks NM55NW 8002	Steam trawler	Unknown	25/2/1908	Fish	uncertain	The stirks, Sound of Mull	☐
Macduff: Ardmore Point, Sound of Mull. NM45NE 8004	Steamship (steel)	Glasgow	20/7/1908	Salt	in transit	Near Ardmore Point	☑
Mary Smethurst: Tobemory Bay NM55NW 8005	Schooner		29/12/1908	Unspecified	uncertain	Tobermory, Mull	☐
Unknown: Sound of Mull NM64NW 8011	Lugger		27/2/1909		uncertain	Sound of Mull	☐

Sound of Mull Archaeological Project

Name	RCAHMS Ref. or other source	Type of vessel/find	Port of registry	Date of incident	Cargo	Purpose in the Sound of Mull	Approximate location of incident	Total loss?
Wharfinger: Lochaline	NM64SE 8008	Steamship (steel) Puffer	Glasgow	21/1/1911	Coal	local/west of Scotland	Lochaline	☑
Shuna: Rubha Aird Seisg,	NM54NE 8004	Steamship (steel)	Glasgow	8/5/1913	Coal	local/west of Scotland	Rubha Aird Seisg	☑
Scarinish: Calve Island, Tobermory Bay,	NM55SW 8003	Ketch	Greenock	11/11/1917	Coal	local/west of Scotland	Inside Calve Island	☑
John Edwards: Tobermory, Sound of Mull	NM55NW 8019		Caernarvon	26/1/1920	Unspecified	in transit	off Tobermory Harbour	☑
Annie Melling: Sound of Mull	NM55NW 8001	Steam trawler		10/8/1922		uncertain	Tobermory Bay; Mull; 'Tobermory, offshore'	☐
Rondo: Deirg Sgeir, Eileanan Glasa	NM54NE 8001	Steamship (steel)	Oslo	2/2/1935	Ballast	local/west of Scotland	Dearg Sgeir	☑
Buitenzorg: Glas Eileanan	NM64SE 8002	Steamship (steel)	Rotterdam	26/2/1941	Pig-iron, rubber, tea	in transit	Scallastle Bay	☑
Margaret Wetherly: Firth of Lorne	NM61NE 8001	Steam trawler (steel)	Granton	5/2/1943		uncertain	Sound of Mull	☐
River Tay: Eilean Rubha an Ridire	NM74SW 8008	Steam trawler (steel)	Granton	29/11/1943		uncertain	Innimore	☑
Bondja: Tobermory Bay, Sound of Mull	NM55NW 8016	Yacht		19/8/1946	None	local/west of Scotland	Between Rubha nan Gall lighthouse and Tobermory Bay	☑
Avro Shackleton: Scallastle Bay,	NM64SE 8003	Airplane		11/12/1953		local/west of Scotland	Scallastle Bay	☑
Golden Gleam: Sound of Mull	Whittaker, 1998: 293	Motor ketch	Tarbert	27/10/1954		uncertain	Sound of Mull	☑
Hispania: Sgeir Mor,	NM55SE 8005	Steamship	Gothenburg	18/12/1954	General cargo	in transit	Sgeir Mor	☑

Gazetteer of incidents and finds

Name RCAHMS Ref. or other source		Type of vessel/ find	Port of registry	Date of incident	Cargo	Purpose in the Sound of Mull	Approximate location of incident	Total loss?
Evelyn Rose (possibly): Ardtornish Point,	NM64SE 8004	Steam trawler	Grimsby	31/12/1954	In ballast	in transit	Ardtornish Point	☑
Logan: Lochaline Pier,	NM64SE 8006	Puffer	British	15/12/1961	Coal	local/west of Scotland	Lochaline	☑
Johanna: Lochaline Pier,	NM64NE 8002	Motor fishing vessel		29/4/1968		local/west of Scotland	Lochaline	☑
Carol Ann: An Corr Eilean	NM55SE 8004	Fishing vessel	Belfast	25/11/1971	Shell fish (clams)	in transit	off Drimnin	☐
Ballista: Eilean Rubha An Ridire	NM74SW 8003	Steamship (iron)		6/2/1973	Coal	local/west of Scotland	Eilean Rubha an Ridire	☑
Morning Star: Caisteal Nan Con	NM54NE 8005	Motor fishing vessel	Fraserburgh	16/4/1973	Fish	in transit	Killundine Point, Morvern	☐
Cessna 150: Fishnish Bay,	NM64SW 8002	Airplane		24/12/1975		local/west of Scotland	Fishnish Bay	☑
Girl Sandra: Eilean Rubha An	NM74SW 8009	Motor vessel (wood)		25/10/1981		local/west of Scotland	Inninmore Bay	☑
Strathbeg: Cnap a Chailbhe	NM55SW 8004	Fishing vessel		3/5/1984		local/west of Scotland	Doirlinn a' Chailbe, Calve Sound	☐

N.B The RCAHMS reference is provided to guide readers to more complete versions of the records, showing original sources of information to facilitate further research (at www.rcahms.gov.uk) . Any discrepancies in this gazetteer from the RCAHMS record, or any other source, are the responsibility of this author.

Appendix 4

Glossary

Ships, types, construction and fittings

Anchors – the sheet anchor was a vessel's heaviest anchor, reserved for emergencies. Bower anchors were heavy anchors used for mooring. A stream anchor was a smallish anchor to supplement the bowers or to hold the stern steady. A kedge anchor was used for light work such as swinging the ship around or moving about in harbours (fig. IV.1)

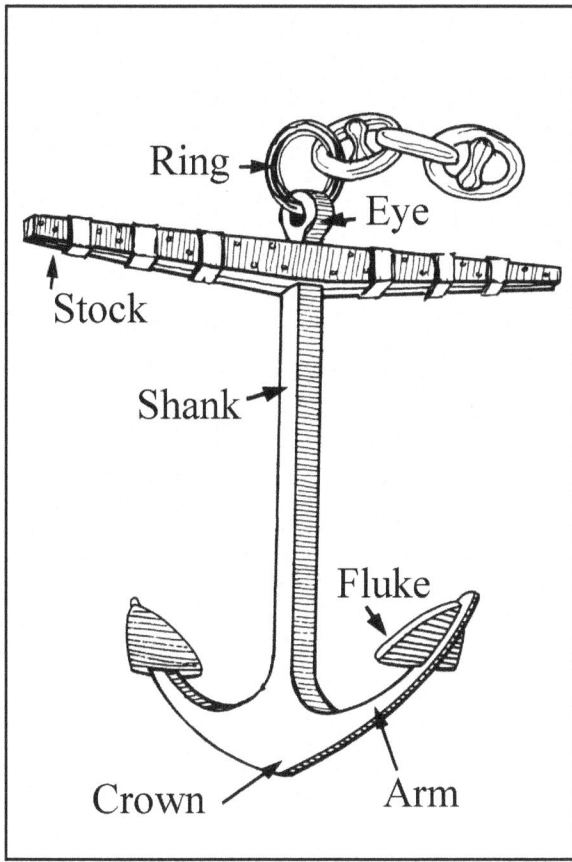

Fig. IV.1   Anchor nomenclature

Barque – a sailing ship with the rear mast fore-and-aft-rigged and the remaining masts square-rigged.

Bowsprit – a spar which projected forward over the bow, more horizontally than vertically. The bowsprit held down guy-lines, called stays, which steadied the foremast. A bobstay steadied the bowsprit itself. The martingale, known in earlier times as a dolphin straker was a forged iron bar which hung from a lug on the bowsprit cap and spread the stays which guyed a jib-boom (an extension to the bowsprit for ships with extra-high topgallant masts).

Capstan – a crank-operated windlass turned on end. Capstans in the forecastle were often used to help with raising the anchor.

Coaming – any vertical surface on a ship designed to deflect or prevent entry of water. It usually refers to raised section of deck plating around an opening, such as a hatch.

Binnacle – a wooden or brass housing for the compass.

Decklights – small, thick, fixed-glass windows set flush in decks with the prism side down to disseminate light below.

Fifth-rate frigate – in the British Royal Navy, a fifth-rate was a sailing frigate mounting 32 to 44 guns, with the main battery on a single deck.

Forecastle – the bow area of the ship, pronounced "fo'c'sle" by the seamen.

Fore-and-aft rig – a sailing rig consisting mainly of sails that are set along the line of the keel rather than at right angles to it.

Gabbart – A long narrow flat vessel or lighter with a hatchway extending almost the full length of the decks, sometimes fitted with masts that may be lowered to pass under bridges. Most Scottish canal craft developed from this typical Scottish sailing barge.

Gudgeon – a female half of a metal hinge fixed to the sternpost.

Keelson – a heavy central timber which lay on top of the floor frames, sandwiching the frames between it and the keel. Keelson, floors, and keel were drift-bolted into one strong unit. A rider keelson, also called a false keelson, lay on top of the keelson in a large craft and it were seated the mast steps, spreading the weight of the spars over the whole structure (Fig. IV.2).

Knees – heavy right-angles of wood or iron, primarily for reinforcing the joins of deck beams to the hull (Fig. IV.2).

Lead apron cover – a piece of moulded lead sheet used to cover the vent of a cannon from the elements.

MFV – Motor Fishing Vessel.

Glossary

Pintle – a male half of a metal hinge fitted to the rudder

Poop – a poop deck is a deck that constitutes the roof of a cabin built in the aft (rear) part of the superstructure of a ship. In sailing ships, with the helmsman at the stern, an elevated position was ideal for both navigation and observation of the crew and sails

Puffer – a type of small steamboat which provided a vital supply link around the west coast and Hebrides islands of Scotland, the puffers developed from the gabbart. The original puffer was the *Thomas*, an iron canal boat of 1856, less than 66 ft (20 m) long to fit in the Forth and Clyde Canal locks, powered by a simple steam engine without a condenser so that it 'puffed' with every stroke.

Quarterdeck – The part of the upper deck abaft the mainmast, including the poop deck when there is one.

Ring-netter – A vessel used for ring-netting. This technique was popular in the herring fisheries, particularly around the sheltered waters of Argyll. The method involved surrounding a shoal of herring with a net and then pulling the ring tight to trap them.

Schooner – A type of sailing vessel characterised by the use of fore-and-aft sails on two or more masts.

Scuppers – drains through the edge of the top deck and out through the vessel's side. The holes were often lined with lead piping flanged at both ends.

Smack – A single masted for-and-aft-rigged boat, often used for fishing

SS – Steam ship. In the early days, a 'ship' was a vessel that had only square sails from its masts, though it could also hang some fore-and-aft sails from stays.

Steering quadrant – popular from around the 1880s, a form of tiller shaped like an arc. Steering ropes or chains kept the pull at the proper angle to the swing of the tiller.

Treenails – wooden pegs, often used where the strength of iron was unnecessary. Treenails made a tight join, expanding and contracting with the surrounding wood.

Winch – a crank operated windlass

Windlass – machine with a horizontal axle, usually for raising anchor

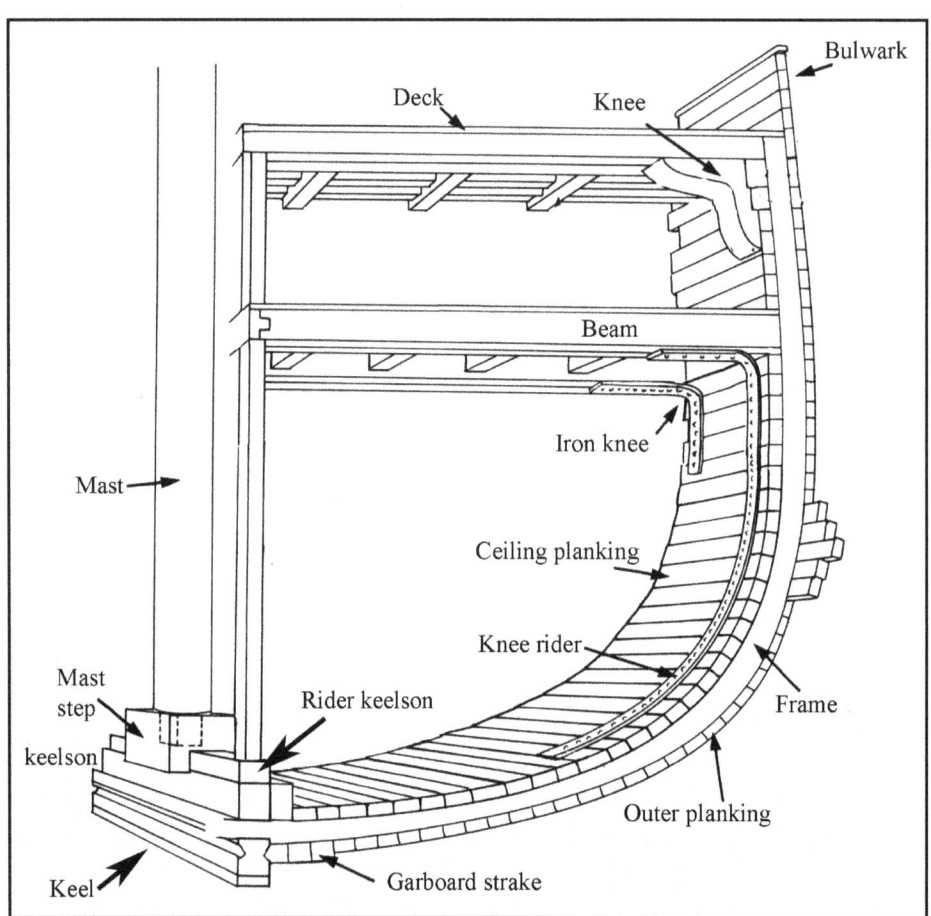

Fig. IV.2   Hull nomenclature

Archaeological survey

Trilateration/ triangulation – are survey techniques which use the geometry of triangles: triangulation uses angle measurements to calculate the subject's location; trilateration uses the known locations of two or more reference points and the measured distance between the subject and each reference point.

Offset – An offset measurement positions a feature using a single measured distance at right angles to the baseline from a known point.

Differential Global Positioning System (DGPS) – is regular Global Positioning System (GPS), but with an additional correction (differential) signal added to enhance accuracy. This differential is added by determining the GPS position of a reference station; this is computed and compared to its surveyed geodetic position. The differential information (some systems use the error in fix position, while others use individual satellite range errors) is transmitted to user receivers by radio or other means.

Multibeam sonar – multiple-beam echo sounders which can measure the seabed surface in three dimensions.

Real Time Kinematic (RTK) – RTK is a positioning technique used in land survey which is capable of centimetric levels of accuracy. It is based on the use of 'carrier phase' measurements of GPS signals where a single reference station is set up to provide real-time corrections.

Side-scan sonar – Archaeologists use these sonar systems to identify seabed detail and the presence of archaeological remains on the seabed surface. A transponder transmits a narrow acoustic beam to the side of the survey track line. As the acoustic beam travels outward, the seabed and other obstructions reflect some of the incident sound energy back to the sonar. The travel time of the acoustic pulses from the sonar are recorded together with the amplitude of the returned signal as a time series and sent to a topside console for interpretation and display.

Others

Mean High Water (MHW) is the average position of the high tide mark.

Mean Low Water (MLW) is the average position of the low tide mark.

Nephrops – The Norway lobster, *Nephrops norvegicus*, (also called Dublin Bay prawn or langoustine), is a slim orange-pink lobster found in the north-eastern Atlantic Ocean and North Sea. The Norway lobster is an important species for fisheries, being caught mostly by trawling.

Scotland's Territorial seas – those waters within 12 nautical miles of the coastal baseline for which Scottish Ministers have devolved jurisdiction under the Scotland Act 1998.

Bibliography

Manuscript sources

National Library of Scotland, Campbell (formerly Mamore) Papers, MS3733.

Maps and Charts

Adair, J., 1703, *A true and exact Hydrographical description of the Sea coast and Isles of Scotland made in Voyage round the same by that great and mighty James the 5th.* Edinburgh.

Huddart, J., Laurie, R., and Whittle, J., 1794, *A new chart of the West Coast of Scotland from the Mull of Galloway to Dunan Point in Sky.* London

Knapton *et al.*, 1728, *A chart of the Coast of Scotland with all its islands: drawn according to the Globular Projection.* London.

Mckenzie, M., 1775, The Sound of Mull, In Murdoch Mckenzie Senior 1776 *A maratim survey of Ireland and the west of Great Britain*, vol. II, Plate XXII .

Mount, J., and Page, T., 1715, *A new chart of the sea coast of Scotland with the islands thereof.* London.

Taylor, A. B., 1980, *Alexander Lindsay, a rutter of the Scottish seas, c.1540. abridged version of a manuscript by the late A.B. Taylor, edited by I. H. Adams and G. Fortune.* National Maritime Museum, London.

United Kingdom Hydrographic Office, Admiralty Charts 2155 (surveyed 1851, published 1852) and 2390 (surveyed 1976, amended 1991).

Printed primary sources

Aberdeen Press and Journal.

Ayton, R., and Daniell, W., 1978, *A voyage round Great Britain undertaken between the years 1813 and 1823, and commencing from the Land's end, Cornwall, with a series of views illustrative of the character and prominent features of the coast.* 2 vols, London.

Boswell, J., 1984, The journal of a tour to the Hebrides in P. L. Levi (ed.) *A journey to the Western Isles of Scotland and the journal of a tour to the Hebrides .* London.

Johnson, S., 1984, A journey to the Western Isles of Scotland, in P. L. Levi (ed.) *A Journey to the Western Isles of Scotland and the journal of a tour to the Hebrides .* London.

Lloyd's List Shipping Intelligence.

Lloyd's Register of Shipping 1863–4.

Maclean-Bristol, N. (ed.), 1998, *Inhabitants of the Inner Isles: Morvern and Arnamurchan 1716.* Scottish Record Society, Edinburgh.

Martin Martin, 2002, *A description of the Western Isles of Scotland, circa 1695, a voyage to St Kilda, with a description of the Occidental, i.e., Western Islands of Scotland.* Edinburgh.

Merchant Shipping Act, 1894, *report of court, No.S.433: s.t. Evelyn Rose O.N. 143857.*

Monro, D., 2002, in Martin Martin, *A description of the Western Isles of Scotland, circa., 1695, a voyage to St Kilda, with a Description of the Occidental, i.e., Western Islands of Scotland*, 299–339. Edinburgh.

The [New] Statistical Account of Scotland, 1845, vol. vii, *Argyleshire.*

Oban Times and Argyllshire Advertiser.

Scott, W., 1998, *The voyage of the Pharos: Walter Scott's cruise around Scotland in 1814.* Scottish Library Association, Hamilton.

The [Old] Statistical Account of Scotland 1791–1799, J. Sinclair (ed.), facsimile edition, I Grant and D Withrington (eds), Wakefield, 1983, vols viii, *Argyll* (mainland) and xx, *Western Isles.*

The Times. London.

Secondary sources

Admiralty, 1952, *Admiralty Manual of Seamanship,* vol. ii. BR67 (2/51). London.

Aldridge, D., 1992, Jacobitism and the Scottish seas, in T. C. Smout (ed.), *Scotland and the sea,* 76–93. Edinburgh.

Baird, B., 1995, *Shipwrecks of the West of Scotland*. Glasgow.

Baker, R., 1999, *The Terror of Tobermory*. Edinburgh.

Barnes, M., 2004, The Story of the Lochaline Silica Mine in P. Martin (ed.), *Exploring Morvern*, 14–19. Morvern Heritage Society.

Brouwer, N.J., 1999, *International Register of Historic Ships*. 3rd edn, London.

Butland, W. E., and Siedlecki, J. K., 1987, *BSAC wreck register, Scotland, 2, West coast [and] Western Isles*, (revised edn), London.

Caruana, A., 1997, *The history of English sea ordnance. Volume 2: The age of the system, 1715–1815*. Rotherfield, Sussex.

Cook, J. K., and Kaye, B., 2000, A new method for monitoring site stability in situ, *The NAS Newsletter* 2000.4.

Currie, J., 2000, *Mull, the island and its people*. Edinburgh.

Cuthbert, A. D., 1956, *Clyde Shipping Company Limited, a history*. Glasgow.

Dean, M., Ferrari, B., Oxley, I., Redknap, M., and Watson, K., (eds), 1992, *Archaeology underwater, the NAS guide to principles and practice*. Dorchester.

Douglass, R., 1988, 'Mull (Kilfinichen and Kilvickeon parish): survey', *Discovery & Excavation in Scotland*, 21.

Douglass, M., 2003, *Lost townships, silent voices: a field study of Mull*. Dunoon.

Duckworth, C. L. D. and Langmuir, G. E., 1987, *West Highland steamers*. Glasgow.

Fergusson, J., 1951, *Argyll in the forty-five*. London.

Finlayson, B., 1998, *Wild harvesters, the first people of Scotland*. Edinburgh.

Flemming, N. C., 1988, review of R. Ballard and R. Archbold, *The discovery of the Titanic, IJNA* 17.2, 198–200.

Foster, S. M., 2004, *Picts, Gaels and Scots*. London.

Friel, I., 2003, *The British Museum maritime history of Britain and Ireland*. London.

Fyfe, J. A., Long, D., and Evans, D., 2003, *The geology of the Malin-Hebrides sea area*. HMSO, London

Gardiner, R. J., and Greenhill, B. (eds), 1993, *The advent of steam, the merchant steamship before 1900*. London.

Gaskell, P., 1980, *Morvern Transformed*. Cambridge.

Greenhill, B., 1988, *The merchant schooners*. London

Haldane, A. R. B., 1995, *The Drove roads of Scotland*. Exeter.

Hewitson, J., 2004, *The Scots at sea, celebrating Scotland's maritime history*. Edinburgh

Holt, P., 2003 'An assessment of quality in underwater archaeological surveys using tape measurements', *IJNA* 32.2, 246–51.

Hunter, C., 2004, *Smuggling in West Argyll and Lochaber before 1745*. Oban.

Jarvis, A., 1993, 'Alfred Hold and the compound engine', in R. J. Gardiner and B. Greenhill (eds), *The advent of steam, the merchant steamship before 1900*, 156–9. London.

Jones, R. C., 2006, *Dinorwic: the Llanberis slate quarry, 1780–1969*. Wrexham.

Larn, R., and Larn, B., 1995, *Shipwreck Index of the British Isles, Vol. 4. Scotland*. London.

Lavery, B., 2001, *Maritime Scotland*. London.

Lenihan, D. J. (ed.), 1989, *Submerged Cultural Resources study: USS Arizona Memorial and Pearl Harbor national historic landmark*. Santa Fe, NM.

Levi, P., (ed.), 1984, Introduction and notes to Johnson, S., *A journey to the Western Islands of Scotland* and Boswell, J., *The journal of a tour to the Hebrides*. London

Liddiard, J., 1999, Wreck Tour 2: the *Hispania, Diver* magazine (April 1999). Available online at http://www.divernet.com/

Liddiard, J., 2001, Wreck tour 21: the *Thesis, Diver* (March 2001). Copy available online at http://www.divernet.com/

Liddiard, J., 2002, Wreck Tour 35: the *Rondo, Diver* (January 2002). Available online at http://www.divernet.com/

Liddiard, J., 2003, Wreck Tour 48: the *Shuna. Diver* (February 2003). Copy available online at http://www.divernet.com/

Lindsay, J., 1968, *The canals of Scotland*. Newton Abbot.

Lloyd's Register, 1934, *Annals of Lloyd's Register*. London

Lynch, J. P., 2001, *An unlikely success story – the Belfast Shipbuilding industry: 1880–1935*. Belfast.

Lyon, D. J., 1974, 'Documentary sources for the archaeological diver. Ship plans at the National Maritime Museum', *IJNA* 3, 3–20.

Bibliography

McCarthy, M., 2000, *Iron and Steamship Archaeology: Success and Failure on the SS Xantho.* New York.

Macdonald, R., 1993, *Dive Scotland's greatest wrecks.* Edinburgh.

Macdonald, R., 2000, *Dive Scotland's greatest wrecks.* Edinburgh.

McLeay, A., 1986, *The Tobermory Treasure: the true story of a fabulous Armada galleon.* London.

Martin, C. J. M., 1978, 'The *Dartmouth*, a British frigate wrecked off Mull, 1690: The ship', *IJNA* **7.**1: 29–58.

Martin, C., 1998, *Scotland's historic shipwrecks.* London.

Martin, C., and Martin, P., 2003a, 'The Coastal Heritage of Morvern', in P. Martin (ed), *Exploring Morvern*, 39–42. Morvern Heritage Society.

Martin, C., and Martin, P., 2003b, 'Marine boathouses of the Sound of Mull', *IJNA* 32.1, 91–110.

Martin, C., and Parker, G., 1988, *The Spanish Armada.* London.

Moir, P., and Crawford, I., 1994, *Argyll Shipwrecks.* Privately published, Inverclyde.

Moir, P. and Crawford, I., 2003, *Argyll Shipwrecks.* Privately published, Inverclyde.

Muckelroy, K. (ed.), 1980, *Archaeology underwater: an atlas of the world's submerged sites.* New York.

Munday, J., 1987, *Naval Cannon.* Aylesbury.

Munro, R. W., 1979, *Scottish Lighthouses.* Stornoway.

Nicolaisen, W. F. H., 2001, *Scottish place names.* Edinburgh.

Ransley, J., 2007, 'Rigorous reasoning, reflexive research and the space for alternative archaeologies. Questions for maritime archaeological management' *IJNA* 36.**2**, 221–37.

Raven, F., 2003, 'Ardtornish Castle', in P. Martin (ed.), *Exploring Morvern*, 24.

Ridley, G., 1990, *Dive North-West Scotland.* revised edn, London.

Rixon, D., 1998, *The West Highland galley.* Edinburgh.

Robertson, P., 2003 'The visitor schemes on the wrecks of the *Swan* and HMS *Dartmouth* in the Sound of Mull, Scotland (UK)', in D. Scott-Ireton and J. Spirek (eds), *Preserving and interpreting our sunken marine* heritage, 71–83. New York.

Roth, R., 1989, 'A proposed standard in the reporting of historic artillery', *IJNA* 18.3, 191–202.

Rule, N, 1989, 'Direct Survey Method (DSM) of underwater survey and its application underwater', *IJNA* 18.2, 157–62.

Smith, R., 1988, 'Towards a typology for wrought iron ordnance', *IJNA* 17.1, 5–16.

Smylie, M., 2001, '*Glen Carradale* CN253', *Fishing Boats* **20**, 39–40.

Stevenson, D., 1980, *Alasdair MacColla and the Highland problem in the Seventeenth Century.* Edinburgh.

Stevenson, D., 2005, *Mull and Iona, a landscape fashioned by geology.* Scottish Natural Heritage, Perth.

Thomas, J., 1984, *The West Highland railway.* 3rd edition, Newton Abbot.

Thornber, I., 2002, (ed.), N. Macleod, *Morvern: A Highland Parish* (originally published as *Reminiscences of a Highland Parish*, 1863). Edinburgh.

Vlierman, K., 1994, 'A note on deck-lights, glasses or prisms from 19th century wrecks in Flevoland, the Netherlands', *IJNA* 23.4, 319–23.

Waine, C. V., 1980, *Steam coasters and short sea traders.* revised edn, Wolverhampton.

Whittaker, I., 1998, *Off Scotland, a comprehensive record of maritime and aviation losses in Scottish waters.* Edinburgh.

Williams, R., 1984, *The Lords of the Isles, the Clan Donald and the early kingdom of the Scots.* London.

Unpublished reports

Bailey, C., Georma, F., Mayger, C. M. G., Micha, P., Sa Pinto, S., Soussi, E., and Taylor, J., 1998, Site report on the cannon site at Scallastle Bay, Sound of Mull Scotland (10–16 May 1998). Unpublished MA dissertation, Dept of Archaeology, University of Bristol.

Cleasby, D., 2001, Survey of an object on the deck of the SS *Thesis*. Unpublished NAS Part II project

Collyer, T., 2000, A sonar and magnetic survey of the Sound of Mull, Argyll. Unpublished BSc dissertation, Geological Oceanography, University of Wales, Bangor.

Diamond., P, 1994, The *Dartmouth*. Unpublished NAS Part 2 project report.

Faux, A., 1994, Slate wreck survey report. Unpublished NAS Part 2 project report.

Fish, A., 2003, Debris Field at the Bow of the SS *Thesis*, Eilean Rubha an Ridire, Sound of Mull. Unpublished NAS Part 2 project report.

Fortey, N. J., Carr, A., Wagner, D. G., and Turner. G., 2005, Mineralogical Examination of Archaeological Samples from the SS *Thesis*. British Geological Survey Commissioned Report for Lochaline Dive Centre (archived in the RCAHMS).

Guest, R., & Guest, J., 2000, SOMAP 2000. Unpublished NAS Part 2 project report.

Lloyd's Register, 1887, *Belfast survey report number 3303 SS Thesis*. Unpublished construction survey (for insurance purposes) by Lloyd's of London. Copy available on application to Photographs and Plans section, National Maritime Museum, Greenwich.

Maddocks, J., 1996, Scallastle Bay cannon site. Unpublished NAS Part 2 project report.

Maddocks, J., 1998, Recording cast iron ordnance underwater. Unpublished postgraduate diploma, Department of Archaeology, University of Winchester.

Pritchard, A., 1994, SOMAP–94, the slate wreck in the Sound of Mull. Unpublished NAS Part 2 project report.

Restell, M., and Restell, R., 2004, SS *Thesis*, a Comparison of Classification survey from historical records with Seabed Measurements. Unpublished NAS Part 2 project report.

Robertson, J. C., and Hagan, H. H., 1953, 'A century of coaster design and operation'. Paper 1176 presented to the Institute of Engineers and Shipbuilders in Scotland 1st December 1953, in National Register of Archives (Scotland) 1982, *The Institute of Engineers and Shipbuilders in Scotland, Glasgow*. Series No 2424

Robertson, P., 2004, Targeted search, survey and site stabilisation work on the HMS *Dartmouth*, Sound of Mull, Scotland. Unpublished licensee report to the Advisory Committee on Historic Wreck Sites.

Robertson, P., 2005, Sound of Mull remote sensing project report. Data structure report for Historic Scotland (Archived with RCAHMS).

Walsh, T., 2003, Site survey of the wreck of the *Pelican*, Calve Island, Sound of Mull. Unpublished NAS Part 2 project report.

Wessex Archaeology, 2004, *Dartmouth*, Sound of Mull: designated site assessment full report Report reference 53111.03m for Historic Scotland

Young, J., 2000, A recording exercise on the *Thesis*: a study towards the NAS Part II qualification. Unpublished NAS Part 2 project report.

Index
Ship's names are given in italics

Albicore	24
Aleksander	30, 104
Amadeo	67
Anna Bhan	iv, 19. 20, 84, 98
Archaeological Diving Unit, University of St Andrews	viii, 1, 11, 58
Ardnamurchan Packet	17, 101
Ardtornish	iii, vii, 3, 5, 7, 8, 10, 11, 24–27, 84, 112
Ardtornish Point	3, 5, 10, 11, 13, 24–27, 41
Argyll	viii, 1, 3, 4–7, 27, 110–112
Armada	5, 17, 112
Aros	ii, 5, 6, 14, 22, 23
Bailemeonach	ii, 6, 14
Ballista	iii, 13, 30, 41, 106
Belfast	10, 28, 67, 70, 77, 81, 82, 87, 90, 111
Betty	6
Bonny Prince Charlie	6
Boswell, James	17, 110, 113
British Fisheries Society	6, 17
Buitenzorg	iii, 10, 28, 43, 44, 84, 85, 105
Calderon	67
Columba	4
Craignure	3, 8, 32, 46
Cromwell, Oliver	5
Dál Riata	4, 5
Dearg Sgeir	iv, 22–24
Duart	ii–vii, 1–3, 5, 6, 11–13, 14, 16, 28, 29, 32, 45, 84, 85
Dukes of Argyll	6, 7
Eileanan Glasa	20, 22, 23
Elizabeth	17, 20, 84, 101, 102, 103
Evelyn Rose	iii, iv, 25, 26, 42, 85, 106, 110
Fishnish	3, 6, 7, 27, 28
Fiunary	4, 20, 24
Fraserburgh	47, 57, 84
Gaelic Rose	ii, vii, 11, 15
Galvanic	70
Glas Eileanan	3, 10, 11, 27, 28
Glen Carradale	24, 97, 112
Grass Point	6
Happy	10
Hebrides	3, 5, 110, 111
Hero	28, 102
Hispania	ii–iv, 11, 22, 23, 37, 38, 40, 84, 85, 105, 111
Historic Scotland	vii, 1, 11–13, 113
HMS *Berkeley*	11, 58
HMS *Dartmouth*	iv, 1, 11, 13, 28, 30, 31, 58, 61, 62, 84, 85, 98, 112, 113
Inninmore Point	2, 3, 11, 28, 31, 67, 71, 81
Ireland	4–6, 17
Jacobites	6, 10, 11
Jane Shearer	28, 102
John Preston	i–v, 11–13, 16, 24, 45, 46–57, 84, 85, 103
Johnson, Dr Samuel	10, 17, 110, 111
Kalafish	24, 103
Kitty	20, 101
Liberty	32, 101
Lighthouses	ii, 8, 15, 41, 84, 112
Lindsay, Alexander	5, 8, 10, 22 110, 111
Lismore	7, 8
Loch Aline	iii, 3, 6–8, 24, 25, 27, 41
Loch Sunart	3, 4, 6–8
Lochaline	ii, iv, vi, vii, 1, 3, 7, 8, 11, 12, 14, 15, 24,25, 27, 46, 47, 58, 111, 113
Lochaline Dive Centre	vi, vii, 1, 11, 12, 46, 113
Logan	iv, 11, 25, 84, 106
Lords of the Isles	5, 112
Louisa	84, 102
Macbrayne, David	17
Macduff	ii, 20, 35, 104
Macleans of Duart	5, 6
Macleod, Norman	6, 10, 112
Margaret	84, 102
Martha and Margrett	32, 97
Martin, Colin	ii–iv, vi, vii, 1, 5–8, 11, 12, 14, 28, 30–32, 41, 58, 64, 112
McKenzie, Murdoch, Senior	6, 10, 11, 20, 24, 27, 28, 32, 58, 110
Menai	84, 104
Menai Strait	57
Middlesbrough	67, 70, 77, 81
Mingary	ii, 5, 6, 14
Monro, Sir Donald	6, 10, 17, 110
Morvern	vii, 1–3, 4–8, 10, 11, 13, 20, 28, 31, 67, 71, 84. 111–112
Mull	i–viii, 1–3, 4–8, 10–13, 14, 15, 17–20,22, 23,28, 32, 46, 57, 58, 67, 70, 81, 84–86. 111–113
Nautical Archaeological Society (NAS)	vi, 1, 12, 13, 46, 69 67, 71, 84, 111–112
Adopt a Wreck Scheme	13, 46
New Blessing	84, 103
Oban	iii, 3, 4, 5, 8, 10, 11, 22, 26, 68, 70, 71, 81
Oban Times and Argyllshire Advertiser	10, 11, 22, 26, 68, 70, 81, 110
Pelican	ii, iv, 12, 17–20, 33, 34, 84, 104, 113
Port Dinorwic, North Wales	iv, 46, 47, 56, 57, 111
Porthmadog	30, 46
Princess Anne	6
Providence of Dumbartane	5
Remote sensing	ii, iii, viii, 1, 11, 15, 19–25, 28, 33–40, 42–45, 49, 58, 65, 69, 80, 85, 86, 109, 112, 113
River Tay	30, 105
Robin	67
Rondo	ii–iv, 23, 24, 39, 40, 84, 85, 105, 111
Rubh'ant Sean Chaisteil	3
Rubha Aird Seisg	3, 20
Rubha Dearg	i, 4, 24, 27, 46, 47, 57
Salen	i, iii, iv, 2, 4, 6, 8, 15, 22, 70
San Juan de Sicilia	5, 97

114

Scallastle	3, 511, 12, 27, 28, 47, 58, 63, 84, 85, 112, 113	*Thomas Graham*	32, 101
Scott, Sir Walter	10, 17, 110, 112	Tobermory	ii, iv, 3, 5–8, 10, 11, 17–20, 22, 30, 25, 80, 84, 111, 112
Shuna	ii, 20–22, 36, 38, 84, 85, 105, 111	*Tolka*	70
Speedwell of Lynn	32, 96	Torosay	3, 7
SS *Breda*	8	University of Bristol	30
SS *Great Britain*	19	University of Dundee	viii, 11
Strathbeg	ii, 20, 35, 106	University of St Andrews	iii, vii, viii, 1, 8, 11, 12, 32, 58
Strontian	6		
Swan	1, 28, 32, 96, 112	University of Wales, Bangor	11
Telegram	17, 102	Vikings	5
Terror	6, 8, 28, 111	*Xantho*	67, 112
Theme	iv, 68, 70, 76, 77, 81, 82		
Thesis	ii–iv, 11–13, 15, 16, 31, 64, 65, 67–83, 84–86, 87–93, 94, 95, 103, 111–113		

www.ingramcontent.com/pod-product-compliance
Lightning Source LLC
Chambersburg PA
CBHW041705290426

44108CB00027B/2858